DATE DUE

The Commu

BRODART   Cat. No. 23-221

THE COMMUNITY ECONOMIC

WILLIAM H. SIMON

Law, Business, and the New Social Policy

DEVELOPMENT MOVEMENT

DUKE UNIVERSITY PRESS : DURHAM AND LONDON 2001 . . . .

© 2001 Duke University Press   All rights reserved
Printed in the United States of America on acid-free paper ∞
Designed by Rebecca Giménez   Typeset in Minion with
Franklin Gothic display by Keystone Typesetting, Inc.
Library of Congress Cataloging-in-Publication Data
appear on the last printed page of this book.

Contents

Acknowledgments

In 1995 Gary Bellow asked me to develop a course for the Harvard Law School winter term to complement the clinical practice of the Community Enterprise Unit at the school's Hale and Dorr Legal Services Center in Jamaica Plain. I've taught the course every January since 1986, and this book is a product of that experience.

The argument incorporates and responds to many comments from the remarkable group of students the course has attracted over the years. I am especially grateful to that first group in January 1996, who responded to my groping efforts with a combination of sympathy, worldliness, and visionary hope that continues to inspire me.

The lawyers at the Hale and Dorr Center, including Jeanne Charn, Brian Ford, Liz Solar, and Vin McCarthy have taught me a lot and provided various forms of support. Arthur Johnson, a CED pioneer who has dedicated himself with integrity and imagination to the Jamaica Plain community for twenty-five years, has been my most important informant. Our collaboration in the Law School's CED course has been invaluable to me.

I got my first taste of CED in 1991 at the Center for Law and Economic Development in Berkeley (now Oakland), where Brad Caftel, James Head, Dave Kirkpatrick, and Jan Stokeley—four more pioneers—shared their knowledge. Since then, I have benefited from many conversations with Kevin Stein of the East Palo Alto Community Law Project and Peter Pitegoff of the State University of New York at Buffalo.

For helpful comments on the manuscript, I'm grateful to Greg Alexander, Susan Bennett, Peter Pitegoff, Mark Aaronson, Joel Handler, Jerry Frug, Fred Block, and Chuck Sabel. I got valuable suggestions and encouragement at a seminar at the Columbia Law School, where I presented drafts of two chapters.

The Copes—Greg, Comfort, Eliza, and Thomas—put me up in Jamaica Plain and offered support of many kinds during some of those cold Januaries. I could not have done it without them.

Norma Tabares provided excellent research assistance. As always, Pat Adan's administrative support was invaluable.

Chapter 1 ⋮ Introduction

Within a five-minute walk of the Stony Brook subway stop in the Jamaica Plain section of Boston, you can encounter the following:

—A renovated industrial site of about five acres and sixteen buildings that serves as a business incubator for small firms that receive technical assistance from the Jamaica Plain Neighborhood Development Corporation (JPNDC), a nonprofit community development corporation, which is also housed there. Known as the Brewery after its former proprietor, a beermaker, the complex is owned by a nonprofit subsidiary of JPNDC.

—A 44,000-square-foot Stop 'n Shop supermarket. The market opened in 1991 after years in which the community had been without a major grocery store. It lies next to a recently renovated community health center and a large high-rise public housing project. The land on which the market and health center sit was developed and is owned by a limited partnership that includes, in addition to a commercial investor, JPNDC and the Tenant Management Corporation of the housing project. Some of the income from the market's and health center's leases goes into the Community Benefits Trust Fund, which supports job training and business development activities.

—A cluster of small, attractive multi-unit residential buildings containing a total of forty-one homes. These units were built with support from the federal Low Income Housing Tax Credit, and most are occupied by low- and moderate-income families at rents limited to 30 percent of family income. The buildings are owned by a limited partnership in which the general partners are a subsidiary of JPNDC and a resident cooperative; the limited partners include five conventional business corporations and a nonprofit corporation with a board composed of prominent government and business figures that promotes housing development throughout the state.

—Two recently renovated apartment buildings—one with eleven units and one with forty-five units—designed with common areas and facilities for medical support for elderly residents. The project benefits from large federal grants. It is owned by JPNDC; the units are leased to the tenants at rents that may not exceed 30 percent of income.

—A wood-frame building containing three apartments recently renovated by JPNDC with support from various public programs. JPNDC then sold the building at a price well below market value to an individual, who, as a condition of ownership set out in the deed, must live in one of the units and rent the others only to people who meet specified income-eligibility conditions at specified rents.

These institutions are products of the Community Economic Development (CED) Movement. Although it is unusual to find so many concentrated in such a small area—there are still more there that I have not mentioned—such projects can be found in most cities; their numbers have increased substantially in recent years, and there will be many more of them if current programs succeed. Such projects figure prominently in the most optimistic and innovative approaches to urban poverty on both the left and the right. They exemplify a kind of social entrepreneurialism that is flourishing across the country.[1] As support for traditional welfare and public housing programs has waned, a corresponding (though far from proportionate) increase in support for CED has arisen. The movement has been fueled by trends toward decentralizing public administration, on the one hand, and channeling the development of local markets along socially desirable paths, on the other. It has also been encouraged by changes in the contours of urban politics, especially new strategies by neighborhood activists.

1. See Harold McDougal, *Black Baltimore: A New Theory of Community* (1994); *Harold Washington and the Neighborhoods: Progressive Government in Chicago 1983–87*, ed. Pierre Clavel and Wim Wievel (1993); Peter Medoff and Holly Sklar, *Streets of Hope: The Fall and Rise of an Urban Neighborhood* (1994) (Dudley Street area of Boston).

Though there are many variations, the core definition of CED embraces (1) efforts to develop housing, jobs, or business opportunities for low-income people, (2) in which a leading role is played by nonprofit, nongovernmental organizations (3) that are accountable to residentially defined communities.[2] Chapter 2 surveys the increasing focus on such efforts in a broad range of public programs.

These efforts are supported by a cluster of convergent policy rationales that, in the most influential perspective, represents at once a theory of local economic development, a strategy of social policy implementation, and a vision of grassroots democracy. These "three logics of community action" are explored in chapter 3.

The CED Movement has brought forth a profusion of legal and institutional innovation. CED institutions are based on traditional, albeit peripheral, legal forms, especially the charitable corporation and the cooperative, but the movement has elaborated and combined them in innovative ways. The popular term "public–private partnership" glosses over the myriad and complex forms that public and private take in these projects.

The heart of the analysis focuses on the institutional contours of CED practice. There are five core themes:

Chapter 4 discusses the theme of the community as beneficiary of economic development. At the modest end of the spectrum, this notion refers to the traditional role of local institutions in regulating to mitigate the negative external effects of development and in taxing property and economic activity to support the provision of public goods, such as roads, police, and schools. At the more radical end, it connotes the idea

2. The average population of a community development corporation (CDC) community was 69,000, and the median was 32,500 in a 1992 study of 130 CDCs: Avis Vidal, *Rebuilding Communities: A National Study of Community Development Corporations* 38 (New School for Social Research, 1992). The range is broad. The Bronx Overall Economic Development Corporation, which coordinates the federal Empowerment Zone program in the South Bronx serves an area of about 100,000 people. The Jamaica Plain Neighborhood Development Corporation, as well as the CDCs I discuss below in East Palo Alto, California, and the Dudley Street area of Boston, have constituencies of about 25,000. Optimal size, of course, depends in part on the types of projects the organization does. Job training tends to be done over larger areas than housing, and CDCs serving small areas may find large real estate projects beyond their means. But generalization is difficult. Marin City, California, whose CDC recently completed a major housing and commercial project, has only about 2,500 residents.

that the community—defined as the collectivity of residents within its borders—is the residual claimant on the proceeds of local development. The more radical interpretations challenge some traditional doctrines of American local government, including constitutional doctrines that limit residential communities' ability to pursue their interests at the expense of property owners and nonresident workers.

Next, there is the theme of the community as agent of economic development, discussed in chapter 5. This notion implies an entrepreneurial role for local institutions that, as applied to nonbusiness institutions, is somewhat novel. A central question for the movement has been how this entrepreneurial role should be institutionalized. The most prominent answer gives a central role to the community development corporation (CDC). Although they are not primarily oriented toward profit, CDCs are in many ways competitive enterprises, and their mechanisms of accountability are a hybrid of those associated with business and government.

Constrained property rights are the subject of chapter 6. CED institutions tend to create property rights that are quite different from the paradigm of private law. Such property tends to be subject to two kinds of constraint—alienation constraints and accumulation constraints. Alienation constraints limit the ability to sell or transfer the property. Accumulation constraints limit the degree of inequality within some group associated with the property. These constraints are most salient in the limited-equity cooperative, a type of organization found in both subsidized housing and business development. Though less visible, such constraints play important roles in other types of organizations associated with CED, including the CDC.

Chapter 7 takes up the theme of induced mobilization. To widely varying degrees, CED projects depend on local participation. In addition to its entrepreneurial side, the CDC has an organizing and representative side. This latter side is encouraged by a growing number of state, regional, and national institutions that provide support for local development that is conditioned on some degree of mobilization. These supporting institutions typically require community applicants to demonstrate at least openness to—and, sometimes, effective encouragement of—resident participation. These programs represent a striking comeback of an idea that has often been pronounced dead since the 1960s. Induced mobilization was central to the "Community Action Program" launched by the Economic Opportunity Act of 1964, but the idea was disparaged on both right and left, and it faded. The new variation has both continuities with and differences from the older one.

The last of the basic themes is institutional hybridization, taken up in chapter 8. CED structures tend to defy conventional boundaries that separate levels of government and types of private organization. They recombine organizational attributes in unfamiliar ways in order better to link such functions as political representation and economic entrepreneurialism.

The focus here is on the institutional configuration of CED practice. I suggest that the movement has developed a set of structures that responds usefully to the social forces emphasized in the three logics of community action discussed in chapter 3. These innovations represent an enduring achievement that promises a broad range of productive applications. This is not, however, a full-scale appraisal of community-based social policy. Such an effort would require a larger body of information than we possess, and it would also have to consider the interactions of the local values and forces emphasized in the CED perspective with competing values and surrounding structures above the local level. Chapter 9 identifies some of these considerations and considers briefly how they bear on the appraisal of Community Economic Development.

Its practitioners think of the CED Movement as a grassroots affair. To begin an account of CED by reviewing national-, regional-, and state-support structures might strike them as looking through the wrong end of the telescope. Yet no one denies that grassroots CED activities depend on an elaborate network of larger-scale efforts. Moreover, the increasing salience of CED in political and policy discourse can be most readily seen in the recent growth of national, regional, and state programs designed to encourage and sustain it.

General Planning: The Revival of Redevelopment and Community Action

Looming over the current CED Movement are memories of two earlier experiments in community development—urban renewal, or Redevelopment (a word I capitalize to indicate that it is a term of art referring to a special legal process), and the Community Action Program. Both are widely regarded as discredited, and to some extent the current movement has been shaped in reaction to their failures. However, in some respects, current efforts might also seem a continuation and vindication of the earlier movements.

REDEVELOPMENT

The Redevelopment process was created by the states under the impetus of the National Housing Act of 1949, which provided for grants and other support for local efforts to revitalize "blighted" areas. The federal grant program came to be called "Urban Renewal." The state process it supported begins with the designation of an area as "blighted." A municipal agency then undertakes with private investors to formulate a plan of public and private investments to improve the area. The agency can draw on municipal powers of spending, eminent domain, land-use regulation, and public finance—with streamlined procedures. The plan often provides for public provision of structural improvements, as well as the condemnation and delivery to private developers of large tracts of land, perhaps at a substantial "write down" (below-cost price). The private developers undertake various improvements on their own account and perhaps build community facilities, such as parks, meeting places, or low-income housing. The plans and ensuing contracts often limit or designate special uses for state and local taxes on the improvements.[1]

The Redevelopment process responds to a problem of coordination pervasive in real estate development that has been thought exceptionally severe in poor or otherwise "blighted" areas. One aspect of the coordination problem arises from the fact that the basic local instruments of economic development—providing tangible public goods such as roads and parks; delivering services such as police and schools; regulating land use; and offering fiscal subsidies, such as targeted tax breaks or favorable credit terms—often involve separate political processes. Bringing them to bear simultaneously on an ambitious development project could be cumbersome. Redevelopment combines the tools in a single, streamlined process.

The other aspect concerns the coordination of investments. The success of a real estate investment typically depends on other investments in the surrounding area, both public investments in public goods and services and private investments that make the neighborhood more attractive or produce beneficial services. In a prosperous neighborhood,

---

1. For overviews with citations to the extensive literature, see Sonya Bekoff Molho and Gideon Kanner, "Urban Renewal: Laissez-Faire for the Poor, Welfare for the Rich," 8 *Pacific Law Journal* 627 (1977); Benjamin B. Quinones, "Redevelopment Redefined: Revitalizing the Central City with Resident Control," 27 *University of Michigan Journal of Law Reform* 689 (1994).

informal coordination or simply shared optimism may be sufficient to induce separate but mutually beneficial investment. However, in a blighted area, public and private investors may need more formal commitments from each other.[2] The Redevelopment process structures negotiation and produces binding contracts intended to create such commitments.

Redevelopment has been harshly criticized for decades. The critics have shown that, over and over, the development facilitated by the process has come at the expense of the initial residents of the communities being developed. In the worst-case scenario, which has been often enacted, it takes the form of "Negro removal"—displacing low-income, minority people by destroying rental housing or commercial buildings they use or occupy and replacing them with upper-income housing or business facilities serving the affluent. The West End in Boston and the Western Addition in San Francisco are two famous examples.[3]

The Redevelopment process encouraged such injustice by weakening democratic constraints on governmental aid to development; by creating various fiscal incentives for localities to undertake it; and by subsidizing the private participants through sweetheart land deals, cheap finance, tax breaks, and publicly provided infrastructure tailored to their investments. There is substantial evidence that the returns in economic growth to public Redevelopment investments have been small or negative and that the distributive effects of the program on balance have been regressive.

In 1974, the federal government ended specific support for Redevelopment and folded these funds into the Community Development Block Grant (CDBG) program.[4] Under this program, resources are not tied to specific projects or types of projects; instead, local governments have discretion to decide how to spend them within broad parameters.

2. A similar premise applies to new or "green-belt" communities being built from scratch and accounts for another category of specialized development procedures applicable to these communities. See, for example, Daniel Mandelker, Roger A. Cunningham, and John M. Payne, *Planning and Control of Land Development* 631–51 (4th ed., 1995).

3. Molho and Kanner, "Urban Renewal," 643–62.

4. Housing and Community Development Act of 1974, Public Law No. 93–383, tit. I, sec. 101, 88 Stat. 633, 93d Cong., 2d Sess. The related Urban Development Action Grant program came on line in 1977 but has since expired.

Nevertheless, Redevelopment did not die. It survived as a state law process. In some states, its use expanded in the 1980s and 1990s under the impetus of efforts to limit property taxes, such as California's Proposition 13. By limiting revenues from the existing tax base, these measures prompted local governments to seek new taxable development. The consequence in California has been called "the fiscalization of land use": Municipalities exercise their regulatory power over land use with a view to enhancing their tax revenues. The Redevelopment process is especially attractive in this regard both because it streamlines large-scale development and because the statutes typically allow local government to keep a larger share of tax revenues attributable to Redevelopment efforts than they keep from revenues arising from conventional sources. Counties, school districts, and other taxing entities claim larger shares of the non-redevelopment tax base.[5]

Federal support remained substantial even after the expiration of the urban renewal program. Although CDBG funds were not tied to Redevelopment projects, local governments that wanted to could so use them. Moreover, the federal tax code has continued to permit localities to issue tax-exempt bonds to finance Redevelopment projects.[6]

The fiscal attractions of Redevelopment are great enough in some areas to prompt local officials to characterize relatively prosperous areas, and even vacant land, as blighted, and in California a lot of Redevelopment projects do not involve low-income neighborhoods. The process continues to attract criticism as wasteful of public subsidy and arbitrary in its effects on taxation. However, assessments of its potential for low-income neighborhoods are far less negative than in the past, and some prominent Redevelopment efforts have been viewed as CED success stories.

Statutory reform has strengthened the requirements of community participation and provided safeguards and remedies for displacement. California, for example, requires the formation of a "project area committee" with representation of residents, community organizations, and

---

5. See William Fulton, *Guide to California Planning* 208–13, 242–261 (1991).

6. 26 USC. 144c. Lynne Sagalyn estimated that the annual value of the tax subsidy for Redevelopment finance in the 1980s considerably exceeded the annual amounts of direct expenditures under the prior urban renewal program: "Explaining the Improbable: Local Redevelopment in the Wake of Federal Cutbacks," 56 *Journal of the American Planning Association* 429, 432 (1990).

businesses. If the project involves displacement or the use of eminent domain, the committee must be chosen through an election publicized throughout the area. The committee is entitled to information from the Redevelopment agency and to consultation on major decisions. While it cannot veto a project, it does have potentially significant voting rights. If the committee votes against the project, then the project can proceed only on a two-thirds vote by the Redevelopment authority, rather than the usual majority.[7] A thick body of judicial precedent also gives residents who oppose projects the right to challenge them in court on a variety of procedural grounds (for example, compliance with environmental-impact-assessment requirements or consistency with the city or county plan).[8]

Since the 1970s, federal law applicable to both federal projects and federally supported state and local projects has given important rights to displaced tenants, homeowners, and businesses. Some states, including California, have enacted similar protections for projects with only state support. For example, in addition to moving expenses, tenants are entitled to payments designed to compensate them for any increased rent they must pay for the next five years in their new apartments. The reimbursement formula potentially compensates the lowest-income tenants by more than the costs of displacement and hence can leave them better off for being displaced.[9]

Finally, if low- or moderate-income housing is eliminated by the

7. California Health and Safety Code 33385–88.
8. Goldfarb & Lipman, *A Legal Guide to California Redevelopment* 87–8 (2d ed. 1994).
9. 42 USC 5301 *et seq.*; 24 CFR 42.350 (standards applicable to projects supported by CDBG and related programs); California Government Code 7260 *et seq.*

The federal standards require protection against rent increases for five years; the California standards require protection for three and a half years. Both federal and California law require that the compensation enable the tenant during the period of protection to pay no more than 30 percent of her income for the new apartment. Moreover, California requires that the compensation be based on the cost of a new apartment that complies with the Sanitary Code. Because many low-income people pay more than 30 percent of their income for housing and most live in sub-code apartments, the formula can leave them better off when they are displaced. However, if the residents are being displaced from the community entirely because no satisfactory housing is available for them, then the payment might be viewed as compensation for the loss not only of the current benefits of residence in the community, but of the opportunity to enjoy the benefits of the new development. From that point of view, it would be less likely to seem excessive.

project, federal and sometimes state law require that localities build comparable replacement housing within a few years.[10] California further specifies that 20 percent of the incremental tax proceeds attributable to the project be used to fund affordable housing development.[11]

Some of these provisions are unenforced, and others can be circumvented or neutralized by a determined Redevelopment agency. But they do make abuse more difficult and increase the likelihood that development will involve grassroots participation and benefit. Here, for example, are two recent examples of Redevelopment activity that seem consistent with CED aspirations:

The city of East Palo Alto, California, is a low-income minority area with about 25,000 residents. It has been desperately short of public revenues since its inception. The city can honestly be described as blighted; it has poor public services, a substantial crime problem, and despite rising land prices, had little private investment for decades. Yet it sits in the middle of booming Silicon Valley and contains large tracts of underdeveloped land. Aside from the fiscal incentives mentioned earlier, the Redevelopment process offers an opportunity to induce greater investment by coordinating public and private efforts and to canalize the development process in a way that allows benefits to be widely shared.

Since the city is relatively small and participation in municipal government is extensive, citywide governmental processes have a community character. The city council sits as the Redevelopment agency, and its activities are closely and widely followed. In the planning for the first of its projects to reach the active development phase—a large commercial center along the highway that separates the city from the rest of Silicon Valley—several community organizations pressed with some success for various community benefits, for example, a "First Source Hiring Ordinance" giving preference to local residents for jobs in the project area and commitments for affordable housing to be built by nonprofit developers. The project area committee and affiliated residents' council were active both in organizing its constituents and negotiating with the Redevelopment agency. The project has displaced 150 families, but they, too, have shared in its benefits. A few have received subsidized units in

10. 24 CFR. 42.375; California Health and Safety Code 33413a.
11. California Health and Safety Code 33334.

the city's first affordable housing project; the rest have received reloca-
tion payments averaging about $70,000—arguably, large amounts for
vacating dilapidated apartments in which they were tenants-at-will.

The Dudley Street Neighborhood Initiative (DSNI) in the Roxbury
area of Boston is another example of a Redevelopment project that
appears to involve genuine community control.[12] DSNI is a nonprofit
corporation devoted to organizing residents around development planning. It operates in a low-income minority neighborhood with a population about the same size as that of East Palo Alto. The neighborhood
has suffered severely from poverty, crime, and disinvestment and, in the
early 1980s, had an appearance of unredeemed physical devastation.
DSNI has sponsored a variety of projects, including social-service programs, a new town common, and a few hundred units of subsidized
housing. It has been credited with improving the delivery of social services and reversing the trend of disinvestment. Its processes are widely
considered a model of grassroots accountability and involvement.

In collaboration with the city of Boston, DSNI has made a striking use
of the Redevelopment process. In accordance with a long dormant authorization in Massachusetts Redevelopment law, the city has delegated
to DSNI various Redevelopment powers, including eminent domain.[13]
DSNI's physical revitalization plans required acquisition of hundreds of
small lots, mostly absentee-owned and many with untraceable ownership. This is a classic case in which eminent domain seems necessary. In
Boston, however, where Redevelopment-driven eminent domain has
historical associations more with liquidation than with revitalization of
low-income neighborhoods, the city's ability to engage in large-scale
condemnation without arousing community opposition is constrained.
By delegating the power to a community-based organization, the city
neutralized much fear and suspicion.[14]

12. See Medoff and Sklar, *Streets of Hope: The Fall and Rise of an Urban Neighborhood*
(1994).

13. Massachusetts General Laws, c. 121A, secs. 3, 11.

14. State "brownfields" programs, which proliferated in the 1990s, should be mentioned
as a specialized but important type of Redevelopment process. The programs are
designed to facilitate remediation and development of environmentally contaminated
sites. They offer prospective developers financial assistance, liability protection, and
relaxation of clean-up requirements. Some explicitly condition benefits on a showing
of community support. Although these programs are not targeted at low-income areas,

Community action agencies emerged from the Economic Opportunity Act of 1964, the controversial centerpiece of the Kennedy and Johnson administrations' War on Poverty. A central provision of this act contemplated the delivery of a range of social services through "community action agencies." The act provided for certification and support by the federal government of a community action agency for any low-income urban neighborhood. Public and private nonprofit agencies could apply, but both were obliged to demonstrate "maximum feasible participation of the residents" of the geographic areas in which they were focused.[15] The agencies were expected to oversee a range of services—most notably, educational enrichment and job training, but also "community economic development."

The Community Action Program was an attempt to force decentralization of urban government. One premise was simply that municipalities were often too centralized and bureaucratic to design and deliver services effectively to poor neighborhoods. Another was that many municipalities were dominated by white political coalitions insensitive to racial minorities. The program responded to the first problem by inducing the formation of neighborhood institutions and giving them responsibilities for social service administration. It responded to the second by setting up relations between these local agencies and the federal government that were substantially independent of local power structures.

The program disappointed the expectations of its designers in two distinct ways. For the most part, the citizen-participation goals were never realized. Turnout at elections tended to be tiny, and ongoing involvement in the program was limited. The agencies tended to be dominated by their staffs or, in some cases, unaccountable boards. At best, these organizations were competent service providers; at worst,

---

many toxic sites are located in such areas, and community-based organizations have occasionally made effective use of the programs to support beneficial development. See Lincoln Davies, "Working Toward a Common Goal? Three Case Studies of Brownfields Development in Environmental Justice Communities," 18 *Stanford Environmental Law Journal* 285 (1999).

15. Public Law 88–452, Title II, Pt. A, sec. 202, 88th Cong., 2d Sess., 1964 *U.S. Code Congressional and Administrative News,* 595–96.

they were inefficient and patronage-ridden. Some community action agencies appear to have been more effective in mobilizing constituents, but they were no more successful as organizations in the long run. Agencies tended to engage in confrontation with established municipal power structures to demand more resources and attention to their communities. Although such confrontation was exactly what some of the program's designers hoped for, the protests from established local Democratic figures came as a surprise to Lyndon Johnson, who had no taste for inner-city mobilization that threatened the party's core constituents. The federal government failed to support activist community action agencies and came to regard them as liabilities.[16]

Unlike Redevelopment, the Community Action Program did not survive in name (though many community action agencies continue as local social service providers), and its activities withered in the 1970s. One small fragment that did survive, however, played a significant role in the CED Movement. In 1968, the Economic Opportunity Act was amended to provide grants to "community development corporations," which were defined as locally initiated nonprofits focused on the problems of low-income areas. More than half of the seats on the organization's governing body were required to be held by residents of the relevant geographical area.[17] After the Office of Economic Opportunity was abolished, this grant-making function went to the Community Services Administration, later renamed the Office of Community Services within the Department of Housing and Urban Development (HUD). The HUD Community Services Program is a small operation, most interesting for its links to the past, though it has continued to support notable projects. Both the Brewery business incubator and the Stop 'n Shop supermarket project in Jamaica Plain benefited from its grants. The Community Services Program was one of several, including the Community Reinvestment Act and others to be discussed shortly, that encouraged community groups that had been founded as protest organizations or social-service delivery agencies to reinvent themselves as economic developers.

Moreover, the federal urban grant programs that succeeded the Community Action Program—most importantly, the CDBG program—continue to mandate "public participation," though more ambiguously

16. See Robert Fisher, *Let the People Decide: Neighborhood Organizing in America* 110–20 (1984).
17. 42 USC 9805, 9807.

and less ostentatiously than in the past. The CDBG program requires that municipalities have a "public participation" plan that includes publicity about plans and opportunities, public hearings, and technical assistance to groups interested in applying for grants.[18] Although this is a far cry from the Community Action Program idea of facilitating the formation of a community-based organization in each poor neighborhood, HUD has encouraged municipalities to consider the option of forming "Neighborhood Strategy Areas," in particular communities that seem to be promising sites for focused assistance. The strategy area idea involves the formation of a community-based development organization with an elected board.[19]

Despite the lowered profile of federal support for community-based organizations in the 1970s and 1980s, this period saw an explosion in neighborhood activism that has been described as a "backyard revolution," a "rebirth of urban democracy," and a "rise of sublocal structures in urban governance."[20] Community groups formed to demand more and better services from city governments. They formed to influence land use and investment decisions, protesting proposed uses with negative external features (dumping facilities, high-density public housing projects, freeways) and pushing for uses likely to enhance the community (parks, schools). Many of these groups were reacting to decades of municipal policies that appeared to lavish investment on downtown areas at the expense of outlying neighborhoods. Some were fueled by political realignments induced by migration patterns that increased the electoral clout of minority neighborhoods (for example, "white flight" to the suburbs followed by the arrival of immigrant groups of color).

State and local policy encouraged such developments by creating new structures designed to enhance community participation in municipal government—little city halls, neighborhood councils, community boards—and new opportunities to participate in land-use and environ-

18. 24 CFR 91.105(a)(2).

19. "Neighborhood Strategy Areas: City of Nashville, Tennessee." Available from: http://www.hud.gov/80/ptw/docs/tn07.html (visited 30 July 1999).

20. Jeffrey M. Berry, Kent E. Portney, and Ken Thomson, *The Rebirth of Urban Democracy* 57–60, 108–14 (1993); Harry Boyte, *The Backyard Revolution: Understanding the New Citizen Movement* (1980); Richard Briffault, "The Rise of Sublocal Structures in Urban Governance," 82 *Minnesota Law Review* 503 (1997).

mental decisions and to challenge them in the courts. Federal policy also played a role. In a study of the "rebirth of urban democracy" in five cities, researchers concluded that in four of the cities, community activism had resulted from local government initiatives encouraged by the federal Community Development Block Grant and related programs, and in the fifth, San Antonio, the grassroots movement that emerged without municipal assistance had been prompted in part by the goal of participating in CDBG allocations.[21] Some states have enacted their own programs of general financial support for "community development corporations," "community preservation companies," or "neighborhood assistance organizations."[22]

With the advent of the Clinton administration, the federal government re-embraced the combination of developmental and participatory themes associated with the War on Poverty in the Empowerment Zone/ Enterprise Community program. Announced at the beginning of the Clinton administration with great fanfare, the program offered an extraordinary package of federal benefits over a ten-year period to a small number of competitively selected Empowerment Zones and a smaller package to a larger number of Enterprise Communities. After an initial application period, HUD designated nine Empowerment Zones in 1994. Impressed by initial reports, Congress then authorized funding for

21. Berry et al., *Rebirth*, 57–60, 108–14. The cities in which the book describes extensive and effective grassroots activism are Birmingham, Alabama; Dayton, Ohio; Portland, Oregon; St. Paul, Minnesota; and San Antonio, Texas. See also Fisher, *Let the People Decide*, 121–52.

Briffault, "Rise of Sublocal Structures," describes the emergence of a different category of "sublocal structures"—tax-increment finance districts, special zoning districts, business-improvement districts, and enterprise zones. With some exceptions, especially the new federally supported Empowerment Zones, these entities are generally oriented toward, and often controlled by, businesses and landowners rather than residents. To that extent, they are not CED in our sense, but they are part of a common trend toward decentralizing municipal governance.

22. Massachusetts General Laws, c. 40F (authorizing Community Development Finance Agency to provide support for "community development corporations"); New York Consolidated Laws Private Housing Finance Law 901 *et seq.* (authorizing state assistance to "Neighborhood Preservation Companies," or "community-based not-for-profit organization[s]"); Virginia Code 58.1–333, 63.1–32 *et seq.* (tax credit for donations to "neighborhood assistance organizations," or 501(c)(3)-qualified organizations providing "neighborhood assistance to impoverished people").

twenty-two more in 1997. Ninety-three "Enterprise Communities" receive the smaller set of benefits.[23]

Empowerment Zone benefits include increased grants for social services and economic development, regulatory waivers, use of tax-exempt bonding authority, and tax benefits for employers, including a credit for wage payments to employees who reside in the zone. Communities with "pervasive poverty" compete for selection by producing "strategic plans" of coordinated public and private efforts at housing, business, and job development. Congress mandated that the "affected community" was to be a "full partner" in the development of the plans. An important criterion in evaluating the plans is "the extent to which the affected community" and its "community-based organizations . . . have participated in [its] development . . . and their commitment to implementing it."[24] Regulations require that applicants identify the community groups participating in the development of the plan; explain how they were chosen to participate; describe their history; show that they are, collectively, representative of the full range of the community; and "describe the role of the participants in the creation, development, and future implementation of the plan."[25]

The Empowerment Zone idea combines themes from both Redevelopment and Community Action while it attempts to respond to the salient criticisms of both. Like Redevelopment, it seeks to encourage coordination of large-scale public and private investment. It has, however, a considerably broader vision of investment that includes social services as well as physical improvements. Most importantly, it defines the goals of the program in terms of benefit to the community, which it identifies with its current residents,[26] and mandates broad community

23. "Empowerment Zone/Enterprise Community Initiative." Available from: http://www.hud.gov/cpd/ezec/ezecinit.html (visited 22 May 2000). The initial round of designates was to receive a total of $1.5 billion in grants and $2.5 billion in tax benefits over a ten-year period.

24. 26 USC 1391(f); 24 CFR 597.201(c).

25. 24 CFR 597.200(d). "What sets this initiative apart from previous urban revitalization is that the community drives the decision-making," HUD's Web site, cited in note 23, asserts. An assessment of early efforts of the first round of designates finds mixed results in terms of community participation: Marilyn Gittell, Kathe Newman, Janice Bockmeyer, and Robert Lindsay, "Expanding Urban Opportunity: Urban Empowerment Zones," 33 *Urban Affairs Review* 530 (1998).

26. For example, 24 CFR 597.201.

participation. The social service themes and emphasis on community participation resonate with the Community Action Program. The programs, however, do not bypass local government to fund community groups directly: Applications for Empowerment Zone status must come from government entities.[27] The program gives state and local governments material inducements to support and cooperate with community groups by making such support and cooperation the central eligibility criterion for benefits. Moreover, in contrast to the Community Action Program, the Empowerment Zone program does not contemplate support for a single organization to mobilize and represent the entire community; it assumes that multiple community-based organizations will be involved, with no one of them necessarily pre-eminent.

A further reassertion of community-action themes at the federal level came with the 1998 revision to the Community Services Block Grant program, which provides funds to local governments for a panoply of social programs. The statute describes the purpose of the program this way: "to provide assistance to states and local communities, working through a network of local action agencies and other neighborhood-based organizations" for poverty alleviation and community revitalization. It prescribes that specific expenditures be coordinated under a general plan formulated with "maximum participation of residents of the low income communities and members of the groups served."[28]

Housing

The model of public housing institutionalized in the National Housing Act of 1937 involved rental housing constructed, owned, and operated by local public-housing authorities (PHAS). The Housing Act created a system of federal financial assistance to local PHAS for building and maintaining such housing under guidelines enforced by federal authorities, currently the Department of Housing and Urban Development. The guidelines restrict eligibility for housing to applicants who meet specified measures of low- or moderate-income status and restrict the rent charged to residents to (currently) 30 percent of the household's income.

In the 1970s, a different model designed to enlarge both tenant choice

27. 24 CFR 597.200.
28. 42 USC 9901.

and private market incentives was introduced. Under the "tenant-based Section 8" program, a local agency distributes certificates to eligible low-income applicants. The certificate obligates the agency to pay a portion of the applicant's rent on a qualifying apartment leased from a private landlord. The portion is currently the difference between an amount intended to approximate the market value of the leasehold and 30 percent of the certificate holder's income. The holder then pays 30 percent of her income to the landlord. The holder has to find a landlord with a suitable apartment willing to accept the certificate and enter into a triangular relation with the holder and the administering agency.[29]

The conventional model of PHA-owned and operated housing has fallen into steadily increasing disfavor since the 1960s. Some of the complaints focus on a particular physical configuration that is now discredited—the large high-rise located in a desolate area of concentrated poverty. Projects of this sort have long been considered breeding grounds for crime and other social pathology. This view has led to a reorientation of public housing design toward smaller, lower, more attractive, and more dispersed projects. Some of the older high-rise projects have been demolished, and HUD is funding the demolition or rehabilitation and redesign of others. PHAs continue to be active in the development of the newer style of projects, and they play important roles in HUD's demolition and rehabilitation programs.

However, another set of criticisms questions the efficacy of PHAS more generally. PHA-owned housing is substantially more costly to build and maintain than comparable private housing, and notwithstanding the greater costs, it is often poorly maintained, sometimes horrendously so. The prevalent explanation points to the familiar limitations of public bureaucracy—poor incentives and information. PHAs have been monopolists largely immune to market pressures and highly vulnerable to political pressures that compromise efficiency. They have been organized in a centralized fashion that concentrates discretion at the top among administrators with limited knowledge of conditions in the projects they manage.

Even though the matter is controversial, many do believe that programs of tenant-based private housing assistance have not performed

29. U.S. Department of Housing and Urban Development, *Opting In: Renewing America's Commitment to Affordable Housing* (April 1999), 1–8.

better.[30] This model does not directly produce new housing, and critics assert that private supply of low-end housing is not strongly responsive to the increased demand induced by the certificates. Moreover, the certificate model has incentive and information problems of its own. The administering agency has to estimate the market value of the leasehold to calculate the proper subsidies. It has no market incentive to get things right, and it has limited information. Because of resource constraints, the agencies set uniform levels across broad geographical areas. They are thus certain to get the figures wrong for many apartments, and may well do so for most. To the extent that the standards underestimate the market value of minimally adequate apartments, the subsidy is not enough to induce landlords to rent to certificate holders. Thus, a substantial number of those awarded certificates—between 20 and 40 percent, various studies suggest[31]—return their certificates unused because they cannot find appropriate housing. To the extent that the standards overestimate market rents, subsidies are excessive, and resources are wasted. "Estimates of the amount HUD pays above market run as high as $1 billion per year."[32] The tenant has no incentive to search or bargain for a lower rent, because the difference between 30 percent of her income and the standard is paid by the program.[33]

The first Bush administration, under HUD Secretary Jack Kemp, and

30. Jenifer J. Curhan, "The HUD Reinvention: A Critical Analysis," 5 *Boston University Public Interest Law Journal* 239, 243–45 (1996).

31. Ibid., 250–51, and sources cited in notes 92–97 therein.

32. HUD, *Opting In*, 22.

33. A third approach is "project-based" private housing assistance. Here the government subsidizes the construction or rehabilitation of privately owned housing in return for an agreement by the owner to rent only to eligible tenants at specified rents for a specified period. Such programs are designed to directly increase supply, but they suffer from information problems similar to and, in some respects, more severe than those in the "tenant-based" approach. In "project-based" assistance, contracts typically run for twenty years or more, rather than the two or three years characteristic of "tenant-based" assistance. If the subsidy turns out to be too low and rents are insufficient to cover costs, the owner, whose obligations are usually nonrecourse and undercollateralized, can insist on a bailout or simply walk away. Thus, in the depressed market of the 1970s, mass defaults and abandonments created a crisis. However, if the subsidy turns out to be higher than necessary, the owner recovers excess profits during the term of the contract, and if there is substantial appreciation, he can escape the use restrictions at the end of the term and capture the appreciation. Thus, in the boom market of the 1990s, HUD faced an "expiring use" crisis. See HUD, *Opting In*, 9–17.

the Clinton administration, under secretaries Henry Cisneros and Andrew Cuomo, responded to the dissatisfaction with these established models with a more or less common approach that looks simultaneously in two quite different directions. One, which looks away from the CED Movement, is voucherization. Vouchers resemble Section 8 certificates in their portability; recipients use them as subsidies in leases negotiated with private landlords. However, they differ from Section 8 certificates in that they provide for payment of a flat amount that does not vary with the negotiated rent and is not measured in terms of an estimate of market value. They are thus administratively simpler, and because the recipient bears full responsibility for the portion of the rent that exceeds the voucher amount, she has an incentive to seek the lowest rent. However, like certificates, vouchers do not directly increase housing supply and are thus unsatisfactory to those who believe the private market is not strongly responsive to demand-side subsidies. Moreover, vouchers operate through individual action by geographically dispersed recipients and thus do not induce the types of institutions and experiences associated with Community Economic Development.[34]

The other tendency in recent HUD programs resonates strongly with CED: A 1997 HUD publication interprets recent policy shifts as an abandonment of "traditional top-down" perspectives in favor a "community-building" approach encouraging "initiatives to create a network of partnerships among residents, management, and community organizations or enterprises."[35]

First, there is an emphasis on tenant participation in PHA projects that dates to the 1960s but has been strengthened in recent years. HUD's declared policy is to encourage resident participation "in all aspects of [a project's] overall mission and operation." HUD mandates that local PHAS recognize and consult with duly organized tenant councils. It stipulates various democratic procedural requirements for such councils and makes available technical assistance and material support for them.[36]

More ambitiously, HUD encourages resident management. Residents

34. Compare Curhan, "HUD Reinvention," arguing against vouchers, with Stephen B. Kinnaird, "Public Housing: Abandon HOPE, but Not Privatization," 103 *Yale Law Journal* 961 (1994), which argues for them.

35. U.S. Department of Housing and Urban Development, *Community Building in Public Housing: Ties That Bind People and Their Communities* v, 14 (April 1997).

36. 24 CFR 964.1–115.

are invited to form resident management corporations to bid to assume management responsibilities from the PHA. The management corporations must be nonprofit corporations that meet specified requirements designed to insure accountability to tenants generally. Again, technical and material assistance is available to qualifying corporations.[37]

In the area of PHA construction, HUD is currently focusing its support on rehabilitation or demolition and replacement of "distressed" projects. Funds are allocated in a competitive process in which one of the requirements is a showing of consultation with tenants regarding the plan.[38]

Second, some HUD programs promote home ownership by low-income people in various ways, including the sale of PHA housing to tenants. The Bush administration entertained the idea of converting most of the PHA stock into ownership, but such plans now seem unrealistic, given the limited financial capacities of low-income people to finance such purchases and maintain the buildings. Nevertheless, some ownership programs continue to operate. The ownership interests created by such programs typically manifest, at least temporarily, the equity limitations characteristic of CED property rights. Moreover, they are most commonly collective ownership interests in which the residents exercise their rights through cooperative corporations or homebuyers' associations.[39]

Third, many HUD programs now combine housing with services or financial assistance designed to help residents achieve economic self-sufficiency. These programs often have a community focus. HOPE VI, the major revitalization program, requires that 10 percent of its grants be used for services such as job training and placement, day care, and substance-abuse counseling. Residents often have responsibility for developing and, occasionally, for administering these plans.[40] HUD's Tenant Opportunity Program provides funding and technical assistance for business activities of residents.[41] Section 3 of the Housing and Urban Development Act of 1968 requires that PHA construction projects ac-

---

37. 24 CFR 964.120–50.

38. 24 CFR 971 *et seq.*

39. See 42 USC 1437aaa–1437aaa8; 24 CFR 92.2, 92.254(a), 572.130.

40. Bennett Hecht, *Developing Affordable Housing: A Practical Guide for Nonprofit Organizations* 262–63 (2d ed., 1999).

41. 24 CFR 964.200.

cord an employment preference to project residents and a procurement preference for resident-owned businesses.[42]

Perhaps the most significant aspect of recent housing policy for the CED Movement is the increased importance of nonprofit (typically, CDC) entrepreneurialism. Since the 1980s, direct federal support for new construction under PHA and project-based private programs has dwindled. Directly supported production is now barely sufficient to replace units being demolished. Net additions to the affordable stock depend on the efforts of private producers.

The major current sources of support for affordable private-housing development make special provision for nonprofit producers. The HOME program legislated in 1992 makes grants to state and local governments that can be put to a broad range of uses in increasing home ownership and affordable housing options for low-income people. The program is budgeted at $1.65 billion for the 2001 fiscal year and is expected to result in the production of 92,064 units of housing.[43] At least 15 percent of HOME allocations within each jurisdiction must be set aside for "community housing development organizations," which are defined as non-profit organizations engaged in affordable housing development that maintain "accountability, through significant representation on [their] governing board[s] and otherwise, to low income community residents, and to the extent practicable, to low income beneficiaries" of its activities. HOME funds can also be used to provide operating support to such organizations.[44]

Other HUD programs also focus support on nonprofit developers. A program enacted in 1990 to preserve privately owned housing constructed with project-based assistance on which use restrictions are expiring makes available funds for the purchase of the housing by applicants who will commit to long-term restrictions. The statute designates nonprofits, along with government agencies and resident councils, as "priority purchasers" who have an exclusive right to bid for an initial period after the project is offered for sale.[45] Under a 1992 provision, residents' councils in PHA projects can apply to HUD to have manage-

42. 12 USC 1701u.

43. U.S. Office of Management and Budget (OMB), *Budget of the United States Government: Fiscal Year 2001*, 496.

44. 42 USC 12704(6), 12771.

45. 12 USC 4110.

ment transferred from the PHA; if private, the alternative managers must be nonprofits or joint ventures with nonprofit participation.[46]

The Low Income Housing Tax Credit, which since 1986 has been the single biggest source of subsidy for affordable housing, also makes special provision for nonprofit corporations. This program involves a tax expenditure, amounting to $3.2 billion and supporting production of 70,000 to 90,000 new units of affordable housing per year.[47] Developers sell the credits to corporate investors, who become limited partners, in return for capital contributions to the projects. Thus, even though nonprofits have no tax liability of their own to offset with the credits, they can make use of the credits in the same manner as for-profit developers. Although the credits offset federal taxes, the federal government allows the states to allocate them. State agencies allot them through a competitive application process in which both private and nonprofit developers are eligible. Seeking to enlarge the role of nonprofit developers, Congress mandated that each state must allocate at least 10 percent of its credits to projects with nonprofit developers.[48] In fact, nonprofit developers have received considerably larger portions of the credits in most areas. In California, for example, nearly half of tax credits were allocated to projects of nonprofit developers in the mid-1990s.[49]

An elaborate structure of intermediaries has grown up in recent years to support community-based nonprofit housing developers. Some of these institutions are government-sponsored entities (GSES)—corporations specially chartered by a legislature with boards that are wholly or partly publicly appointed. There is, for example, the federal Neighborhood Reinvestment Corporation and, typical of many state examples, the Massachusetts Housing Finance Corporation.[50] Other such institutions are nonprofits operating across many communities. Especially notable examples are the Enterprise Foundation and the Local Initiative

46. 42 USC 1437(w), (c), (f), (m).

47. HUD, "A New HUD: 1997 Consolidated Report." Available from: http://www.hud. gov./conrept.html; U.S. OMB, 216.

48. 26 USC 42(h)(6).

49. California Tax Credit Allocation Committee, *1993 Annual Report* (April 1994), 8. (Forty-three percent of federal credits and 50 percent of credits under affiliated state-funded programs were awarded to nonprofit sponsors in 1993.)

50. 42 USC 8101 *et seq.;* Massachusetts Special Laws, ch. S7, sec. 1 *et seq.*

Support Corporation.[51] Such institutions channel public funds or private charitable donations to provide financial and technical assistance to community-based developers. Sometimes they participate as equity partners; sometimes they make loans or grants for specific projects. They often make loans or grants for general organizational support. Sometimes they act as financial intermediaries in pooling or reselling securities issued in connection with affordable housing development.

The net effect of these initiatives is that community-based organizations now play a critical role—in some areas, the dominant role—in affordable housing development. For example, in New York City, PHAS account for about 3,000 new units per year; conventional for-profit developers account for 1,500 to 2,000 more, and 6,000 to 10,000 units are produced by "an infrastructure of nonprofit development groups, intermediaries, community development lending institutions, small private developers, homebuilders, and contractors—all of whom share a neighborhood focus, work on a small scale, and utilize a blend of public and private resources."[52]

Banking and Credit

Poor people's limited access to credit might be viewed as an unremarkable consequence of their poverty. Since the 1960s, however, credit insufficiency has come to be viewed in urban policy as in part a cause, rather than solely a consequence, of poverty. The availability of credit in low-income areas seems mediated by three distinct problems.

The first is race discrimination. "Redlining"—categorically restricting or precluding residential lending in minority neighborhoods—was openly practiced by banks and government agencies prior to the Fair Housing Act of 1968. Despite that statute and the subsequent Equal Credit Opportunity Act of 1975, studies continue to find that people of color, or people who reside in predominantly minority neighborhoods, are less likely to have success in applying for credit than white people and people in white neighborhoods in otherwise comparable economic

51. For an extensive list, with descriptions, see Hecht, *Affordable Housing,* 121–203, 212–19.

52. Kathryn Wylde, "The Contribution of Public–Private Partnerships to New York's Assisted Housing Industry," in *Housing and Community Development in New York City: Facing the Future* 77–78 (Michael Schill ed. 1999).

circumstances.[53] The findings are controversial because it is difficult to control for comparable economic circumstances, but they have been convincing to most within the CED Movement. The studies are amplified by a massive body of anecdotal evidence from people of color who have had bad experiences with the credit system.

There have been few major enforcement actions against lenders under the civil-rights statutes. Enforcement is limited by problems of proof. The same difficulty of separating economic from racial influences that troubles researchers constrains the courts. Moreover, the conventional *prima facie* case of credit discrimination involves a showing that minority applicants have been denied while economically similar, non-minority applicants have been approved. Thus, lenders that simply discourage minority applications—for example, by locating their branches far from minority communities or maintaining hours inconvenient for low-income working people—are hard to reach.[54]

The second problem is coordination. Because real estate investments support one another through local externalities, each lender has a material incentive to lend where others are lending and to avoid areas shunned by others. (The coordination problem explains only why some neighborhoods are shunned, not why they tend to be minority neighborhoods. Thus, if we credit the disparity studies, coordination seems more a complementary than an alternative explanation to racism.) We have seen that the Redevelopment process is designed to induce investment by eliciting complementary commitments, but this process is expensive and exceptional. Where there is no mechanism for insuring complementary investments, poor impressions of a neighborhood can become self-reinforcing.

The third explanation concerns information. People with capital to lend tend to be socially distant from low- and moderate-income people and the neighborhoods they live in. This distance may make it difficult for the lenders to assess the creditworthiness of these applicants and the

---

53. Douglas S. Massey and Nancy A. Denton, *American Apartheid: Segregation and the Making of the Underclass* 50–7, 105–9 (1993).

54. There have been suggestions that branching decisions that discourage minority credit applications may trigger Equal Credit Opportunity Act liability, but they are controversial. See the discussion of the *Chevy Chase* decree in Jonathan Macey and Geoffrey Miller, *Banking Law and Regulation*, 207–10 (2d ed. 1997).

value of their collateral.[55] Of course, lenders can hire people to make such judgments for them, but the same social distance that impedes their assessment of credit applicants may make finding such agents difficult for them. Through research and experimentation, a lender can acquire the knowledge of a socially distant community she needs to make reliable judgments of creditworthiness. She may be reluctant, however, to invest in such research and experimentation for fear that she will not recover its costs. If others can observe the results of her efforts, and hence get the benefit of them without contributing to the cost, they can compete away her gains.

These three perspectives suggest that an effective response to credit scarcity in poor communities should not depend on difficult matters of proof, should encourage coordination and the focusing of multiple investments, and should address the exceptionally severe asymmetries of information that impede assessment of creditworthiness in such communities. The two most important recent initiatives in this area take important steps toward these goals. These are the Community Reinvestment Act, enacted by Congress in 1977 and strengthened by new implementing regulations in 1995, and the Community Development Banking and Financial Institutions Act of 1994, one of the most touted elements of the Clinton administration's domestic program. Each of these measures has supported the trends and institutions of the CED Movement.

Whereas the support of the Community Development Banking and Financial Institutions Act is direct, that of the Community Reinvestment Act (CRA) is circuitous. The CRA ascribes to any bank that receives federal deposit insurance a "continuing and affirmative obligation to help meet the credit needs of the local communities in which [it is] chartered." The obligation applies to "the entire community, including

---

55. There is a coordination problem with respect to information, too. To be useful, collateral has to be valued. With real estate collateral, one of the most important types of information about the value of a particular property is the value of surrounding properties. Thus, real estate appraisals, like real estate investments, generate positive externalities. The more appraisals we have of neighboring properties, the more reliably we can value the property we are interested in. This is another reason that banks like to lend where others are lending: Michael Klausner, "Market Failure and Community Investment: A Market-Oriented Alternative to the Community Reinvestment Act," 143 *University of Pennsylvania Law Review* 1561, 1569–70 (1995).

low- and moderate-income neighborhoods, consistent with the safe and sound operation of such institution." The statute, however, does not further specify the obligation, simply directing the regulators to "assess" each institution's compliance.[56]

The regulations provide some structure to the assessment. Banks must define an "assessment area" that includes their major activities and does not gerrymander out minority and low-income communities. Ratings are based on lending, investment, and service activities within the area, with lending activities weighing twice as much as the other two. Among the factors considered in assessing lending are the ratio of loans made within the assessment area to deposits (the "loan-to-deposit ratio"), the percentage of loans in the assessment area (the "concentration ratio"), the percentage of census tracts within the assessment area in which loans were made (the "penetration ratio"), and the percentage of loans made to low- and moderate-income borrowers and to borrowers within census tracts with low or moderate average incomes. The "investment test" measures the bank's support either through grants or through equity investments to institutions focused on the needs of low- and moderate-income residents of its assessment area, such as credit unions, small-business–loan funds, and affordable housing developers. The "service test" looks at such factors as the accessibility of branches and ATMs in low- and moderate-income neighborhoods and the provision of specialized services, such as credit counseling or homebuyer education, to low- and moderate-income customers. All these factors are added up to provide an overall numerical score, which is then translated into one of five ratings ranging from "Outstanding" to "Substantial Noncompliance."[57]

Notwithstanding the quantitative scores, the rating process depends largely on debatable qualitative judgments, and the regulators are often accused of inconsistency, arbitrariness, and favoritism. Uncertainty is further increased by the statute's failure to specify a definite sanction for poor CRA performance. The statute provides only that the regulators consider such performance in deciding on a bank's application to open or relocate a branch, to merge with or acquire another bank, or to establish a bank holding company.[58] With pervasive restructuring in the

56. 12 USC 2901(a)(3), 2903(1).
57. 12 CFR part 25; Kenneth Thomas, *The CRA Handbook* 379–419 (1999).
58. 12 USC 2902(3), 2903(a)(2).

industry, such regulatory approvals have been often sought in recent years. Few applications have been denied on the grounds of poor CRA performance.[59] However, the stakes in such proceedings are often so large that even a tiny probability of denial, or even of delay, has proved enough to motivate many banks to strive for a respectable CRA rating. The motivation was intensified by the 1995 regulations, which appeared to signal an intention by the regulators to enforce more vigorously.

By one estimate, the CRA induced $35 billion in lending and investment in traditionally under-served communities between its enactment in 1977 and 1993.[60] This figure was dwarfed by a series of CRA commitments in following years. In 1998, Treasury Secretary Robert Rubin estimated total CRA commitments in the preceding four years at $355 billion. Shortly after he spoke, a single CRA agreement, arising from the merger of Nationsbank and Bank of America, produced a $350 billion commitment over ten years for low- and moderate-income lending and investment.[61]

For our purposes, two aspects of the CRA structure are most notable. First, the duties CRA creates are explicitly to "local communities" and "neighborhoods," understood in the precise CED sense to mean primarily the residents of small, geographically bounded areas. Second, the vague and indirect enforcement structure of the act creates a vital role for community-based organizations. Community groups organized around economic development issues are, aside from the banks, the major source of information for and pressure on the regulators in the ratings process. These groups can intervene in regulatory application proceedings to raise CRA issues. They also use low CRA ratings to generate bad public relations for local banks. Kenneth Thomas describes the

59. Of 105,000 applications between 1977 and 1993, only 31, or .03 percent, were denied on CRA grounds, though the rate rises to about 1 percent if one considers only contested applications. Thomas, *CRA Handbook*, 87–92.

60. Senate Banking, Housing, and Urban Affairs Committee Report no. 103–69, 28 October, 1993; *U.S. Code Congressional and Administrative News* 1881, 1891, 103d Cong., 2d Sess. (1994).

61. Paul Grogan and Tony Proscio, *Comeback Cities: A Blueprint for Urban Neighborhood Revival* 58, 110 (2000); Alex Schwartz, "From Confrontation to Collaboration? Banks, Community Groups, and the Implementation of Community Reinvestment Agreements," 9 *Housing Policy Debate* 631 (1998).

CRA process as a regulatory "triangle" consisting of regulators, banks, and community groups.[62]

The CRA prompts many banks to engage in a variety of routine, ongoing negotiations and collaborations with community-based organizations, but its most visible consequences can be seen in settlements connected to regulatory applications for mergers or acquisitions in which consortia of groups agree not to oppose the application in return for community development commitments. Such settlements can involve promises to lend specific amounts or to make loans on specified terms in low- and moderate-income neighborhoods, to open or refrain from closing branches or ATMs, to make investments or contributions to economic development projects, and to provide support to community-based organizations. An example is the commitment made by Washington Mutual in its contested acquisition of Great Western Bank in 1997. In apparent response to the efforts of two consortia of community-based organizations, the Greenlining Coalition and the California Reinvestment Committee, Washington Mutual promised to lend at least $70 billion over ten years on specified conditions with low- and moderate-income neighborhoods in its post-merger assessment areas; to make charitable contributions amounting to at least 2 percent of its pretax income; to close branches in low- and moderate-income areas only under specified conditions; to meet regularly with leaders of community-based organizations over CRA issues; and to introduce in one area a new checking account without fees or minimum balances.[63]

Thus, a critical byproduct of the CRA's effort to enhance credit in low-income neighborhoods is the empowerment of community-based organizations. From the community's perspective, because CRA benefits correlate with the strength of community-based organization, the act creates a strong inducement to form and support such organizations. From the organization's point of view, the act makes it possible to extract resources from the banks that support the organization directly, when the resources go to it and its projects, and indirectly, when it gets local credit for bringing resources to the community.

The second of the two recent major federal initiatives is the Commu-

62. Thomas, *CRA Handbook,* ix.
63. Ibid., 119–20. Schwartz, "Confrontation," discusses anecdotal and statistical evidence that CRA agreements between banks and community groups have increased credit in disadvantaged neighborhoods.

nity Development Financial Institutions Fund (CDFI). The fund's main activity is providing grants, loans, equity capital, and technical assistance to "community development financial institutions." Such institutions are defined as nongovernmental entities committed to community development that serve "an investment area or targeted population" and "maintain, through representation on [a] governing board or otherwise, accountability to members of its investment area or target population." Among the factors to be weighed favorably in considering applications is the extent to which the applicant is "community-owned or community-governed."[64]

In enacting the bill, Congress mentioned the following types of institutions as embraced by its CDFI definition:[65]

—Community development banks. These are insured depositary institutions with lending strategies oriented toward community development goals. The best-known bank of this kind is South Shore Bank in Chicago, a widely admired institution credited with turning around a declining working-class neighborhood.

—Community development credit unions. Credit unions, as we will further discuss later, are financial cooperatives; in community development credit unions, the majority of the members are low-income people. Congress estimated that about 150 such institutions existed when it passed the act.

—Community development loan funds. These are nonprofit organizations funded by donations or capital provided on favorable terms by socially conscious lenders or investors to make loans for affordable housing or for job or business development in distressed communities.

—Micro-enterprise funds. This is another type of nonprofit fund specializing in modest loans to very small businesses.

—Community development corporations. This broad term embraces institutions engaged in planning, entrepreneurial, or management activities involving community economic development. Congress specifically mentions "multi-bank community development corporations," in which banks pool funds to make CRA loans and investments, some of which they may be prohibited from making directly.

64. 12 USC 4702(5)(A), 4706(a)(11).

65. Senate Report 103–69, at 1894–6. See generally Rochelle Lento, "Community Development Banking Strategy for Revitalizing Our Communities," 27 *University of Michigan Journal of Law Reform* 773 (1994).

The basic premises of the CDFI program are those of the CED Movement. CDFIs are defined in terms of a focus on a community and accountability to its members. The core CED conception of a community defined in terms of residence and geographical proximity is included in the definition of CDFI, though the definition ranges somewhat more broadly to include communities defined in terms of a target population with shared social or economic characteristics, as well as in terms of a geographical area. It is also possible that a community focused on a particular area might include nonresidents—for example, employees and business owners. For-profit organizations and nonprofits are eligible. In practice, most beneficiaries of the program have been organizations with a geographical focus or that provide assistance primarily to organizations with a geographical focus, often defined in terms of residence. The majority have been nonprofits.[66]

A less prominent but still important federal player in this field is the Small Business Administration, which administers a range of programs providing credit, technical assistance, and procurement preferences in federal contracting or federally subsidized state contracting. (Procurement preferences take various forms. They can allow the relevant agency to award a contract to a preferred bidder even though her bid is not the lowest, require a general contractor to award a specified percentage of the project to preferred subcontractors, or provide a financial reward for awards to preferred bidders.) Eligibility for some of these programs is defined principally in terms of business size; other programs require an additional showing of "economic and social disadvantage." Although these criteria are not specifically framed in CED terms, they do include some CED activities. Community development corporations are specifically designated as eligible intermediaries for support in the Small Business Administration's Microloan Demonstration Program,[67] and they benefit from an exception in the federal procurement-preference program for "socially and economically disadvantaged" people.[68] An applicant for certification as an enterprise qualifying for the preference must normally show that the individuals who control the enterprise meet the criteria of social and economic disadvantage. However, an enterprise

66. See the CDFI fund's Web site. Available from: http://www.treas.gov./cdfi/ (visited 6 June 2000).
67. 13 CFR 120.701(e) (1).
68. 13 CFR 124.3, 124.105–6, 124.111.

controlled by a community development corporation need not make this showing. A CDC is defined for this purpose in part as a nonprofit organization "responsible to the residents of the area it serves."[69]

At the state level, there are several agencies analogous to the federal CDFI, including, for example, the Illinois Community Development Finance Corporation,[70] the Massachusetts Community Development Finance Agency, [71] and the Urban and Community Development Program of the New York State Urban Development Corporation.[72] A broad range of private nonprofit organizations provide similar support.

Job Training and Placement

Job training and placement efforts for low-income people became salient in the 1990s, as federal welfare reform sought to eliminate long-term eligibility for employable applicants and shunt them into jobs.

American job training and placement programs have not performed well. The most salient criticism is a failure to coordinate these efforts with demand in the job market.[73] The programs have been poorly informed about private-sector job opportunities. They have tended to teach skills for jobs that are not the ones in demand, or to teach skills that are too abstract or too narrow to fit usefully with employers' needs.

The main responsibility for delivering training has been given to local public institutions—high schools and community colleges. Such institutions have had trouble coordinating their programs with private employers. This may reflect an ambivalence within these institutions about the commitment to vocational education, as opposed to preparing students for four-year liberal-arts colleges. It may reflect a suspicion on the part of private employers of government.

The need to induce more private-sector participation prompted Congress in 1982 to mandate "private industry councils" representing

69. 13 CFR 124.3. In addition, the CDC must have received assistance under the Community Services Program of 42 USC 9805, which is available only to organizations addressing the "problems of low-income neighborhoods."

70. Ch. 315 Illinois Compiled Statutes Annotated 15/2.

71. Massachusetts General Laws, c. 40F.

72. New York Consolidated Laws, Unconsolidated Laws sec.s 6254, 6255.

73. Paul Osterman, *Employment Futures: Reorganization, Dislocation, and Public Policy* 92–107 (1988).

local employers in the design and implementation of federally supported job training programs. But private-industry participation has
proved neither as easy to get nor as invariably productive as was once
expected. Opening the program to employer participation does not
guarantee that the employers who participate will be those with the
most attractive jobs or the ones whose training needs provide the most
benefits to trainees. Some types of training are more beneficial to employers than employees. This is notably true of training in skills narrowly relevant to only a single job or firm, as opposed to more general
skills relevant to a broad range of jobs. Some employers may prefer to
steer programs to narrow skills because that is what they need, even
though workers would benefit more from general training. Moreover, a
danger exists that employers will use the program not to increase training resources, but to substitute for training they would otherwise have
to do, and pay for, themselves.[74]

Another limitation of traditional institutions arises from the fact,
emphasized in the social science literature of recent years, that formal
training and certification play a far less important role in the allocation of many jobs than informal referral and vouching by incumbent
workers. These workers are in a good position to know about openings
and to vouch credibly for the reliability of the relatives and acquain-
tances they refer to the employer. This process typically rests on kin or
ethnic networks from which some groups, especially African Americans, are excluded. A public program aspiring to introduce previously
bypassed groups into such jobs would need to develop fairly thick
knowledge and relationships with both job-seekers and employers. It
seems doubtful that the community colleges have either the aptitude or
flexibility to do this.[75]

Community-based nonprofits supported by public funds have
achieved the most noted job training successes of recent years, usually in
alliance with community colleges or other public agencies and private

74. Bennett Harrison and Sandra Kanter, "The Political Economy of States' Job-
Creation Business Incentives," 46 *Journal of the American Institute of Planners* 424, 429
(October 1978).
75. For a discussion of the problem of isolation from job-allocation networks and of a
moderately successfully attempt by a CDC to remedy it, see Philip Kasinitz and Jan
Rosenberg, "Missing the Connection: Social Isolation and Employment on the Brooklyn Waterfront," 43 *Social Problems* 180 (1996).

employers. The nonprofits typically play a coordinating role with respect to government and for-profit participants and provide or design a kind of training better tailored to both the needs of individual trainees and the shifting demands of the job market than public institutions have been able to offer.[76] Perhaps the most highly regarded example is the Center for Employment Training (CET) in San Jose, California, which has developed a training model that has been replicated with federal support in several other places and adduced as a model in the Clinton administration's welfare-reform initiative. The basic idea behind CET is to create an individually customized program that combines general education, in-class skills training, and sheltered work experience.

However, CET has not played a further role that the labor economist Paul Osterman has suggested community-based organizations might play in the labor market: bringing political pressure to bear on local employers to improve wages and working conditions. Osterman suggests that market conditions leave some employers with a range of options as to how to use and compensate workers and that local political pressure can sometimes influence them to adopt the strategies more beneficial to workers, those that involve higher compensation and more training and responsibility. He thinks that CET cannot play this role because its community base is too weak. By contrast, he points to Project QUEST, an employment program in San Antonio, Texas, affiliated with Communities Organized for Public Service, a network of community organizations that has achieved citywide political clout. QUEST has successfully negotiated with local employers for commitments, not only to employ graduates of its programs, but also to improve the compensation of the jobs involved.[77]

Recent federal legislation acknowledges and encourages the role of community-based organizations by mandating that state plans under federally supported training programs reflect their participation.[78]

76. Bennett Harrison, Marcus Weiss, and Jon Gant, *Building Bridges: Community Development Corporations and the World of Employment Training* (Ford Foundation, 1995).
77. Paul Osterman, *Securing Prosperity: The American Labor Market: How It Has Changed and What to Do about It* 136–39, 165–66 (1999).
78. See 29 USC 2832(b)(2), which requires that states establish "local workforce investment boards" to oversee various federally supported training programs with representation from, inter alia, "community-based organizations."

Welfare Reform

For decades, the welfare system was charged with inducing a kind of addictive dependence, sapping the ambition and initiative of its beneficiaries. The claim, always prominent in popular discussion, received support from a large body of academic literature in the 1970s and 1980s, though the experts remained divided.[79] Popular opinion became overwhelmingly committed to this portrayal and led to the dramatic cutbacks and restructuring in 1996.

One interesting aspect of the growing discontent with welfare is that it was partially embraced by some prominent leaders of minority and poor communities. Few supported the cutbacks, but many expressed sympathy for the dependency critique and spoke with sympathy about the importance of cultivating a "work ethic" among inner-city young people. Moreover, the attacks on welfare throughout the 1970s and 1980s emphasized how vulnerable political reliance on welfare made poor communities. Thus, discontent with welfare was associated with increased interest in efforts to expand work and business opportunities.[80]

The most important of the 1996 reforms turned the major cash assistance program—Aid to Families with Dependent Children (AFDC)—from an entitlement program committed to funding benefits at a specified level for anyone meeting the eligibility standards into a fixed block-grant program ostensibly giving states more discretion with respect to implementation but subjecting them to heightened requirements for moving recipients into work.

From the perspective of the CED Movement, the reform was significant in two respects. First, it channeled administrative effort and resources away from providing cash assistance toward job training and development, and even business development. Second, it enlarged state discretion to conduct poor support through community-based organi-

79. My own view is that the claims are largely implausible for reasons set out in Joel Handler, *The Poverty of Welfare Reform* (1995).

80. For example, Floyd Flake, former congressman and pastor of the Allen African Methodist Episcopal Church in Queens, New York, a major CED player, told his congregation, "There was a time when we lived without [welfare], and if they take it away, we can live without it again." Flake argues that the self-esteem that comes with a "good work ethic" is one of the best defenses against the psychological pressures of racism. James Traub, "Floyd Flake's Middle America," *New York Times Magazine* (19 October 1997), 60.

zations. The reform legislation provided that all services and benefits under the successor program to AFDC could be provided either directly or "through contract with charitable, religious, or private organizations."[81] The explicit legitimation of contracting with religious organizations was the most controversial aspect of this provision. Whatever one thinks of its merits, it reinforces the trends associated with CED, because religious organizations are usually strongly community based.[82] In companion legislation revising the Community Services Block Grant program to complement welfare reform, Congress explicitly emphasized the centrality of "local action agencies and other neighborhood-based organizations" as providers and mandated "maximum participation of the residents" of the communities served.[83]

As with housing, however, another current in the welfare-reform debate flows away from CED themes. This current includes proposals for employment subsidies that supplement wages, such as the present Earned Income Tax Credit, "individual development accounts" that match savings, and relatively unconditional "stakeholder" grants.[84]

81. 42 USC 604(a).

82. On the religious-organization provision, see Paul Ambrosius, " 'The End of Welfare as We Know It' and the Establishment Clause," 28 *Columbia Human Rights Journal* 135 (1996). The tendency of churches to organize on a community basis is discussed in chapters 5 and 6.

83. 42 USC 9901 (Community Opportunities, Accountability, and Training and Educational Services Act of 1998, sec. 201, 112 Stat. 2702.)

84. Wage supplements reward work by paying benefits in proportion to wages earned within a specified, usually low-income, range. The Earned Income Tax Credit is an example. See Edmund Phelps, *Rewarding Work* (1997).

"Individual development accounts" reward savings by matching amounts put aside by the beneficiary. Typically, the accounts must be intended and used for housing, business investment, or post-secondary education. A variety of small-scale experiments are under way. See the Corporation for Enterprise Development's Web site at http://www.cfed.org. In connection with welfare reform, Congress authorized the states to use federal welfare grants to support such programs run by either public agencies or nonprofits. 42 USC 604.

"Stakeholder" grants contemplate a one-time transfer of a large sum to the beneficiary at the outset of adulthood. Their use is less restricted or supervised than that of individual development accounts, and the grant is not conditioned on work or savings. Bruce Ackerman and Anne Alstott, their most ambitious proponents, would have the state give every citizen $80,000 at age eighteen as long as she has graduated from high

These programs typically contemplate relatively centralized government administration, and they are not designed to strengthen the recipients' ties to a local community. Anne Alstott associates them with "mobility policies" intended to enhance recipients' ease of exit from their present communities into new ones.[85]

Community Health Care

A variety of public and private programs support delivery of health care through community-based organizations in low-income communities.[86] Among the rationales for this approach, two are especially pertinent. First, people in low-income areas seem especially vulnerable to neglect and abuse by for-profit health care providers. Such communities have difficulty attracting able physicians, and their members' relatively low levels of education and limited experience with health care impair their ability to negotiate with and monitor their doctors individually. Nonprofits sometimes have an advantage in attracting doctors motivated to give good care and have greater incentives to monitor certain aspects of quality.

Second, limited education and perhaps non-mainstream cultural backgrounds often lead poor people to seek preventive care less often than is desirable. They tend to rely on emergency care in ways that are both more expensive and less conducive to good health than certain patterns of preventive care. Thus, outreach and education are an exceptionally important part of the health care needs of poor communities. This requires various types of local knowledge—to identify health needs, design programs that are accessible to clients, and coordinate with institutions such as schools and workplaces. These tasks may be especially

---

school and does not have a serious criminal record. Bruce Ackerman and Anne Alstott, *The Stakeholder Society* (1999).

85. Anne Alstott, "Work versus Freedom: A Liberal Challenge to Employment Subsidies," 108 *Yale Law Journal* 967, 1007 (1999). Although these general-reform proposals imply centralized administration, a potential role for community-based nonprofits exists in "demonstration" projects, such as those authorized by Congress in 1998. Several community-based nonprofits are experimenting with them.

86. Lewis Solomon and Tricia Asaro, *Community-Based Health Care: A Legal and Policy Analysis,* 24 *Fordham Urban Law Journal* 235 (1997).

difficult for large, mainstream institutions to the extent that local residents are culturally distant from the mainstream. Community-based organizations have long specialized in developing such knowledge.

The most salient of the various community health efforts is the federal government's Community Health Center program, which provides grants and loan guarantees to nonprofit institutions that provide outpatient care to the residents of "medically underserved" geographical areas. To qualify as a health center, the organization must have a governing board that is representative of its service area and in which a majority are patients.[87]

Unlike the situation in the other policy areas discussed earlier, interest in community-based practice has not grown dramatically in health care in recent years. Nevertheless, the older programs continue, and some predict that disillusion with the current for-profit, managed care models will lead to a revival of interest in provision of health care by nonprofit community organizations.

Support for community health sometimes plays a significant role in community economic development. For example, the Stop 'n Shop supermarket developed by the Jamaica Plain Neighborhood Development Corporation shares its building with the Martha Eliot Health Center, which is supported by a Boston hospital and various federal and state programs. The inclusion of the health center made the project more attractive to various supporters, including the city of Boston, which donated the land, and the center drew on its own sources of support to share in the development and construction costs.[88]

87. 42 USC 254b(a), (b), (j)(3)(H). In 1996, Congress changed the designation of the supported institutions from "Community Health Centers" to "Health Centers," but it did not change the substantive requirements mentioned earlier.
88. The Brownsville Community Development Corporation of Brooklyn used novel economic-development practices, including an unprecedented use of state bond finance, in the course of establishing a major community health center. See Brian Glick with Matthew J. Rossman, "Neighborhood Legal Services as House Counsel to Community-Based Efforts to Achieve Economic Justice: The East Brooklyn Experience," 23 New York Review of Law and Social Change 105, 123–33 (1997).

Chapter 3 : Three Logics of Community Action

CED institutions have three salient functional characteristics:

—Relational density and synergy. CED efforts are designed to multiply the contexts and roles in which people confront one another. As the political process links political activity to residence, so CED links economic development to residence. By striving to internalize control over economic processes within the community, CED increases the number of linked roles that residents potentially play. People who might otherwise encounter one another only as neighbors now meet as well as employers and employees, sellers and consumers, property owners and property occupiers, planners and citizens, administrators and service recipients.

—Geographic focus. At the most mundane level, the physical community is a focal point, a convenient space to bring people together for multiple, varied encounters. More ambitiously, residential community can give physical expression to a sense of distinctive common culture. The new social policy now emphasizes the call of modern urbanism for space with "detail, identity, and a sense of place," as opposed to, for example, "the anonymity of much public housing that is divorced from its surroundings."[1]

1. U.S. Department of Housing and Urban Development, Office of Community Planning and Development, *A Guidebook for Community-Based Strategic Planning for Empowerment Zones and Enterprise Communities* 13 (Jan. 1994).

—Face-to-face encounters. CED efforts tend to replace remote impersonal relations—for example, between absentee owners and tenants or customers or distant bureaucrats and their charges—with face-to-face relations. In doing so, they extend to economic development generally a basic principle of city planning: that the physical structure of the urban environment should be configured so that "face-to-face interactions at the neighborhood level will be enhanced."[2] For example, Jane Jacobs's four principles of land-use planning—mixed use, short blocks, buildings of varying age, and density—are all designed to increase the number and variety of face-to-face encounters.[3]

There is no single dominant theory of CED. Rather, these programs rest on a variety of convergent rationales. They can be grouped in three clusters—economic, social, and political.

Economic

CED programs arise in part from dissatisfaction with bureaucracy. The principal economic complaint about bureaucracy is that bureaucrats have poor incentives and poor information. Because they do not have strong personal stakes in their decisions, their motivation to perform well is weak. Because power tends to reside at the top, while critical information is dispersed at the bottom, the key decision makers tend to be poorly informed.

The economist's stock alternative to bureaucracy is the market. But economists acknowledge that markets have incentive and information problems too, and they are more likely than bureaucratic organizations to be thwarted by difficulties that can be called coordination problems.[4] Market limitations with respect to incentives, information, and coordi-

2. Ibid.

3. Jane Jacobs, *The Death and Life of Great American Cities* 143–222 (1961). Short blocks are valued because they disperse foot traffic through areas that would otherwise be empty; old buildings are valued because they increase the range of economically viable uses and, hence, the diversity of people attracted to them.

4. On market failure in employment and business, see generally Paul Milgrom and John Roberts, *Economics, Organization, and Management* (1992); Paul Krugman, *Geography and Trade* 35–67 (1991). On market failure in housing, see Duncan Kennedy, "The Effect of the Warranty of Habitability on Low Income Housing: Milking and Class Violence," 15 *Florida State University Law Review* 485 (1989); Rolf Goetze, *Understanding Neighborhood Change* (1979).

nation seem especially important in the principal areas of CED activity—housing, job training, and job and business development in low-income communities. So the turn to CED reflects as well a sense of the limits of conventionally understood markets.

The market's ability to provide efficient incentives does not apply to externalities—the costs and benefits of activities that are not reflected in the prices faced by those who engage in them.

Externalities are unusually important in housing. According to some people, they are the whole ballgame. Real estate agents insist that the three most important determinants of the value of a residence are "location, location, and location," which implies that the value of your house depends more on what your neighbors do with their property, how they behave, and who they are than on any decision you make.

The unpriced consequences of property maintenance and investment decisions include conduct as well as physical conditions. For example, the "broken windows" approach to crime control asserts that even minor visible physical deterioration can have a psychological effect that encourages deviant behavior (which in turn feeds back to reduce maintenance and investment further).[5]

"Factor externalities" are another category. They involve activities that affect the costs of labor or supplies to businesses. When community colleges and private employers train workers in generally useful skills, they potentially lower the costs of other employers by enhancing the supply of qualified workers. Businesses often benefit from the local presence of workers with needed skills or of other businesses that supply needed services or products. They also benefit from the presence of other businesses in the same field to the extent that the businesses collectively can attract a better labor pool or a larger field of suppliers to the locality. The larger number of workers and suppliers may mean lower costs because of greater supply or economies of scale; it also creates possibilities of technological spillovers through knowledge shared either through cooperation or as workers move from firm to firm. Industrial districts such as Silicon Valley and the automobile manufacturing areas of De-

---

5. George Kelling and James Q. Wilson, "Making Neighborhoods Safe," *Atlantic Monthly* (February 1989), 46.

troit illustrate these phenomena. To a limited extent, such externalities seem susceptible to influence by public goods and land-use policy.

A notion related to but distinct from externality is complementarity. Individual investments are complementary when the productivity of each is greater when they are made simultaneously. An individual's efforts to get rid of cockroaches in an urban apartment or weeds on a suburban lawn will be more effective to the extent that neighbors make similar efforts. An investment in software that will improve the operation of a particular machine may increase the returns to investment of the machine.

Like externalities, complementarities involve benefits or costs to people other than the primary actor, but they differ in requiring that the beneficiary make investments of her own in order to capture the benefits, and increasing her incentives to make such investments. Externalities and complementarities may overlap, and it may be hard to distinguish the two phenomena. If your neighbors paint their houses, you will benefit simply because the neighborhood is more attractive (an externality effect); it may also be true that the benefit from painting your house will now be greater than it would have been if they had not painted theirs (a complementarity effect). This might be true because people value a house's consistency with the esthetic norms of the neighborhood.

An investment with complementarities has a potential leveraging effect by inducing complementary investments.

INFORMATION

I noted in chapter 2 the evidence that there are creditworthy people in low-income neighborhoods who cannot get mortgage loans. Probably the same point is true about business loans. There are also able workers who cannot get available jobs. These facts may reflect discrimination, but they may also reflect the difficulty lenders and employers have in distinguishing these people from superficially similar applicants who are not creditworthy or able. Lenders and employers have this problem with all credit and employment applicants, but it may be exceptionally difficult with low-income and minority applicants for two reasons:

1) These applicants have few assets. To the extent that an applicant can post assets as security for loan commitments, the lender has less need to rely on assessments of her reliability. Assets perform an infor-

national role, as well. An applicant who puts her own assets at risk by investing in a house or business or in training that fits her for particular jobs signals to others the seriousness of her belief that the investment is a sound one and her intention to act to make it work. Poor people are less able to substantiate their commitments in this way.

2) Lenders and employers may have more difficulty evaluating the applications of poor people because they are more socially distant. Their credit and employment histories look different, and superficially similar events may have different meanings for poor applicants than for more mainstream ones.

COORDINATION

Externalities and complementarities mean that the values of local investments are interdependent, and this means that protecting them often requires coordination. Painting my house will do little to improve its value if my neighbors all allow theirs to peel. In prosperous neighborhoods, informal coordination or shared optimism may be sufficient to induce optimal behavior. In poor neighborhoods, anxiety and pessimism often inhibit spontaneous coordination.

Indeed, poor neighborhoods are sometimes vulnerable to a kind of negative coordination—panics or downward spirals of disinvestment. People lose confidence and start to withdraw their capital or leave simply for fear that others will do the same. "Studies have shown that property owners are extremely sensitive to small signs of physical deterioration. . . . With every additional property owner who decides not to invest, it becomes increasingly likely that others will reach similar decisions, even if they would otherwise be disposed to maintain their buildings. At some point, a threshold is crossed, beyond which the pattern becomes self-reinforcing and irreversible."[6] Although everyone would prefer that all remain and continue to invest in the neighborhood, in the absence of some mechanism to insure each that the others will do so, people exit for fear of being the last one left behind.

The mirror image of the downward spiral of disinvestment is the speculative bubble in which prices spiral upward, as investors buy in the hope of a quick resale to other investors. Prices are driven, not by

6. Douglas S. Massey and Nancy A. Denton, *American Apartheid: Segregation and the Making of the Underclass* 131–32 (1993).

fundamental assessment of the value of the property to a user or occupier, but by expectations about what other speculators will be willing to pay. Bubbles can be temporarily self-sustaining in the manner of Ponzi schemes, but like Ponzi schemes, they must collapse at some point. The process does not cause physical deterioration directly, but some believe it deters tangible improvement and even maintenance. It may do so by bringing in purchasers with a short-term mentality who are interested solely in gain through financial transactions. In addition, the economic instability induced by bubbles makes calculating the profitability of investments difficult, so people may be inclined to defer projects until conditions settle down. Bubbles involve large transaction costs, and they can cause displacement of tenants.

Not all, or even most, housing-price inflation has the quality of a speculative bubble. Bubbles seem most likely to be operating when sharp increases are followed by sharp declines. Many observers of the Boston housing market have interpreted developments at various times in recent decades as at least partly bubbles.[7]

Bubbles are a kind of coordination problem. On average, people would be better off if everyone declined to participate. However, from any individual's point of view, if the others are going to participate, it may be hard to pass up an apparent opportunity to profit by selling before the burst. Moreover, the prospect of a burst may cause a downward spiral. At the same time that outsiders are rushing to buy before prices rise further, insiders, who may be more averse to risk and less affluent, may rush to sell before the crash.

Education also suffers from a well-known coordination problem: Employers may be reluctant to train workers for fear that the workers will leave before the costs of training have been recaptured. Workers may be reluctant to pay for training for fear that they will not find a job or will not keep one long enough to recover their costs.

AN EXAMPLE: SOUTH SHORE BANK

CED programs do not respond to these difficulties by abandoning markets or reverting to conventional bureaucracies. They create structures

7. Karl Case, "The Market for Single-Family Homes in the Boston Area," *New England Economic Review* (May–June 1986), 38; Peter Medoff and Holly Sklar, *Streets of Hope: The Fall and Rise of An Urban Neighborhood* 11–14 (1994); Goetze, *Understanding Neighborhood Change*, 11–26.

that combine and rearrange a variety of organizational attributes. However, at the center are usually community-based organizations characterized by multistranded relations, geographical focus, and face-to-face relations. These characteristics have some capacity to mitigate the problems of incentives, information, and coordination. They do so by facilitating informal negotiation and collective action. The geographical focus means that the membership will include people with tangible stakes in each other's activities and investments. Multistranded relations create economies of scope in the development of information; information generated through one strand can often be used in another strand. Face-to-face dealings enhance possibilities for both gaining information and negotiating coordination.

As an example of a CED institution that seems especially responsive to these economic problems, consider the South Shore Bank, founded in 1972 in what was then a seriously distressed neighborhood of Chicago.[8] A group of social activists was able to raise $3.2 million in philanthropic support to buy an existing commercial bank. The activists then proceeded to reorient the bank's practices to support a CED strategy.

The bank is owned by a nonprofit holding company that controls several for-profit subsidiaries and nonprofit affiliates. The City Lands Corporation, a for-profit company, develops residential real estate projects. The Neighborhood Institute, a nonprofit, operates training and social services programs. The institute has a subsidiary of its own, TNI Development Corporation, which also develops affordable housing. The Neighborhood Fund, a for-profit, is a minority-enterprise, small-business investment corporation licensed and supported by the Small Business Administration. Shorebank Advisory Services, a for-profit, provides consulting on development banking issues.

The bank's lending strategy has four especially interesting features. The first is "concentrated lending": The bank focuses its real estate lending on a specific community and within the community on specific areas targeted for development.[9] Second is "leverage": The bank tries to focus unsubsidized lending in a way that complements its affiliates' subsidized housing development. It makes loans to private, preferably small and

8. Ronald Grzywinski, "The New Old-Fashioned Banking," *Harvard Business Review* (May–June 1991), 87; Harvard Business School, *Shorebank Corporation* (No. 9–393–096, 27 April 1994).

9. Grzywinski, "New Old-Fashioned Banking," 94.

local, developers to build or rehabilitate housing near the subsidized projects its affiliates are developing. Development activities occur in mutually reinforcing "concentric rings" of private and NGO-led effort.[10]

Third, in addition to being geographically targeted, some of the bank's private lending is conditional. The bank initially limited its purchase-money lending for rental properties to borrowers planning to live on the premises. It eventually relaxed this requirement, but it has continued to insist that the borrower commit to rehabilitate the property. It will not lend to landlords who simply want to hold the property for speculative purposes or milk it to maximize short-term returns while permitting it to deteriorate.[11]

Finally, the bank's affiliates provide technical assistance to its local landlord borrowers on such matters as construction, maintenance, regulatory compliance, and accounting. Many of these borrowers are new landlords entering their first business venture. Experience in the training programs has developed face-to-face, mutually supportive relations among them. Two ethnically based networks of small landlords—one comprising African Americans; the other comprising recent Croatian immigrants—have developed; they maintain and continue to invest in small-scale, moderate rental property. The bank's founder insists that these people could not have been identified through conventional business methods: "Had we conducted a market survey in 1973 to get a sense of how many potential entrepreneurs we had in the community . . . the answer would have been 'none.' [These people were] invisible, and now they're an industry—the core of the South Shore's recovery."[12]

Here we have an institutional structure designed to facilitate coordination among private investments, of private with public investments, and of real estate investment with training opportunities. It also strives to canalize for-profit activity in ways most likely to produce positive externalities. And it generates the kind of multistranded relations that create economies of scope in information.

10. Ibid., 95.

11. New York City's "Neighborhood Entrepreneurs" program, which sells property acquired by the city through tax foreclosure to small private landlords, requires that the buyers be "based in one of [the low- and moderate-income] neighborhoods targeted by" the program. David Reiss, "Neighborhood Entrepreneurs Program in New York City," 5 *Journal of Affordable Housing and Community Development Law* 325, 330 (1996).

12. Ibid., 96.

Social

The sociologist's complaint about bureaucracy and markets is that they engender alienation—a sense of disconnection and ineffectuality. The remedy for alienation is empowerment—a pervasive term in CED rhetoric. The ideal of community associated with empowerment is significantly different from the romantic conception that influenced the 1960s left. The romantic conception connotes intimate, indiscriminate altruism. But the community of the CED Movement has more sober and restrained connotations. The most important of these connotations are captured in the sociological themes of "social capital" and the "Protestant ethic."

SOCIAL CAPITAL

Robert Putnam popularized the term "social capital" in a study vindicating de Tocqueville's claim about the democratic importance of associational life.[13] Comparing the performances of Italy's regional governments, he found that the large variation in quality correlated strongly with the scope and density of a region's associational activity. Regions with many broadly participatory civic institutions were able to induce a high level of governmental performance; those without them, were not.

The CED strategies are responsive to this notion. Multistranded relations induce people to encounter one another repeatedly in different but related capacities—as citizens, employers and employees, landowners and residents, business owners and customers. Each encounter is an opportunity to develop collaborative capacities, and there is a synergy among the relations. People's self-confidence, their knowledge of their neighbors, and their capacities for negotiation and deliberation spill over from one sector to another and hence develop cumulatively with collaboration across different areas. Moreover, CED strategies tend to increase the expectation of consistent repeat dealings among people whose encounters would otherwise be sporadic. This encourages collaborative effort by increasing the likelihood that particular acts of collaboration can be reciprocated, or particular acts of trespass sanctioned, by the beneficiary or victim in the future.

13. Robert Putnam, *Making Democracy Work* (1993); see Alexis de Tocqueville, *Democracy in America* 485–89 (J. P. Mayer and Max Lerner eds. 1966 [1835]).

As noted, the geographic focus of CED strategies creates a focal point for collaborative effort and gives physical expression to a sense of common interest and identity.

The face-to-face theme in CED is sometimes associated with a romantic celebration of the intrinsic superiority of personal over impersonal relations. More often, we see face-to-face relations valued as conducive to social capital. Part of the idea is that one is likely to be more understanding of and respectful toward the interests of people of whom one is personally aware. Another part is the suggestion that the sense of being observed creates a potentially healthy pressure to conform to local norms. This is the basis of Jane Jacobs's notion of "eyes on the street," the primary goal of her planning precepts. Safe and attractive neighborhoods are neighborhoods in which people are actually or potentially watching each other. The sense of safety comes in part from the probability that others will give assistance in the event of crisis. But it also rests in part on the belief that the experience of being watched itself inhibits deviance.

The CED strategies apply this principle to economic relations. They assume that one will be more scrupulous in fulfilling duties that are associated with face-to-face relations and they try to induce such relations. Consider the "peer lending" feature of the famous Grameen Bank, the widely replicated Bangladesh microcredit program that has a 98 percent repayment rate on loans to a huge class of rural women who had been written off as uncreditworthy by mainstream lenders. To apply for a loan from Grameen, an applicant has to assemble a group of five to ten comparably situated (though not necessarily previously acquainted) people. Loans are made to group members one at a time; all group members guarantee repayment of each loan, and no member can receive a loan until all prior ones are repaid. This structure works by converting an impersonal duty into a personal one.[14]

14. Lewis D. Solomon, "Microenterprise: Human Reconstruction in America's Inner Cities," 15 *Harvard Journal of Law and Public Policy* 191, 193–202 (1992) (describing the Grameen Bank); http://www.grameen-info.org (visited 23 June 1999). For examples of American microenterprise programs using peer-lending models, see the descriptions of the Womens' Self-Employment Project in Chicago in Solomon, "Microenterprise," at 202–6; and of the network of local programs in the Northeast supported by Working Capital. Lisa J. Servon, *Bootstrap Capital: Microenterprise and the American Poor* 67–73, 102–13 (1999).

THE NEW PROTESTANT ETHIC

Putnam speaks of social capital in the liberal rhetoric of solidarity and respect, and this rhetoric has been influential in the CED Movement. However, much CED rhetoric has a more hortatory tone. This rhetoric calls to mind less Putnam's bland liberalism than Max Weber's description of the Protestant ethic, in which an ethic of self-restraint links an exigent religious faith to economic acquisitiveness and initiative.[15]

Weber's successors have demonstrated that the Protestant ethic is neither pervasive in Protestantism nor unique to it.[16] But the idea that the spiritual orientation he identified can support capitalist economic activity seems powerfully illustrated in contemporary CED. It is no accident that faith-based organizations are among the most prominent CED activists. They are associated with Islamic and Catholic as well as with Protestant institutions. And the moral themes associated with the Protestant ethic have influenced secular CED practitioners, as well. These themes are discipline, surveillance, personal formality, and the valorization of wealth.

Weber emphasized that capitalist development required deferral of gratification and resistance to impulses. In a well-known elaboration, Clifford Geertz pointed out that this meant a constraint not only of selfish impulses, but also of altruistic ones. In a study of two Indonesian towns, he found economic development inhibited in one by the short-sighted aggressiveness of its merchants, and in the other by the strong sense of duty to share income on the part of the elite, which precluded capital accumulation.[17] Both these perspectives were represented in the "culture of poverty" literature on the American inner city. In the view that became popular among conservatives, the key problem was impulsive selfishness.[18] In an alternative view, the problem was a disposition to share, coupled with the pervasiveness of economic misfortune, which meant that some friend or relative always had a compelling claim on

15. Max Weber, *The Protestant Ethic and the Spirit of Capitalism* (Talcott Parsons trans. 1958).

16. Kurt Samuelsson, *Religion and Economic Action* (1957); Maxime Rodinson, *Islam and Capitalism* (1978).

17. Clifford Geertz, *Peddlers and Princes: Social Change and Economic Modernization in Two Indonesian Towns* (1963).

18. For example, Edward Banfield, *The Unheavenly City* (1970).

one's resources.[19] Either perspective lent itself to the conclusion that these communities might benefit from something like the norms of the Protestant ethic.

The culture of poverty debate and, indeed, virtually all critical discussion of culture and norms among the poor became anathema to liberals in the 1960s. It came to seem unacceptably paternalistic and imperialistic for professionals to prescribe moral norms to poor people. However, this liberal posture was undermined, first, by the coming to prominence of conservative social-policy elites who felt no such inhibitions, and second, by the embrace of critical moralism by some of the most effective leaders of poor communities.

Many of these leaders have been pastors. The Weberian rhetoric of discipline is prominent in their pronouncements. Summarizing an interview with Eugene Rivers of the Azusa Christian Community in Dorchester, Massachusetts (Rivers is famous for his work with indigent young people), George Packer writes, "For Rivers, discipline is everything, and it depends on faith."[20]

This theme is equally prominent in many secular projects. The first of the four principles of the Grameen Bank is "discipline."[21] (The other three are "unity, courage, and hard work.") The principles are elaborated in subsidiary precepts, the "16 Decisions," that make clear that discipline means a deferral of selfish gratification—for example, by saving and educating children—and a willingness to hold one's peers accountable. Members of peer borrower groups in Grameen-style micro-enterprise programs are made guarantors of one another's loans precisely so they will hold one another's feet to the fire.

HUD's manual "Community Building in Public Housing" insists on the importance of "enforcing community standards," then proceeds to give speedy eviction of derelict tenants as an example.[22] Amendments made in 1966 to the federal public-housing statutes encourage PHAS (public housing authorities) to institute an eviction policy called "One

19. Elliot Liebow, *Tally's Corner: A Study of Negro Streetcorner Men* 65–6 (1967); Carol Stack, *All Our Kin: Strategies for Survival in a Black Community* (1974).

20. George Packer, "A Tale of Two Movements," *The Nation* (14 December 1998), 19. See also Robert Worth, "Amazing Grace: Can Churches Save the Inner City?" 30 *Washington Monthly* 28 (January/February 1998).

21. Solomon, "Microenterprise," 218, n. 160.

22. HUD, *Community Building in Public Housing* 53–54 (April 1997).

Strike and You're Out" under which tenants who engage in criminal activity are promptly evicted; they are also encouraged to institute tough screening procedures to eliminate people with recent criminal convictions at the application stage.[23] They also mandate that PHAS require residents to perform six hours a month of uncompensated community service.[24]

Discipline is one of the principal themes of the job-readiness training provided by the widely replicated STRIVE program for disadvantaged youth. During the first half of the program, The clear message [is] "stick to the rules or leave." Some infractions [are] punished by small fines, but those who present . . . continuing problems [are] terminated ("fired" in the parlance of STRIVE) to maintain a sense of responsibility.[25]

Cooperative Home Care Associates, the worker-owned health care provider whose members are mostly former welfare recipients, has disciplinary rules that rival in severity those of the strictest capitalist employers:

> [Members] are warned once for allowing unknown visitors into a patient's home, then fired for a second infraction. They get one warning for failing to show up for work at a patient's home; missing a second appointment is cause for dismissal. In cases where less than standard care is noticed by supervisors, or called to their attention by patients, the firm has a four-step discipline procedure. One breach prompts informal supervisory encouragement to improve. If the problem happens a second time, members are warned in writing. If the same problem happens a third time, the paraprofessional is dismissed, subject to an appeal. [Members] are fired immediately for theft, substance abuse, or falsifying a time sheet.[26]

Related to the theme of discipline is that of surveillance. CED institutions extend the experience of being observed by one's neighbors and colleagues. This is quite explicit in Jacobs's "eyes on the street" principle for physical structure design, but it is equally apparent in the design of

23. Housing Opportunity Program Expansion Act of 1996, sec. 9; 104th Congress, Public Law 104–20.

24. 42 USC 1437j(c)(1)(A).

25. Harvard Business School, *STRIVE* (Case No. 9–399-054, 24 November 1998), 5.

26. Frank Adams, Fred Gordon, and Richard Shirey, *Cooperative Home Care Associates: From Working Poor to Working Class Through Job Ownership* 8 (Industrial Cooperative Association, 1995).

institutions, such as the Grameen Bank or Cooperative Home Care, that repeatedly bring people into personal contact with one another.

The rhetoric of surveillance occasionally arouses discomfort. "Eyes on the street," which to Jacobs connotes safety, has some kinship to Michel Foucault's "panopticism," which connotes repression.[27] The pervasive face-to-face relations and their pressures for cooperation may remind some of the stifling, repressive quality of small-town life portrayed by writers such as Sinclair Lewis and Sherwood Anderson.

Jacobs, however, insists that the sort of community that typifies vital urban neighborhoods is quite different from the small-town and suburban varieties.[28] She argues that multistranded relations with the local knowledge and trust needed for collective activity do not necessarily entail intrusiveness or repressiveness. Such relations are denser by definition than are impersonal single-stranded relations, but in city contexts, there is a natural limit to their density: "A good city street neighborhood achieves a marvel of balance between its people's determination to have essential privacy and their simultaneous wishes for differing degrees of contact, enjoyment, or help from the people around."[29]

Ideally, the city street, which for Jacobs is both a locus of social practice and a school in which people acquire social skills, brings people into contact with a range of others with whom they cannot expect to become personally intimate. Iris Young emphasizes this when she defines a conception of community close to Jacobs's as "the being together of strangers."[30] Repeated contact encourages various forms of social interaction and collaboration. People watch out for one another's children and property, give directions, help with parcels, hold their keys. But both the large number of people and cultural norms preclude routine intimacy. The needed number of collaborations could not be sustained if each entailed a high degree of intimacy. Jacobs contrasts city

27. Michel Foucault, *Discipline and Punish: The Birth of the Prison* 195–228 (1977).

28. Jacobs, *Great American Cities,* 58–68. Actually Jacobs avoids the word "community," probably precisely because of its connotations of intimacy and pervasiveness. Nevertheless, her theory links urban vitality to multistranded social relations, and consequent trust and local knowledge, of the sort for which CED practitioners generally use the term "community."

29. Ibid., 59.

30. Iris Young, *Justice and the Politics of Difference* 237–38 (1990); for elaboration, see Jerry Frug, "The Geography of Community," 48 *Stanford Law Review* 1047, 1049–55 (1996).

neighborhoods to suburbs, where, because of the absence of casual street contact and cultural norms of impersonal collaboration, people are ambivalent about collaboration. There, the prospect that any particular act of assistance will involve you deeply in the beneficiary's life makes it seem more demanding and risky.

Jacobs's view of community is more cosmopolitan than that of many CED proponents. It is quite hostile to the inclination toward neighborhood autarchy one occasionally finds in this literature. Urban communities differ from small towns in being part of a large, closely connected fabric, and that means that the routine presence of outsiders in one's own community and the routine experience of being an outsider in other people's is an important defining quality. To the extent that the CED Movement adopts Jacobs's view, it seems a powerful response to concerns about privacy and regimentation.

As the CED Movement imports ideals of equality and participation from the political to the economic sphere, it also brings from the business sphere to the political one norms of orderly, goal-oriented behavior. Thus, personal formality is another dimension of the new Protestant ethic. In terms of organizational structure, CED institutions are informal. But at the level of face-to-face interaction, they are often moderately formal. Formality is valued because it facilitates orderly collaboration, because it protects individuals from enforced intimacy, and because it is associated with norms of respect accorded actors in mainstream institutions. CED is serious business, its practitioners emphasize. They spend a good deal of time teaching members and others to read balance sheets and conduct meetings in accordance with Robert's Rules of Order.

Romantic communitarians are troubled by the fact that local currency systems of the sort I will discuss in chapter 5 monetize exchanges, at least some of which would have occurred informally without the system. But Edgar Cahn, a local currency proponent, defends this formality not only as necessary to increase the level of exchange, but also as a good in itself. By associating labor exchanges with mainstream economic transactions, local currency enhances the sense of dignity and worth of these transactions, he insists.[31]

31. Michael Shuman, *Going Local: Creating Self-Reliant Communities in a Global Age* 142 (1998).

The insistence on personal formality reaches an extreme in the practice of Saul Alinsky's Industrial Areas Foundation, which has played an important role in community organizing since the 1940s. Alinsky's ostentatious toughness often seemed out of sync in the 1960s, when a more sentimental style was in vogue, but it fits well with the trends of the 1990s. Alinsky organizers make a point of repudiating "friends and neighbors politics" in favor of a "self-consciously businesslike" approach: "Organizers encourage members to deal with one another in a professional manner. A visitor notices an air of brisk efficiency about the organization's office. Members typically address one another, as well as their opponents, by surname; and tend not to socialize with one another. These organizations are definitely not conceived as fellowships bound by all-inclusive loyalties against a hostile environment."[32]

Many CED practitioners regard the Alinsky style as unattractive, but hardly any would embrace the opposite extreme, which equates community with pervasive intimacy and spontaneity. All would agree that the repertory of CED skills includes tactics for maintaining social distance and imposing structure on relations. Between the extremes, a broad range of styles is possible.

A final theme in the new Protestant ethic is the valorization of wealth. In Weber's portrayal, early Protestantism exalted wealth as a sign of God's favor. It gave an altruistic, communal dimension to acquisitive success. Success was a form of tribute to God as well as to the entrepreneur. It also benefited the community, both because the wealthy would have charitable obligations to their fellows and because God's favor would be likely to spill over to the larger community.

There is a contemporary analogue to this view in the recent policy literature that urges support for efforts to increase private wealth among minorities, especially African Americans.[33] The communitarian rhetoric of the 1960s was suspicious of wealth and contemptuous of ambitions for it. The more recent literature rejects these attitudes and criticizes traditional social policy for focusing on income support and employment training to the exclusion of savings, investment, and entre-

32. Peter Skerry, *Mexican Americans: The Ambivalent Minority* 151 (1993).

33. Melvin Oliver and Thomas Shapiro, *Black Wealth, White Wealth* (1997); Michael Sherraden, *Assets and the Poor: A New American Welfare Policy* (1990); Jessie L. Jackson Sr. and Jessie L. Jackson Jr., *It's About the Money!* (1999).

preneurialism among low-income groups. It urges wealth creation in minority communities as an important social goal. Although wealth sometimes means public or collective assets, these writers also suggest that private, individual wealth has social benefits. Wealthy individuals are a potential philanthropic base for their communities. They are role models that give hope to others in the community. They serve as positive images to counter negative stereotypes of outsiders about group members. While the old Protestant ethic valued wealth as a sign of God's favor, the new ethic values it as a sign of mainstream society's favor.[34]

The social perspective typified by the Protestant ethic, and its Catholic, Islamic, and secular analogues, is strongly congruent with the functional themes of CED. By insisting on the link between spiritual orientation and economic activity, these accounts are on their face theories of multistranded relations. Economic relations are also spiritual relations, they insist, and it is unlikely that one dimension of such relations can be transformed without change in the other. Geographic focus is less inherent in these ideas; it is only one potential focus for the establishment of multistranded relations, but it is a prominent one. Because political life and, as is elaborated in chapters 5 and 6, much of religious life are organized on a geographical basis, it offers a relatively thick structure on which to build.

Finally, the face-to-face encounter seems an important premise of those who focus on spiritual and moral change as an aspect of economic change. For example, the "Ashcroft provisions" of the 1996 welfare-reform bill authorizing states to subcontract for the provision of assistance through religious as well as secular nonprofits was inspired by "historian Marvin Olasky's book *The Tragedy of American Compassion,* which argues that government-run charity lacks the *personal dimension* of religious charity and thus is inevitably powerless to change the behavior of the poor."[35]

---

34. The IRS has upheld the charitable character of some programs that provide business assistance to beneficiaries in low-income neighborhoods who are neither poor nor victims of discrimination by using strikingly Calvinist rhetoric: "The recipients in such cases are merely the instruments by which the charitable purposes are sought to be accomplished": Revenue Ruling 74–587, 1974–2 *Cumulative Bulletin* 162.

35. Paul Ambrosius, "The End of Welfare as We Know It and the Establishment Clause," 28 *Columbia Human Rights Law Review* 135, 145 (1996). Emphasis added.

Political

The political intuitions that underpin the CED Movement can be distinguished in terms of an interest-group perspective and a republican perspective.

THE INTEREST-GROUP PERSPECTIVE

From the interest-group perspective, CED looks like a strategy by poor communities to increase the resources they extract from outside institutions. The importance of multistranded relations, geographic focus, and face-to-face encounters is that they facilitate more cohesive and assertive organization that can exert greater pressure, especially against municipal government. This is very much the view of Alinsky and the Industrial Areas Foundation,[36] and although most CDCs have a more collaborative orientation, they would recognize his view of political bargaining as part of what they do.

However, the idea that CED is a potentially powerful strategy of poor people's politics contradicts a critique that was previously quite influential and remains of interest. The political discourse of the 1960s tended to be suspicious of poor people's organizations. Conservatives suspected them of demagoguery; radicals suspected them of co-optation. Both portrayed them as likely to generate leaders who would sell out their constituents. They might do so by accepting personal favors from outside officials or businesses in return for inducing their followers to accept or support projects of little or even negative value to the community. Or they might scare away potentially beneficial projects by inciting their followers to make impossible demands. Or they might trade off the interests of the community as a whole in order to favor the interests of a subgroup of friends and supporters. No one doubts that such activities occurred in the past and continue to do so today, but at one time their likelihood in poor neighborhoods was widely thought to be so great that it made almost any effort to encourage local organizing dubious.

One of the most influential expressions of this view from the left came in two books by Richard Cloward and Frances Fox Piven.[37] They

---

36. *Mexican Americans*, 144–61; Saul Alinsky, *Reveille for Radicals* (1946).

37. Richard Cloward and Frances Fox Piven, *Regulating the Poor* (1970), Richard Cloward and Frances Fox Piven, *Poor Peoples' Movements* (1977). The intense fear of co-

argued that the key political resource of the poor is their capacity to disrupt. Disruption might take the form of electoral rebellion, excessive welfare claims, strikes, or simply rioting. In their view, fear of disruption was the principal motivation of elites in yielding benefits to the poor. In order to sustain this fear, it was important that disruption occur with some severity and frequency. In this situation, organizing is inherently co-optive because, by its very nature, it tends to dampen disruption. The process of organizing itself might be disruptive, but once an organization stabilized, the leaders, even if well-meaning, would consider it their business to channel the behavior of their constituents along orderly paths. In doing so, they would undermine their principal resource; the elites, no longer anxious about disruption, would concede less. Moreover, once organizations began to stabilize, the "iron law of oligarchy" would kick in, and leaders would feather their own nests at the expense of the rank-and-file.

Among several objections to this argument, one is of particular interest. The argument involves a non sequitur. Organizing is considered inherently bad because it mitigates disruption, but according to the argument, it is not disruption itself but the fear of disruption that induces the elites to provide benefits. Moreover, the inducement must involve not just the fear of disruption, but the expectation that concessions will reduce disruption that would otherwise occur. And because disruption has a cost to the poor as well as to the elites, it is in their interest to disrupt only when the benefits from elite anxiety exceed these costs. It is thus not in the interest of the poor to maximize disruption. But without organization, why should they be able to discern or approach the optimal level of disruption? Without organization, they cannot deliberate collectively on the matter. They cannot credibly promise the elites to limit disruption in return for benefits. And in many circumstances, the threat of disruption may be less credible from a diffuse mass than from an organized group. Piven and Cloward portray the poor as engaged in a kind of bargaining with the elites, but they focus exclusively on the costs of organized bargaining and largely ignore the costs of

---

optation from organization also appears in Alinsky's work. Although Alinsky was more sympathetic than Piven and Cloward to poor people's organization, he encouraged suspicion that any form of collaboration with government would lead to co-optation. Thus, he vehemently opposed the Community Action Program. See "The War on Poverty: Political Pornography," 21 *Journal of Social Issues* 41 (1965).

disorganized bargaining.[38] Even under Piven and Cloward's dark assumptions—a zero-sum negotiation, selfish elites, weak leadership or organizational capacity among the poor—an important, potentially valuable function for organization remains in cutting deals exchanging acquiescence for resources. If we relax the dark assumptions, we can see additional functions, such as those emphasized by the economic rationales: mobilizing voluntary effort, aggregating information about community needs, and coordinating projects.

We cannot say more than that these are potential benefits. It is surely true that people sometimes do worse with organization than without. Even in such cases, however, the problem might better be understood as a matter of too little organization rather than too much. A promising hypothesis holds that the returns to outside investment in a community will be highest when the level and density of organization in the community is either relatively low or relatively high. Returns to the outside investor are high when organization is slight because the investor encounters little opposition and can design his project to maximize his own interests. Returns to the community are high when organization is great. At high levels of organization, the community has the capacity not only to prevent disruption that impairs the investment, but also to facilitate support for investment and to bargain for a share of the returns. An organized community can promise credibly that the property will not be vandalized, that neighboring parks will be maintained, or that job training will be configured to complement investment in a new business. Although returns are thus likely to be highest at the poles of the organization spectrum, the distribution of those returns will vary from pole to pole. At the low-organization end, the outside investor captures most of the returns. At the high-organization end, the returns are divided between investor and community.

At intermediate levels of organization, however, the hypothesis pre-

38. Piven and Cloward attempted to show historically that the poor did better in times of disorganized disruption than in times of organized bargaining. The demonstration was being contradicted empirically, however, as they wrote. As they later acknowledged, under the Nixon administration, well after the subsiding of the disruptive protests of the 1960s on which they had pinned their hopes, social-welfare benefits underwent their greatest expansion since the New Deal. See Frances Fox Piven and Richard Cloward, "The Historical Sources of the Contemporary Relief Debate," in Fred Block et al., *The Mean Season: The Attack on the Welfare State* 3–39 (1987).

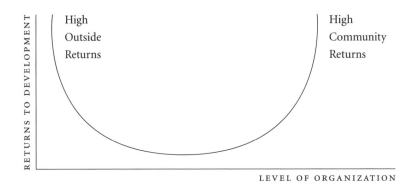

Figure 1

dicts that returns—and hence, investment—will be lowest. We might visualize the situation as a U-curve (see Figure 1).[39] Returns are lowest at intermediate magnitudes of organization because here organizations are strong enough to raise large costs but not strong enough to provide large benefits. Moderate levels of organization are sufficient to bring a lawsuit, or pack a meeting of the zoning authority, or mount a couple of demonstrations, or encourage vandalism. However, they are not strong enough to bind the community in ways that would assure a prospective investor that he will not face disruption or will receive support. The disorganized community cannot credibly promise that there will be no demonstrations, lawsuits, or vandalism. It cannot assure police protection or job training or complementary investments.

Moreover, at intermediate levels of organization, the danger that an organization will pursue narrow group interests at the expense of the larger community may be highest. As an organization expands to include more community interests, this becomes harder to do. The closer the organization comes to including the entire community, the less the potential that the organization will see its own interests as different from those of the community. The problem of the "iron law of oligarchy" can be mitigated as the organization's internal processes strengthen. Thus, when we see organizations selling out the community or their own members, the most plausible diagnosis will sometimes be too little, rather than too much, organization.

39. I have taken the U-curve and the accompanying intuition from an analysis of labor relations by Joel Rogers in " 'Divide and Conquer': Further Reflections on the Distinctive Character of American Labor Laws," 1990 *Wisconsin Law Review* 1, 32–37.

Piven and Cloward's diagnosis seemed to reflect a common assumption of 1960s radicalism that the best that the poor could hope for from the capitalist state was a decent welfare system. The favorable response they anticipated to unorganized disruption was increased welfare benefits. Of course, this strategy no longer seems politically viable, and it is not attractive to many of the people it was supposed to benefit. To the extent that poor communities are looking for investment, many forms of disruptive protest seem transparently counterproductive. Disorder in lower-class neighborhoods leads quickly to private *dis*investment, and even a public sector that feels the kind of pressure to placate the poor on which Piven and Cloward relied would not respond by putting resources into long-term projects that could pay off only with local collaboration.

THE REPUBLICAN PERSPECTIVE

Republican political thought gives another perspective on the CED Movement. Republicanism has its origins in antiquity; it received its canonical modern formulations in the Renaissance and the seventeenth century, and was strongly influential in eighteenth- and nineteenth-century American thought. Some of the most distinctive themes of the thought of Jefferson and Lincoln and of the Knights of Labor and the People's Party are best understood in the light of Republicanism.[40] The CED Movement has arisen during a period that has also seen a Republican revival in political theory, and the rhetoric and practices of CED resonate with Republican themes.

Republicanism is an exceptionally strong form of democracy, one with a preference for small, geographically based political units. It exalts qualities of civic virtue and deliberation that have some resemblance to the sociological notion of social capital. Like economics, it also has an interest in material incentives, though it is primarily concerned with incentives for political rather than economic activity. The most distinctive political contribution of Republicanism is its insistence that democracy entails powerful constraints on property arrangements.[41] Property

---

40. J.G.A. Pocock, *The Machiavellian Moment: Florentine Political Thought and the Atlantic Republican Tradition* (1975); Bruce Laurie, *Artisans into Workers: Labor in Nineteenth-Century America* (1989).

41. See William H. Simon, "Social-Republican Property," 38 *UCLA Law Review* 1335

is important to Republicans because it confers power. The Republicans deny any strong distinction between the kind of power property confers and political power. It follows for them that the egalitarian values that all democrats apply to the political realm must also be applied in the economic realm.

One implication of this view is a preference for economic self-sufficiency and a concern about nonresident, "absentee" ownership. Integration into broad-based markets subjects the community to forces beyond the reach of self-government. And because property confers power, outside ownership of property undermines the political autonomy of the community. In nineteenth-century American republican thought, the railroad was a paradigmatic nemesis of self-government. The railroad was controlled by outsiders, but it had enormous power over local affairs. Its monopolistic decisions over rates and scheduling could spell life or death for small agricultural communities. At the same time, the railroad, by fusing once isolated local economies into far-flung markets, subjected them to volatile product-price swings that undermined stability and independence. Republicanism thus favored both institutions that afforded local communities some autonomy from outside economic pressures and, at the regional and national planes, institutions that would subject these broader pressures to democratic control.

The Republican political ideal also had implications for property arrangements within the community. As it calls for economic autonomy at the community level, Republicanism calls for propertied independence at the individual level. In this view, self-government requires that the citizen have a stake in the polity that links her fate to that of her fellows. The stake makes it likely that the individual will share in both the successes and failures of collective decision; it is both an inducement to participation and bond against recklessness. In former times, the paradigmatic Republican stake was landed property. The immobility of land holds people in place and binds them to their neighbors. Landowners, the French Republican Anne Robert Jacques Turgot wrote, "are attached to the land by virtue of their property; they cannot cease to take an interest in the district where it is placed. . . . It is the possession of

---

(1991); Gregory S. Alexander, *Commodity and Propriety: Competing Visions of Property in American Legal Thought* 21–88, 211–40, 248–76 (1997).

land . . . which, by linking the possessor to the State, constitutes true citizenship." By contrast, proprietors of liquid, mobile capital "belong to no place."[42] Thus, politics takes a geographical form; geographically contiguous property constitutes people as a collective with a common identity.

As the space for yeoman farmers in the American economy shrank in the nineteenth century, Republicans recognized that they had to adapt their vision to accommodate a more integrated system with larger production units. They responded with two sorts of proposals. At the local level, they favored the organization of production in terms of cooperatives—a form of egalitarian worker ownership. Above the national level, they favored programs supporting small business and shielding it from big business. Shielding took the form of antitrust and related laws. Support took the form of government programs providing credit and technical assistance and facilitating collaboration among small businesses to attain economies of scale in the purchase of inputs, research and development, and the marketing of their products. A panoply of New Deal programs in the agricultural sphere represent the most fully elaborated, ambitiously implemented example of the modernized Republican vision.[43] The Republican vision continues to be reflected in public policies that favor home ownership, in part on the ground that the economic independence it fosters makes for better citizens. The income-tax exemption for interest on home mortgages—the largest housing subsidy—is sometimes justified in Republican terms. HUD secretary Jack Kemp argued for a shift from rental to ownership subsidies on the ground that owners "vote more regularly and become more engaged in the democratic process."[44]

In nineteenth-century America, the Republican commitment to propertied independence had both reactionary and radical implica-

---

42. Quoted in William Sewell, *Work and Revolution in France: The Language of Labor from the Old Regime to 1848* 127–28 (1980).

43. See Grant McConnell, *The Decline of Agrarian Democracy* (1953).

44. U.S. Department of Housing and Urban Development, *Home Ownership and Affordable Housing: The Opportunities* (1991). Survey research shows a significant correlation (controlling for income, age, education level, and the length of time a person has remained or expects to remain in the community) of home ownership with membership in nonprofessional organizations, knowledge of local political leaders, voting, and self-reported local political activity. Denise DiPasquale, "Incentives and Social Capital: Are Homeowners Better Citizens?" 45 *Journal of Urban Economics* 354 (1999).

tions. On the one hand, an exclusionary interpretation concluded that self-government required the disfranchisement of those who lacked property. On the other, an inclusionary interpretation held that self-government required the redistribution of some minimal amount of property to all citizens. Senator John Calhoun's insistence that property-less laborers were unqualified for political participation was solidly grounded in Republican premises; so was General Sherman's insistence that meaningful emancipation would entail giving each former slave "40 acres and a mule."

There is a modern version of this dialectic. As political-participation rates decline, scholars are again interested in what motivates people to participate and are again considering the role of property. Robert Ellickson has emphasized an important limitation on the incentives on non-owner residents—tenants—to participate in local political processes. Many collective improvements to the community, such as better schools, parks, or policing, increase private property values by an amount proportionate to the general valuation of the improvements. Public benefits are thus privately appropriated through real estate appreciation. Ellickson points out that this limits the incentives for tenants to participate in local politics, for property value increases tend to be passed on to them in the form of higher rents. To the extent that public achievements translate into rent increases, tenants cannot benefit from participation.[45]

The prescriptions Ellickson draws from this observation are in the tradition of Calhoun—disfranchisement of nonowners. (This is constitutionally impossible in general elections, but Ellickson favors the remission of governmental functions to private associations or special-purpose districts constituted exclusively of owners.) For its part, the CED Movement would respond in the tradition of Sherman. As we will see in detail in chapter 6, it proposes to create and extend a set of ownership interests that depart from conventional private property in some respects but that are adequate for the Republican purpose of grounding and motivating responsible participation.

From a more general perspective, Republicanism gives a political cast

45. Robert C. Ellickson, "Cities and Homeowners' Associations," 130 *University of Pennsylvania Law Review* 1519, 1547–54 (1982); idem, "New Institutions for Old Neighborhoods," 48 *Duke Law Journal* 75, 92–5 (1998). Ellickson's analysis is based in part on the assumption that local governments have little capacity to redistribute wealth. The CED Movement contests this, as I discuss in chapter 4.

to the three defining themes of CED. By insisting on linking political and economic roles, Republicanism prescribes a form of relational density as a vindication of democracy. By taking ownership of real property as the critical economic underpinning of local democracy, Republicanism also adopts a geographical focus. And by insisting on the importance of direct participation, it gives priority in political terms to face-to-face relations.

Specific CED practices also resonate with the Republican program. CED is an effort to subject economic forces to democratic control. Economic self-sufficiency is an important background value in much CED discourse. Its emphasis on security of tenure and, sometimes, home ownership can be seen as a form of propertied independence. Its characteristic business programs provide credit and technical support to small, locally controlled businesses in the manner of late nineteenth-century Republicanism. The Republicans' favorite business form—the cooperative—makes a frequent appearance on the CED landscape. Moreover, as we will see, the charitable corporation, especially in the form of the CDC, manifests many Republican themes.

The Republican prescription of local economic self-sufficiency seems naive and anachronistic in many respects. It would be implausible to deny that the most important responses to poverty and racial injustice require national policies and political coalitions. But we have noted that there are economic rationales for local development initiatives, and the Republican perspective seems responsive to at least two current practical political contingencies.

The first is the political lesson of two decades of welfare cutbacks culminating in a reckless dismantling of the core public-assistance programs led by a liberal democratic administration. The lesson many inner-city leaders have drawn from this experience—that reliance on welfare involves dangerous political vulnerability—resonates with Republican principles. These principles condemn dependence on economic favors of the state as incompatible with political independence.[46] Something like this seems to be the prevalent view among many inner-city leaders. Dependence on welfare now seems too fragile a basis for

46. Compare, for example, the eighteenth-century English Republican attack on the dependence of Whig "placemen" on wealth accumulated in connection with government bonds in Pocock, *Machiavellian Moment*, 425–6, 477–86, with Alinsky's attack on welfare dependence in poor communities in "Political Pornography."

stable community life, since shifting political coalitions can wipe out these programs. Like traditional Republicans, these leaders see a potentially more stable basis in private wealth and economic activity. To be sure, private property is no less a creature of state and national government policy than welfare benefits. There is no natural definition of private property rights. We depend on government to delineate their boundaries. And the value of these rights depends substantially on the capacity of the state to enforce them against violators. However, legal and cultural norms give private property higher normative priority than welfare property, and institutional arrangements protect it more strongly.

The second political reality with which the Republican view resonates is that some poor communities have greater political than economic power. By definition, poor people tend to have little or no capital, income, or marketable skills and only the most uncertain claims on the society to improve their condition through redistribution. On the other hand, basic constitutional norms require that political power be apportioned with formal equality. Formally equal political power is not always worth anything, but sometimes it is. To the extent that it enables poor communities to influence elections in broader jurisdictions, they may be able to trade it for resources. To the extent that it gives them direct power over the use that outside owners make of property within the communities, they can use their power to generate economic benefits they could not attain through market processes. Much CED can be seen as an effort to translate political into economic power, and in circumstances in which disadvantaged groups have more of the former than the latter, this may be a plausible strategy.

Conclusion: The Mural Test

A mural that covers the side of a building on Dudley Street depicts some of the major figures in the Dudley Street Neighborhood Initiative's remarkable efforts to revitalize the community. The impressive new construction in the neighborhood sits amid many older, still deteriorated buildings that have a good deal of graffiti on them. Although the mural is painted on one of the old, unrenovated buildings, DSNI staff emphasize to visitors that there has not been a mark of graffiti on it in the several years since it was created.

Here is a vivid illustration of all three logics of collective action. The mural's pristine state reflects at once informal coordination that enhances the value of an economic investment, social capital, and collective discipline that enhances bargaining power with outsiders. A community group that can credibly promise this type of support can thereby induce significant investments both by its own members and outsiders.

Chapter 4   The Community as Beneficiary

of Economic Development

The Local Perspective

Not all local economic development, even when successful, is Community Economic Development. The CED Movement seeks a kind of development that benefits the community in four distinctive ways. First, it provides benefits to residents. Possible benefits include housing, services, job or business opportunities, public goods such as parks, or increased tax revenues that can be used to fund public goods. It is important, however, that the benefits be accessible to residents.

To appreciate this criterion, imagine, first, a series of investments in a neighborhood that dramatically improve its attractiveness as a place to live. Property values then rise. Because most of the original residents are tenants, they find that their rents increase proportionately. They have difficulty paying the higher rents and gradually move out, to be replaced by higher-income newcomers.

Gentrification of this sort may be economic development, but it is not CED as the term is understood by those who practice it. Community economic development connotes development for the benefit of the community—defined in terms of its residents at the time a project is undertaken.

Next, suppose a new job training program is coordinated with business investments that bring new jobs. Incomes of many residents rise substantially. They respond by moving to a more attractive neighborhood and are replaced by newcomers with less income than they. Few CED practitioners would dispute that such stories should often be regarded as successes, but it is not what their projects seek to accomplish. Benefiting the community means benefiting its residents as members, not just as individuals. Successful CED strengthens the group, thickening its ties and fostering continuity in its membership.

The second criterion of good CED is that it involves beneficial linkages or synergies with other local activities or institutions. If it is a business, for example, it might do this by purchasing its inputs from a community supplier or by providing inputs to some other local producer. Public infrastructure and social service investments can link with each other and with private investments. A job training program should link to local employers. An investment in a park might complement programs for youth activities in the park or law enforcement efforts designed to keep it safe.

Disfavored are institutions that forgo local in favor of outside ties. For example, in a CED appraisal of national fast-food chain outlets, such as McDonald's, Christopher Gunn and Hazel Gunn emphasize that the chains organize their outlets' purchases of services and supplies on a national basis, typically from remote outsiders, and that they rarely make collateral investments within the community. At the same time, they undermine through competition more locally oriented businesses.[1]

An obvious but sometimes elusive synergy involves matching training programs for the unemployed with the hiring needs of local business. The Chicago Manufacturing Institute was established by Chicago Commons, a community-based social service agency in collaboration with a group of small and medium-size businesses in various light-industrial fields, especially metalworking and plastics processing. The institute provides training to inner-city youth designed to qualify them for openings in the businesses and technical assistance to the businesses. Though it is a noncharitable corporation, the institute's affiliation with Chicago Commons, a charitable corporation, allows it to take advantage of job training and social service grants restricted to charitable organizations. Its relation with the businesses gives it the local industrial

1. Christopher Gunn and Hazel Gunn, *Reclaiming Capital: Democratic Initiatives and Community Development* 25–37 (1991).

knowledge it needs to configure its training to their needs. Small businesses often depend on public institutions or trade associations to keep up with technical knowledge. The institute achieves economies of scope by combining this function with its training. It has thus been able both to provide a highly effective training program that places disadvantaged young people in relatively attractive jobs and to support a vulnerable set of businesses that had been having trouble finding qualified employees and access to new technical knowledge. Its structure divides control between its nonprofit sponsor, which has a governing board with representation from the city's low-income communities, and the businesses.[2]

The third CED criterion requires that negative environmental externalities within the community, such as pollution and traffic congestion, be minimal. The tendency to focus solely on benefits, especially jobs or tax revenues, without adequately considering negative externalities accounts for some spectacular failures. The city of Albert Lea, Minnesota, for example, spent $3 million of its own money and procured more than $30 million in subsidies from the federal government to induce Seaboard Corporation to reopen a local pork-processing plant in 1990. The city built a massive sewage treatment plant; provided new roads, water lines, and a parking lot; and contributed toward a new building for the plant. The jobs turned out to be unattractive to residents, so Seaboard had to recruit low-wage workers from the Southwest and Central America. Their influx created a low-rent housing crisis (a kind of adverse forward linkage). The sewage treatment plant proved inadequate. Seaboard demanded increased subsidies as a condition to remain. Waste from the plant impeded drainage, caused water contamination, and suffused the local air with stench. Within two years, Seaboard abandoned its Albert Lea operations, having moved some to an Oklahoma community that had offered a fresh subsidy package (to its eventual regret).[3]

Jacobs's notion of "eyes on the street" draws attention to a distinctive category of environmental externality—pedestrian effects. A project that attracts people to streets at times that they otherwise would be

---

2. Peggy Clark and Steven L. Dawson, *Jobs and the Urban Poor: Privately Initiated Sectoral Strategies* 11–15 (Aspen Institute, November 1995).

3. Donald L. Bartlett and James B. Steele, "The Empire of the Pigs," *Time* (30 November 1998), 52–64.

empty has important collateral benefits. A project that drains pedestrians out of side streets to concentrate them in a central location inflicts serious external costs.[4]

The fourth criterion is that the project reinforces—or, at least, does not undermine—a stable, independent community structure. Or to put it slightly differently, it is consistent with community control. This is the least defined of the criteria. It is easiest to describe the situation it is designed to exclude—the company town in which residents are at the mercy of a single, large, absentee-owned employer that dominates the community's institutions either directly or through threats of disinvestment and downsizing. Desirable social structure is associated with local ownership. Local owners are thought more likely to hire locally and make collateral local investments, as well as slower to lay off and disinvest in event of downturn.[5]

Another relevant theme is diversification, mixed use, and what the administrators of the Empowerment Zone program call "balance": "Balanced economic development means diversifying the job base rather than becoming dependent on any single employer or market—public or private. It means creating jobs at many scales: local and corporate, service-oriented and export-oriented. It means supporting new start-up businesses as well as preserving existing establishments."[6]

Part of the idea here is to reduce vulnerability to firm-specific or industry-specific economic distress. Another part is to mitigate the dangers of political domination by a particular industry. Fiscal considerations are important in some jurisdictions. Low-income municipalities feel driven to seek commercial uses to expand their tax bases. Finally, balance is celebrated as a way to bring together a diverse array of people and activities to make the community a more stimulating, cosmopolitan place. In general, the CED practitioners are skeptical of subsidies for industrial plants owned by large corporations.

It is not obvious that a strategy based on these criteria is a good idea. One concern is competence. In an article titled "The Myth of Commu-

---

4. See Jane Jacobs, *The Death and Life of Great American Cities* 143–222 (1961).

5. Bennett Harrison and Sandra Kanter, "The Political Economy of States' Job-Creation Business Incentives," *AIP Journal*, October 1978, 424–33.

6. U.S. Department of Housing and Urban Development, Office of Community Planning and Development, *A Guidebook for Community-Based Strategic Planning for Empowerment Zones and Enterprise Communities* 14 (January 1994).

nity Development,"[7] Nicholas Lemann argued that poor communities are not adept at economic development and that four decades of federal effort to equip them to do it have failed.

Another concern is parochialism. To the extent that a community succeeds in capturing the benefits of local development for its residents, it precludes benefits that would have spilled over into other communities. If everyone does this successfully, then everyone loses the benefits that would have spilled over under a less autarchic regime. Efforts spent simply to internalize benefits rather than maximize them may prove wasteful. Moreover, because communities can fully internalize benefits only of fairly small projects, the strategy might produce an undesirable bias against projects that need to be large in order to attain economies of scale. The CED vision threatens an undesirable balkanization.

We see the dark side of the CED strategy in the NIMBY ("Not in My Backyard") phenomenon, in which community groups that we tend to call "homeowners' associations" but might equally be called "community development corporations" mobilize thoughtlessly against multi-family housing, social service facilities, or large scale commercial facilities that would benefit outsiders but not them.

These disadvantages might lead one to suggest that prosperity would be greater if localities made less strenuous effort to internalize development benefits and that, as long as the resulting benefits are distributed with what Justice Holmes called an "average reciprocity of advantage,"[8] each jurisdiction would be more than compensated for the loss of benefits from local development by benefits spilling over from other jurisdictions. In fact, such concerns are among the principal rationales for various limitations that we will shortly consider on the power of local government to pursue economic development. One might question whether, even within these legal limitations, the strategy proposed by the CED Movement is too parochial.

We can briefly consider both Lemann's competence objection and the objections from economic parochialism in turn. On examination, the competence objection dwindles remarkably. In fact, the record of urban economic-development programs is mixed, and many strategies that have failed have been revised in the light of experience. Public

7. Nicholas Lemann, "The Myth of Community Development," *New York Times Magazine* (9 January 1994), 27.

8. *Jackman v. Rosenbaum*, 260 U.S. 22, 30 (1922).

housing, for example, has produced many successful projects, and the kinds that have failed consistently—notably, dense high-rises in desolate areas—are no longer being built. Lemann ultimately acknowledges this; it turns out that his pessimism about economic development does not include housing. Nor does it include education, job training, land-use regulation, or policing. All it really includes is business development within the community, and even here the claim is ambiguously qualified to acknowledge that some businesses ("sweatshops and minor provisioners") may be viable in most communities, and many may be viable in some (blue collar neighborhoods).[9]

The claim that inner-city neighborhoods will find attracting large businesses that bring extensive community benefits difficult may be true for some places—Dudley Street, for example, has yet to attract any large business investment—but there are many counter-examples, including Jamaica Plain and East Palo Alto.[10]

The more important point, however, is that even if it were true, it would affect only a narrow range of CED activity. Other than housing development, most CED activity is focused on the traditional activities of local government—land-use regulation and the provision of social services and other public goods. The extraordinary turnaround at Dudley Street began with a campaign to pressure the city to stop illegal garbage dumping in the city. This, of course, is a routine function of municipal governance. It is also a fundamental form of community economic development. A neighborhood that tolerates a large open-air garbage dump at its center puts itself on a trajectory that limits both the amount and nature of the economic activities within its borders. Cleaning up the area changes this trajectory and opens new possibilities. To some extent then, the CED perspective simply calls for greater sophistication and broader participation in the exercise of traditional local-governance functions.

With respect to the parochialism objection, three points should be made. First, the idea of local self-government implies at least some

9. Lemann, "Myth," 38, 54.

10. Jamaica Plain has induced successful development of a major supermarket. East Palo Alto recently brought in a major retail complex anchored by a Home Depot that is generating substantial tax revenues and local employment. Michael Porter gives many examples of successful inner-city businesses, some fairly large. "The Competitive Advantage of the Inner City," *Harvard Business Review* (May–June), 1995, 55.

measure of legitimate pursuit of local self-interest. It would be hard to motivate people to participate in local public affairs, and perhaps even to structure discussions effectively, if it were not appropriate for the group to pursue its own interests within a significant range. It is partly the collective self-interest of the community that differentiates its members from outsiders and hence constitutes them as a coherent, independent entity.

Second, some modes of economic development exist that depend on intensive collaboration that is facilitated by commitment to a community. A community striving for locally beneficial economic development is sometimes in a position to coordinate, for example, land use and social-service decisions more effectively.

Finally and most importantly, the CED movement is motivated by the perception that the norm of an "average reciprocity of advantage" in the distribution of the spillover effects of local economic development has not been realized. Arguably, CED merely extends to poor communities a perspective that more affluent ones have long routinely applied to the disadvantage of their low-income neighbors. In the case of suburban communities, this may not be apparent. When a community zones its entire area for large-lot residential use, its activity is not always considered economic development; more often than not, however, both the effect and the intention is to maximize homeowners' return on property investments. Restrictive suburban zoning practices have important external effects on outside communities, because they both inhibit access to outsiders and intensify pressures elsewhere for the prohibited uses.

Within large cities, the CED Movement arose substantially from perceptions that economic resources had been focused on the downtown at the expense of lower-income neighborhoods; that the lower-income neighborhoods had received more than their share of waste dumps, correctional facilities, and streetcar barns; and that whole populations were subject to removal in the interest of upper-income groups. The common theme of these observations is that, in the absence of popular participation, the local political process is too biased against lower-income and minority groups, and too weak in relation to capital and big business, to produce a fair distribution of the benefits of economic development.

Part of the case for the CED perspective, then, is defensive and remedial. It is an approach designed for disadvantaged communities. A major goal is to enable low-income people to use their political power in ways that compensate for the lack of economic power. Although many CED practices are routinely used by affluent communities, some would be far less desirable and defensible in such communities. So to some extent, CED involves a double standard, pushing for strategies in low-income communities that it would oppose in upper-income communities. It is not clear how controversial the double standard is. For example, as we will soon see, the Supreme Court, which is by no means uniformly sympathetic to the legal premises of CED, tacitly accepts that poor communities have more discretion than others to use local hiring preferences.[11] The tendency documented in chapter 2 to enhance the ability of low-income communities to undertake economic development has been accompanied by a less prominent one that has restricted the ability of affluent communities to ignore the interests of outsiders in their economic-development decisions. Statutes and court cases that impose pressure on affluent communities to permit some high-density housing and state commissions on the siting of various public facilities with power to overrule local zoning are examples.[12] The first tendency enhances the autonomy of poor communities; the latter restricts that of affluent communities. Both are commonly supported by CED practitioners; there is no contradiction between the CED perspective and efforts to curb the effects of local parochialism to the extent that CED is defensive and remedial.

The Community as Residual Claimant: Development Rights

The CED Movement tends to think of the community—residents as a collectivity—as the owner of the developmental potential of its area and, hence, as entitled to the net benefits of development. Two sets of boundaries delineate the notion of community entitlement. Most fundamentally, there are the boundaries of the residential neighborhood. Residents are considered the collective owners of the opportunities of the neighborhoods in which they live. However, these neighborhoods are

11. *United Building and Construction Trades Council of Camden County v. Camden,* 465 U.S. 208, 222–23 (1984) (economic distress is a prerequisite to use of local employment preference under the privileges and immunities clause).

12. See Daniel Mandelker, Roger Cunningham, and John Payne, *Planning and Control of Land Development* 371–446 (4th ed. 1995).

typically situated in larger political jurisdictions, and some of the most valuable development opportunities within these broader boundaries are in non-residential areas—downtown business centers or, occasionally, industrial districts. It follows from the premise of resident ownership that development claims on these areas belong not to those who own land or work there, but to the city as a whole, which means its residential communities, on a pro rata basis. City governments are expected not only to provide centralized public goods, but also to channel the benefits of nonresidential development to residential neighborhoods.[13]

Such claims have a normative and a strategic dimension. The normative dimension sees the community as the most important creator of economic wealth and suggests that it is entitled to appropriate what it creates. The strategic dimension points to the fact that members of many low-income communities have more political than economic power. Community economic development provides an opportunity to use this greater political power to enhance economic resources.

Although it is well rooted in American intellectual traditions, the idea of the community as residual claimant is in strong tension with other mainstream notions of distributive justice. Some of these competing notions are embodied in law, including constitutional doctrine, that constrains the pursuit of the CED ideal. The Constitution includes protections of "property" rights that are sometimes interpreted to vary widely from the CED conception. Moreover, there is no denying the drafters of the Constitution aimed consciously to inhibit the use of political power by disadvantaged minorities to achieve economic benefits. How these eighteenth-century concerns should be interpreted in the circumstances of contemporary America, however, is a matter of intense controversy. Here we examine the CED conception of commu-

13. Moreover, some assets of extraordinary value are considered to belong to the municipality as a whole even when located in or near residential neighborhoods. In 2000, a coalition of community-based organizations sued the city of Boston to stop an arrangement that allocated most of the public proceeds of a major waterfront development to the adjacent neighborhood of South Boston. The plaintiffs charged violation of the civil-rights laws because the effect was to benefit a white, working-class neighborhood at the expense of the city's minority residents. They argued both that the relevant waterfront area had not been traditionally considered part of the South Boston neighborhood and that, even if it had, it would be unfair to allow a single neighborhood to claim the proceeds of such an extraordinarily valuable resource.

nity ownership in confrontation with doctrines designed to protect three competing groups—landowners, nonresident seekers of jobs, and prospective immigrants. In each case, the tendency of the doctrine is to call into question the legitimacy of the ideal of community entitlement and to impose obstacles to its pursuit. The strength of the obstacles, however, is ambiguous.

LANDOWNERS: EXACTIONS

The CED idea of local property embraces the traditional opposition to private appropriation of land rents associated in nineteenth-century America with Henry George. Land is a distinctive form of property: It is not created through human effort, and its supply is fixed. Price increases in land do not reward owners' efforts, and they do not induce increase in supply. They simply reflect the scarcity of land relative to demand, which arises from inextricably mingled efforts of many members of the community. It follows that the returns on landowning—rent—"represents a value created by the whole community" and thus "necessarily belongs to the whole community."[14]

George's followers especially resented the prospect that, as the society becomes more prosperous, the scarcity rents to land would increase proportionately, thus constituting what they regarded as a massive and unjust private appropriation of the fruits of the efforts of society's productive members. He thus proposed that government be financed through a "single tax" on land designed to confiscate the entire rental value (exclusive of buildings and improvements, to which the basic analysis did not apply).[15]

George's ideas have become less prominent as forms of wealth other than land have assumed greater importance in the economy. Nevertheless, some of George's basic point remains viable both on efficiency and

14. Henry George, *Progress and Poverty* 365–66 (1954) [1879].

15. For an appraisal of George's theory, see Stewart Sterk, "*Nollan,* Henry George, and Exactions," 88 *Columbia Law Review* 1731 (1988); for a discussion of efforts to implement the land tax, see Donald Hagman, "The Single Tax and Land Use Planning: Henry George Updated," 12 UCLA *Law Review* 762, 767–80 (1965). George's proposal differed from the more familiar current forms of real property tax in that (1) it was proposed as the exclusive means of public finance; (2) it applied only to land and not to buildings and other improvements; and (3) the rate was supposed to approximate 100 percent.

distributive grounds, and his claim that land values are "created by the whole community" can be amplified with the arguments of the CED Movement. Local public policy is a major influence on land values. The collective decisions a community makes about matters such as roads, parks, schools, zoning, and criminal-law enforcement are all important determinants. In urban communities, especially low-income ones, this success is unlikely to be due predominantly to the efforts of landowners. It is due to the collective activity of all the political participants in the area, including tenants. Even to the extent it is due to landowners, the contribution of each owner would not approximate the value of his land. Yet in the absence of some modification of conventional property rights, the increased values due to these policy decisions are appropriated principally by landowners and in proportion to their landholdings rather than to their political participation.

A further influence on the value of any given parcel of land is private investment in neighboring parcels. This, of course, is the point of the maxim, "location, location, and location." The external benefits of individual private investments cannot be captured by the investor through conventional private-property rights, and they are not individually measurable. Yet they constitute a major proportion of land value.

Finally, property values also reflect diffuse, informal patterns of behavior, which themselves are the aggregate effects of myriad individual micro-decisions. Recall, for example, Jacobs's suggestion that the single most important determinant of the safety and attractiveness of sidewalks and public spaces is "eyes on the street," the continuous presence of a critical mass of users. Similarly, an attractive commercial district is the aggregate consequence of myriad individual tastes and purchasing decisions. City planners and businesspeople try to influence such micro-decisions through public and private investments, but they cannot fully determine them. Spontaneous behavior plays a role, and its aggregate effects are another constituent of value that is collectively created but that, in a conventional property regime, is captured by landowners.

Of course, all local governments impose some charges on landowners to reflect collectively provided benefits. It is no accident that the property tax is one of the most important forms of municipal finance, and municipalities sometimes impose "special assessments" or "impact fees" on owners whose property benefits disproportionately from public improvements.[16] Nevertheless, a premise of the CED Movement is that conventional governance and property-rights regimes are likely to allocate the returns to land excessively in favor of owners at the expense of the community as a whole. This belief is especially strong with regard to low-income communities, where most residents are usually tenants and owners are often absent.

Over the years there have been proposals in the Georgian tradition that development rights—rights to change or intensify the use of the land—be treated as public and sold for their full economic value. In one variation, the owner of the current-use rights gets an exclusive option for the development rights, but he must negotiate a price acceptable to the public authority.[17] In another, the authority puts the rights up for auction; anyone can bid, and if someone other than the current-use owner buys and fails to negotiate an agreement with the current-use owner, the government will take the land by eminent domain and transfer it to the successful development bidder.[18] The distributive idea, in both cases, is "to assure [that] publicly created values in land accrue to the public."[19]

Although an outright public assertion of ownership and sale of development rights would be viewed as radical and enjoined as unconstitutional, local governments may have the practical ability to accomplish something approaching this goal. As Madelyn Glickfeld puts it, "Many jurisdictions use techniques which make development 'as of right' a rare event. Almost every development comes under the specific review and approval of a local agency. We already have, in effect, an ad hoc development-permission system." Writing in 1978, Glickfeld suggested that it would not be a big step from this situation to one in which the public auctioned development rights. The Redevelopment process, which is specifically designed to encourage competitive proposals among

16. For a comprehensive account of devices to "recapture" the benefits of public improvements from landowners, including a variation on the Georgian land tax, see Donald Hagman and Dean Misczynski, eds. *Windfalls for Wipeouts: Land Value Capture and Compensation* (American Society of Planning Officials, 1978).

17. Lynton K. Caldwell, "Rights of Ownership or Rights of Use? The Need for a New Conceptual Basis for Land Use Policy," 15 *William and Mary Law Review* 759 (1974).

18. Marion Clawson, "Why Not Sell Zoning and Rezoning? (Legally, That Is)," 2 *Cry California* 9 (winter 1966–67); idem., "Should Your Town Sell Zoning?" 5 *Nation's Cities* 19 (September 1967).

19. Caldwell, "Rights of Ownership," 771.

prospective developers, could facilitate such an auction (though the results to date have most often involved net transfers of resources away from, rather than to, the public sector).[20]

Local governments have a variety of tools for channeling the benefits of economic development to communities. We will look at this repertory in chapter 5, but for now we can focus on the most direct: exactions. Exactions are conditions on public approvals, most typically land-use permissions, needed for private development. They take the form of a requirement that the applicant provide some benefit to the community either in kind or in cash.

Exaction programs became popular in the 1970s and 1980s, often in response to complaints in large cities that downtown commercial development had provided few public benefits, especially to low-income residents and neighborhoods. Exactions can take the form of financial contributions for, or promises to provide directly, parks, affordable housing, day-care, road or transportation improvements, community facilities, and job training, among other benefits. For example, Boston's "linkage" program has required that developers of large office buildings downtown make payments of $5 per square foot to a fund that supports affordable housing and of $1 per square foot to a fund that supports job training. For a typical building, this has yielded about $2 million for housing and $300,000 for job training.[21] From the CED perspective, exactions should be set as high as possible without deterring desirable private investment. They would thus operate as a Georgian land tax, redistributing the "rents" of development.[22]

The CED project runs up against a strong competing notion of property rights that is at least partly expressed in the Constitution and prominent in popular political discourse. This competing view makes the landowner the residual claimant subject only to restrictions designed to

20. Madelyn Glickfeld, "Sale of Development Permission: Zoning on the Auction Block," in Hagman and Misczynski, *Windfalls*, 376, 377.

21. Boston Zoning Code, art.s 26–26B; Boston Redevelopment Authority, *Building Bridges of Opportunity: Linkage* 1–3 (winter 1988).

22. Georgian and mainstream economics agree that the exaction will usually be borne mostly by the landowner rather than by the developer herself or the ultimate user of the development. The supply of land is fixed, whereas the supply of development services and the demand for and supply of the products of development—apartments, offices, etc.—are somewhat elastic in relation to price. One would usually expect the group with inelastic supply or demand to bear such a cost disproportionately.

mitigate specific negative external effects of the development and to taxation under broad-based programs and general rules. This conservative conception of property has three general themes. First, it appeals to tradition, particularly the suspicion of the use of government for redistribution—the "tyranny of the majority"—that influenced the drafting of the Constitution. Second, it tends to be more willing to see landowners, rather than the community, as responsible for land values. Third, it tends to be suspicious of the process whereby community property rights might be defined and enforced. Even if the Georgian efficiency and distributive claims are true in theory, it might be impossible in practice for communities to distinguish rents from returns to investments in improvements or to determine the level of exaction that would be consistent with desirable economic development. Moreover, the appropriation of benefits by the community will induce activism by people who want to share in them. Although this activism is a plus from the CED perspective, it is a negative in the conservative view. At best, it leads to meetings that waste time and resources; at worst, it leads to the dissipation of benefits to support the particular interests of well-organized but self-seeking groups.

The conservative conception of local property has stronger support in constitutional doctrine than the progressive, or CED, conception. However, it is unclear to what extent the Constitution imposes practical constraints on state and local institutions' ability to pursue policies based on the progressive conception. With respect to exactions, the constitutional question is, When does a condition on a regulatory permission constitute a "taking" of private property, which under the Fifth and Fourteenth Amendments can be mandated only if the landowner is compensated for it. To the extent that exactions are "takings," they cannot be used for redistribution.

The range of positions can be visualized this way (Figure 2): In the box at the left are the traditional governmental powers to regulate to minimize externalities and to tax and spend to provide public goods. The economic loss to private individuals resulting from the exercise of such powers is not a taking of property requiring compensation. In the box at the right are the traditional incidents of private ownership—the rights to occupy, exclude people from, and transfer the property in its current use and condition. Any direct and substantial impairment of these rights is likely to be deemed a taking. In the middle box is the

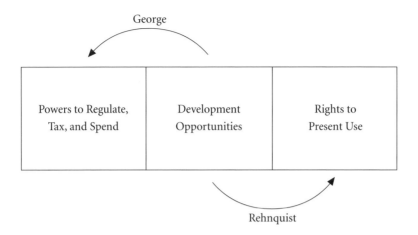

Figure 2

intermediate category of development potential—opportunities to alter the condition of the property for new uses. The doctrinal question is whether development rights should be assimilated to the traditional sphere of public power on the one hand or private rights on the other.

The first option, of course, is the one supported by the Georgian and CED perspectives; the second, the one supported by the conservative perspective. Constitutional doctrine has tended toward the conservative view. In principle, it permits uncompensated restriction of private-property use to limit negative externalities, but condemns efforts to limit property rights in order to appropriate the positive external effects of community activity. This doctrine, however, is not necessarily a strong constraint on local action, such as exaction programs. The strength of the takings constraint depends, first, on how strictly courts review local claims of negative externalities; second, on whether communities can get away with tacitly imposing conditions that would be unconstitutional if they were explicit; and third, whether communities can more formally accomplish the goals of prohibited exactions through more general tax or fee programs.

Recent developments with respect to the first consideration—review of externality claims—clearly attempt to strengthen the constraints on exactions programs, but despite their strong ideological salience, the cases seem to have limited practical effect. The question of how strictly courts review claims of negative externalities from private development is important because, given the pervasiveness of externalities from private-land use decisions, local government can almost always cite them. One position, which might be called the "New Deal position," suggests that courts should uphold exactions, without intense scrutiny, as long as they are supported by any non-frivolous claim that they mitigate an externality. For several decades, something close to this position seemed pre-eminent. However, the Rehnquist Court changed the landscape with its decisions in *Nollan v. California Coastal Commission*[23] and *Dolan v. City of Tigard.*[24]

Nollan involved an effort by the Coastal Commission to condition the allowance of a permit for the expansion of a beach house on the owner's granting a public easement to facilitate access to the beach. The externality cited as the basis for the condition was that the expansion would obstruct the public view of the beach. The Court found the condition a constitutionally prohibited taking, holding that there must be a "nexus" between the external harm on which the condition is grounded and the benefit it exacts. It found no such nexus between the harm of diminished view and the benefit of enhanced access. It saw the public as asking for something unrelated to any burden the proposed private developer imposed on it. The nexus requirement adds a significant restriction to exactions strategy. For example, it calls into question programs such as Boston's "linkage" program that explicitly impose exactions on downtown development in order to "direct the benefits of downtown growth to Boston's neighborhoods."[25] Perhaps the city might satisfy the requirement by showing that new downtown office space creates new jobs, which in turn induce migration that increases housing demand and prices throughout the city, though the case does not indicate how tight the nexus and how strong the showing of it must be.[26]

The *Nollan* nexus test has been amplified by the "rough proportionality" requirement of *Dolan.* That case arose from an application by a landowner to expand the size of her hardware store and the surround-

23. 483 U.S. 825 (1987).
24. 512 U.S. 374 (1994).
25. Boston Redevelopment Authority, *Building Bridges,* 1. Only 10 to 20 percent of the payment is spent in the area "adjacent to the project."
26. It is considerably harder to imagine a "nexus" between the job-training linkage exaction and any externality of office construction.

ing parking lot. The city granted the permit on the condition that Dolan transfer to it a strip abutting a creek amounting to about 10 percent of the lot. The city proposed to use the strip as part of a bicycle way. It defended the condition on the basis of two negative externalities anticipated from the development. First, the larger store and parking lot would bring more traffic and threaten congestion on nearby streets. Second, the enlarged paved surface on the lot would increase run-off of rainwater into the creek, aggravating the risk of flooding. The exaction would mitigate the traffic problem by contributing to the bicycle way, which would encourage bicycle use instead of car use, and it would mitigate the runoff problem by insuring that there would be no construction on a major portion of the dedicated strip.

The Supreme Court, in an opinion by Justice Rehnquist, held the exaction a taking even though it accepted that there was a nexus between the required conveyance and the externalities of congestion and runoff. The problem now was that the city had failed to show some "proportionality" between the magnitude of the exaction and that of the externalities. With respect to runoff, the requirement that the land be transferred seemed disproportionate because the same mitigation could be achieved less intrusively by a prohibition of building on that portion. With respect to congestion, the Court insisted that "the City must make some effort to quantify its findings in support of the dedication for the pedestrian/bicycle pathway beyond the conclusory statement that it could offset some of the traffic demand generated."[27]

Dolan thus lends constitutional support to the view that development opportunities belong to landowners and that a community cannot achieve directly any net collective benefit through the exercise of its power to regulate land use. In this view, a community's efforts to redistribute wealth and develop collective assets must take place through its taxing and spending powers, rather than through its land-use regulatory power. This would be a powerful limitation on CED because taxing and spending power are often less effective for CED purposes. Taxing power is less flexible than a land-use power unconstrained by *Nollan* and *Dolan* would be; it lends itself less to individualized application. Most importantly, local governments and community organizations

27. 512 U.S., 374, 395.

have considerably less discretion and influence over tax policy, which tends to be fairly rigidly specified at the state level, than over land use.

The practical effect of *Nollan* and *Dolan,* however, is limited, though the extent of the limit is unclear. A lot depends on how the courts interpret the requirement that "some effort" at quantification be made. In particular, it depends on who has the burden of proof (risk of non-persuasion) once the city makes a plausible initial showing. Because externalities are often unprovable and are rarely provable with any degree of confidence, the party with the burden is under a major disadvantage.[28] Even with such issues uncertain, the ability to bring judicial challenges under these cases to exactions, and hence cause delay and expense, gives landowners and developers significant leverage, especially when they are better financed than the municipalities or community groups with whom they are dealing.

Nevertheless, the practical import of the cases is subject to two major limitations. First, the *Nollan–Dolan* constraints address particularized decision making over land use, rather than decision making under general rules. How this distinction will play out remains to be seen. Although the Supreme Court characterized the decision in *Dolan* as "adjudicative," it was in fact based on a scheme of some generality.[29] It may be that an exaction based on a fairly rigid formula such as the one in Boston that requires a fixed sum per square foot on all office space would not have to satisfy the *Nollan–Dolan* test and would be reviewed under the loose New Deal standard. The more general and formulaic the exaction rule is, the more the exaction looks like a traditional tax, which continues to be reviewed loosely under the New Deal approach.[30]

Nevertheless, the generality requirement could prove to be a significant limitation on a Georgian exactions strategy. A well-organized com-

28. Some read the case to turn on the fact that the exaction took the relatively uncommon form of a demand for a conveyance of property; they suggest that the looser scrutiny associated with the New Deal perspective would apply in the case of a cash exaction. However, this view has been rejected in several jurisdictions. See, for example, *Ehrlich v. City of Culver City,* 911 P.2d 429, 442–45 (Cal. 1996).

29. 512 U.S. at 385.

30. See the discussion of this point in Justice Mosk's concurrence in *Ehrlich v. City of Culver City,* 911 P.2d at 454–59, and for a general discussion of *Nollan* and *Dolan,* see Molly McUsic, "The Ghost of *Lochner:* Modern Takings Doctrine and Its Impact on Economic Legislation," 76 *Boston University Law Review* 605 (1996).

munity with control over land-use regulation would prefer to preserve its bargaining flexibility to increase or lower demands in particular situations depending on the clout of the developer and the community benefits from the projects. The generality requirement might restrict this flexibility.

A second limitation on the practical effect of the *Nollan–Dolan* constraints is that they apparently apply only to explicitly conditioned permissions, not to denials of permission. A municipality's decisions to set general limits on development and its decisions to deny variances from these limits are still reviewed under the New Deal standard.[31] It has no duty to justify either the general rule or the refusal of the variance by showing with the specificity required by *Nollan* and *Dolan* that the negative externalities of the prohibited development are of any particular type or magnitude. Apparently then, the municipality can avoid *Nollan–Dolan* by denying requests until the developer volunteers a plan with sufficient community benefits.

In this situation, the best overall strategy for a community trying to maximize public benefits may be to enact a general scheme of very strict controls, then engage in only implicit bargaining with developers over waivers, denying applications until the developer volunteers adequate concessions. If the community benefits are part of the developer's proposal, the regulatory authority can obtain them without any explicit conditions on its approval. Whether the courts would tolerate such a strategy if it were evidently and widely adopted is not clear, but it seems consistent with the most recent pronouncements.[32]

In some jurisdictions, the conservative view of property plays a more important role in the political realm than it does as constitutional constraint. State statutes and common law sometimes enact constraints of the *Nollan* and *Dolan* variety,[33] and local governments sometimes decline to enact aggressive exactions schemes, even where constitutionally

31. See, for example, *Montgomery County v. Woodward and Lothrop, Inc.,* 376 A 2d 483 (Md. 1977) (New Deal review of general limits); *City of Monterey v. Del Monte Dunes,* 119 S. Ct. 1624 (1999) (*Dolan* does not apply to denials).

32. Indeed, the facts recited in detail and without comment by the court in *Monterey Dunes* suggested that such a strategy was being pursued there.

33. For example, *Municipal Arts Society of New York v. City of New York,* 522 NYS 2d 800 (N.Y. 1987).

permitted, on the basis of arguments grounded in the conservative view. The contest between the progressive and conservative views is re-enacted continuously in innumerable specific debates over land-use rights.

COMMUTERS AND NONRESIDENT JOB SEEKERS:
LOCAL PREFERENCES

In one extreme view, a political jurisdiction is merely a setting where independent individuals interact on an equal basis. The government's job is to facilitate basic norms of fair interaction among them. For this purpose, there is no reason to distinguish members or citizens from others, and to do so would compromise the principle of equal treatment.

Unqualified, this atomistic view seems incompatible with the idea that members or citizens have special rights to control a jurisdiction's government. It is implausible that members could be expected to exercise such control without regard to their own interests to the extent that they differ from those of outsiders. Moreover, the collaboration required for democratic decision-making requires some degree of special mutual concern among the decision makers. Without such special concern, it seems unlikely that government could work, and with it, it seems unlikely that decisions would not sometimes favor members over nonmembers. In the communitarian view, this is both inevitable and desirable.

Modern governments at all levels incorporate both the atomistic and communitarian views, often in ambiguous measures. We tend to define membership politically. Voting rights are the most important indication of membership, and residence is the most important criterion for the allocation of voting rights. Often we expect and allow those who have voting rights to favor themselves over those who do not, but we limit their ability to do so.

The Supreme Court considers that the federal structure of the Constitution implies rights of interstate mobility that are inconsistent with encompassing notions of local citizenship. Its doctrines limit a state's ability to prefer its residents or, where preference is permitted, to make residence too difficult to acquire. The doctrines—based on the equal-protection, commerce, and privileges-and-immunities clauses—apply to local as well as state government, at least to the extent that disfavored nonresidents include out-of-state as well as in-state people.[34] State law also has doctrines limiting the ability of local governments to prefer their constituents.

No state or locality could have separate laws about contract or theft for citizens or residents on the one hand and noncitizens or nonresidents on the other. Nor could any American jurisdiction deny outsiders the use of its roads or refuse to provide them with police protection against crimes within the jurisdiction. On the other hand, American jurisdictions can and do confine distribution of some benefits to members. This is the case with schooling and welfare benefits. Jurisdictions may not make acquiring membership excessively difficult. More than minimal durational residency requirements are constitutionally suspect. But for a range of benefits, a requirement of residence *tout court* is permissible and customary.

Between the realm where members are clearly prohibited from favoring themselves and the realm where they clearly may do so, there is a chasm of ambiguity. For example, state courts have divided on the question of whether, as a matter of state constitutional law, municipalities may restrict on-street parking in specified areas to residents. Some treat a parking space like use of the streets for transit—a benefit that must be provided to insiders and outsiders alike; some treat it like a welfare payment—a benefit that can be confined to insiders.[35]

---

34. This qualification may make the doctrines inapplicable in some jurisdictions. The court's leading cases on local hiring preferences arose in Boston and Camden, New Jersey, both of which are situated near neighboring states and obviously involve multistate labor markets. To what extent they would apply to a place such as East Palo Alto, which is hundreds of miles from the nearest neighboring state, is less clear.

35. Compare *People v. Greeman,* 137 NYS 2d 388 (1952) (holding preference invalid) with *California v. Housman,* 210 Cal. Rptr. 186, 163 Cal. App.3d 43 (1984) (holding preference valid).

The United States Supreme Court settled a disagreement between the state supreme courts of Massachusetts and Virginia over whether local resident parking preferences violated the federal Constitution, holding that they did not. *County Board of Arlington v. Richards,* 434 U.S. 5 (1977). The Court upheld them against a due-process challenge on the ground that they furthered the general public interests in reducing traffic congestion and air pollution. Although it upheld the preference, the Court implied that an outright purpose on the part of the community to benefit its own members would not be a legitimate basis for it.

Job and business opportunities fall into this intermediate chasm. From a CED perspective, economic opportunities generated by development efforts belong to the community; members should have first crack at them. Thus, community groups typically favor "First Source" hiring or subcontracting laws or agreements by which developers or businesses agree to give preferences to local applicants.

Federal law occasionally mandates local hiring preferences. For example, a federal statute requires public-housing authorities to provide "to the greatest extent feasible" training, job, and business opportunities in connection with federally subsidized projects to residents of the project on which work is done.[36] The federal Empowerment Zone program provides a bounty instead of a requirement: Employers within the zone receive a tax credit for each zone resident they hire.[37]

Congress's ability to enact such preferences seems clear. At the state and local levels, however, there are obstacles. Some states prohibit municipalities from requiring that their employees be residents or from giving preference to residents.[38] These provisions, which seem to have been passed at the behest of public-employee unions, are typically supported by arguments that being a member of a community should not situate a person differently in regard to opportunities of this sort.[39]

Such statutes probably do not preclude most First Source local-development provisions. The statutes apply to government jobs, and most First Source provisions focus on private opportunities generated as a result of publicly supported development. Local First Source provisions are restricted, however, by federal constitutional decisions. These decisions show another line of tension between the CED idea of the community as residual claimant and constitutional conceptions of citizenship.

36. 12 USC 1701u. There appears to have been little enforcement of this provision. See Brad Caftel and Arthur Haywood, "Making Section 3 Work: Employment Training and Job Opportunities for Low-Income People," 27 *Clearinghouse Review* 1336–41 (March 1994).

37. 26 USC 1396.

38. For example, California Constitution, Art. XI, section 10(b).

39. The prohibitions are sometimes explained as measures to insure that the most qualified people are hired, but this leaves open the question of why a locality should not be permitted to trade off quality in order to hire locally if it wishes (or why residence is not a plausible predictor of quality in jobs that benefit from community ties).

The Supreme Court's analysis was first articulated in a case arising from an Alaskan statute mandating that the state's oil leases require that lessees hire Alaska residents in preference to others.[40] The Court has since applied the doctrine to municipal hiring preferences.[41]

The Court begins by suggesting that, to be constitutional, a state or local hiring preference must be responsive to some problem or "evil" that the government has a right to address and concedes that poverty and unemployment are such problems. It then insists that the class disfavored by the preference—nonresidents—be a "peculiar source of the evil."[42] Whether they are such a "peculiar source" turns on whether local residents benefiting from the preference are qualified for the jobs; otherwise, the Court asserts, the source of the problem is not outsider competition but lack of insider skills. Once the state has demonstrated that its unemployed are qualified, some preference is justified, but its reach must be limited. The Alaskan preference applied not only to those contracting with the state, but also to subcontractors and suppliers of contractors and subcontractors. The Court objected to the extent of this ripple effect; binding contractors and their subcontractors appears to be acceptable, but going further may not be.

The requirement that the preference be responsive to an appropriate evil such as unemployment seems uncontroversial. Presumably this would make it much harder for a relatively affluent jurisdiction to adopt such preferences. Although affluent jurisdictions have not shown interest in preferences of such kind, it seems plausible that they should have less authority to benefit their residents at the expense of less affluent outsiders.

However, the remainder of the Court's "peculiar evil" formulation seems odd. The issue is whether a locality may legitimately prefer its own residents in allocating jobs from its development efforts. Whether nonresident applicants should be regarded as a peculiar source of the evil of local unemployment should depend on whether they are entitled to compete on an equal basis for local jobs—the very question that the

40. *Hicklin v. Orbeck* 437 U.S. 518 (1978).

41. *United Building and Construction Trades Council of Camden County v. Camden,* 465 U.S. 208 (1984); see also *White v. Massachusetts Council of Construction Employers,* 460 U.S. 204 (1983).

42. *Hicklin,* 437 U.S., 525.

Court invokes the "peculiar evil" phrase to answer. The Court implies that they are not entitled to equal treatment as long as preferred insiders are qualified. This contention is surprising for two reasons. The Alaskan statute, like nearly all local hiring preferences, explicitly applied only to qualified residents.[43] Thus, it could not have had any effect if there were no qualified unemployed residents. So the demand that the state demonstrate that unemployed residents are qualified as a prerequisite to its validity seems superfluous. Moreover, the Court never explains why the federalism provisions of the Constitution permit preferences for qualified but not for unqualified residents. The distinction does not seem grounded in federalism concerns.

The practical consequence of these cases for hiring preferences is similar to that of *Dolan* for exactions. The Court implicitly rejects the communitarian view of membership, insisting on some more general rationale than simply the community's desire to favor its members. However, it is unclear how much of a burden the community must shoulder to substantiate the rationale once it articulates the acceptable one. Localities are left with a vaguely defined procedural burden, thus creating uncertainty and litigation opportunities for outsiders but leaving the decision to the lower courts as to how demanding the burden will be. Whatever its practical effect, the cases exemplify the discomfort of elite legal culture with communitarian conceptions of membership.[44]

43. Ibid., 520, n.2.

44. A different set of concerns about local preferences arises in affluent communities. Here such preferences are likely to be in tension with the goals of aiding the disadvantaged and promoting racial integration. Objections based on these competing values are especially likely to be pressed in connection with residents' preferences for affordable housing. Local housing agencies are inclined to prefer local residents, and Congress has countenanced such preferences in federally supported programs. However, Congress insists that resident preferences yield, when necessary, to income criteria. Compare 42 USC 1437f (authorizing "local preferences" in Section 8 programs) with 42 USC 1437n (at least 75 percent of Section 8 certificates must be awarded to "low-income families"). Moreover, when a resident preference disproportionately disqualifies minority applicants, it may run afoul of civil rights laws. Preferences adopted by largely white communities, where applicants include substantial proportions of non-local minority-group members, have been struck down. *Comer v. Cisneros,* 37 F.3d 775, 793–96 (2d Cir. 1994); *U.S. v. Housing Authority of Chickasaw,* 504 F. Supp. 716 (S.D. Ala. 1980).

RENT CONTROL

Rent control is another mechanism designed to vindicate the ideal of the community as residual claimant on the fruits of development. A typical rent control regime operates on Georgian principles. It limits the lawful rent to an amount intended to allow the landlord to recover his investment in improvements and his operating costs but to transfer a major portion of the scarcity returns ("rents" in the economist's sense) to the tenant.

Rent control has features resembling both exactions and local hiring and business preferences. Like exactions, it allocates the benefits of community improvement that would otherwise take the form of increases in property values to residents. As the community improves, the tenant is entitled to retain her home without a consequent rent increase. The effect of rent control in redistributing from landowners to residents will often be stronger than that of exactions. In most communities, some residents are homeowners, but by definition, no tenant is.

The benefits of rent control are more individual than those of exaction. The latter go—at least, in the first instance—to the community as a whole, whereas the tenant's right to occupy at a below-market rent goes to her individually. The right, however, is quite different from a conventional private-property right in that it is tied to the community. The tenant cannot sell it or take it with her out of the community. It is thus subject to community-reinforcing constraints of the sort explored in chapter 6.

The resemblance of rent control to local hiring and business preferences lies in its effect on outsiders who would like to enter the community. Rent control makes it harder for prospective entrants to secure apartments in the community or it offers them less advantageous terms than incumbent residents enjoy. Outsiders cannot outbid residents for occupied apartments, and precisely because of the illiquid, immobile nature of the tenant's benefit, vacancies will occur less frequently under rent control. Rent control may inhibit production of new housing that would be available to outsiders. Seeking to avoid this result, most rent control models exempt new construction, but this means newcomers pay higher rents for comparable housing than incumbents. Thus, rent control is another variety of local preference for tenants.

Rent control has been criticized extensively in recent years. It has been accused of deterring housing investment and maintenance and of bringing about arbitrary redistribution, especially where tenants are affluent. Although these criticisms are plausible in some contexts, they have been overstated.[45] Some of the undesirable supply and mainte- nance effects can be strongly mitigated through regulatory design. And although the redistributive effects are superfluous or perverse in some areas, they are strongly justifiable in others.

Indeed rent control sometimes seems to be a critical component of CED, especially where gentrification exerts strong pressure. Where higher-income outsiders have shown an interest in entering a low- income community, there is a risk that successful development will lead to displacement through higher rents. Anticipating this, tenants who have political power will oppose otherwise desirable development. By securing some of the benefits of development to community members, rent control can facilitate community support for development.

East Palo Alto, California, for example—a poor community sur- rounded by affluence—has tremendous potential for gentrification. A surprisingly large portion of its predominantly low-moderate–income residents own their own homes; another large portion are tenants in buildings owned by nonresidents. Without rent control, the tenants would have less reason to support development, and the types of de- velopment they would support might be quite different from those supported by homeowners. Although they might support reforms that would bring resources into the community without making it more attractive to upper-income groups—say, industrial uses that would en- hance tax revenues—they might be inclined to oppose the projects most favored by homeowners. Rent control has the potential to mitigate such conflicts of interest.

Like exactions and preferences, rent control also challenges conser- vative notions of property. Although the constitutional restrictions announced so far are not strong, the courts have upheld rent con- trol against "takings" challenges by landlords only in the rhetorically strained manner found in the exactions and local-preference cases. The cases suggest vaguely that the redistributive and community-preserving effects of the regulations, which from a CED perspective are their most

45. Molly McUsic, "Reassessing Rent Control: Its Economic Impact in a Gentrifying Market," 101 *Harvard Law Review* 1835 (1988); Phillip Weitzman, "Economics and Rent Regulation," 13 NYU *Review of Law and Social Change* 975 (1984–85).

important rationales, would be constitutionally illegitimate or insufficient. They go on to characterize rent control as a response to a social emergency or problem—severe rent inflation—for which landlords are in some sense responsible. Thus, rent ceilings are viewed as a kind of exaction designed to mitigate externalities caused by the landlord.[46]

Practically, the most important obstacles to rent control are not constitutional; they are statutory and political. Municipalities typically lack the power to enact rent control without state legislative authorization, and in many states they have not been given authorization. In two of the states with the most extensive rent control activity—California and Massachusetts—the legislatures have recently provided for the curtailment or phasing out of local rent control authority as currently controlled units become vacant.[47] Even when statutory authority was wider, few municipalities adopted rent control. One of the main arguments put forward by political opponents of rent control appeals to conservative notions of property rights against more collective ones that the CED Movement draws on.

Local Trade: Self-Reliance and Import Substitution

CED rhetoric sometimes connotes economic autarchy or self-sufficiency. The preference for dense, multistranded relations predisposes practitioners toward trade relations in which local businesses—that is, locally owned or locally staffed—sell goods to local consumers (and perhaps even purchase their supplies from local suppliers).

Sometimes CED rhetoric suggests that local demand is an entitlement, not just an opportunity, of local entrepreneurs. When residents shop outside the community, they speak indignantly of money "leaking out of the community." In noting that the typical fast-food–chain outlet is owned by outsiders and purchases supplies from outsiders, Gunn and Gunn call such a business "a suction pump extracting the essential material basis for further development."[48]

46. See *Block v. Hirsch* 256 U.S. 135 (1921); *Pennell v. City of San Jose*, 485 U.S. 1 (1988), especially Justice Scalia's dissent at 19–24, analogizing rent control to an exaction of the sort considered in *Dolan v. City of Tigard*.
47. Massachusetts General Laws, c. 40P; California Civil Code 1954.50 *et seq.*
48. Gunn and Gunn, *Reclaiming Capital*, 34. For a survey of ideas and practices associ-

Some community development corporations (CDCs) engage in general local business promotion of a sort associated with chambers of commerce in more affluent communities. The Dudley Street Neighborhood Initiative has a "Dudley Dollar" program that distributes coupons to members entitling them to discounts at local stores. Its publicity exhorts the community to shop locally as a matter of civic virtue. Its motto is, "The buck stops here!"

In this spirit, some municipal governments have enacted procurement preferences for local businesses. Detroit requires that all of its departments and agencies award at least 30 percent of the market value of their contracts to businesses that are either small (under industry-specific SBA definitions) or Detroit-based. Chicago mandates that a bid from a local firm be preferred to an outside bid unless the local bid exceeds the outside bid by more than 2 percent.[49]

CED practitioners tend to look first to local consumer demand in discussing possibilities of local business development. Indeed, some CDCs have developed businesses to produce goods they themselves purchase. OICW, the job training center in Menlo Park, California, operates the Bell Ringer Cafe, which employs trainees to produce meals primarily for other trainees and the employees of the center. New Community Corporation, the Newark CDC, established the Fashion Institute, a for-profit subsidiary that employs local residents to produce uniforms, sheets, draperies, and other specialized textile products for the schools and enterprises affiliated with it and its sponsor, the local Roman Catholic diocese. It is establishing an auto repair business to take care of the one hundred vehicles it and its affiliates own. It is also building a factory to produce modular housing for its housing-development affiliates.[50]

These starting premises of CED somewhat resemble the strategy of import substitution, which was widely recommended to developing nations in the 1950s and 1960s and adopted by many, especially in Latin America. Jacobs has explicitly urged variations of such strategies for city

---

ated with local self-sufficiency, see Michael Shuman, *Going Local: Creating Self-Reliant Communities in a Global Age* (1998).

49. Emily Palacios, "Detroit's Public Contracting Policies: Is It Time for a Change?" 9 *Journal of Affordable Housing and Community Development Law* 242, 244–46 (2000); Joseph Persky, David Ranney, and Wim Wiewel, "Import Substitution and Local Economic Development," 7 *Economic Development Quarterly* 18, 21 (1993) (Chicago).

50. See http://www.newcommunity.org/busop (visited 31 March 1999).

(though not necessarily community or neighborhood) development.[51] In its stronger forms, import substitution is regarded as discredited today, and many of the objections to it on the national level apply even more powerfully to locally based strategies. Nevertheless, it seems worth visiting here briefly because aspects of both the strategy and the critique seem pertinent to CED programs.

Proponents of import substitution denied that it was in the interest of a developing nation to adapt its development strategies passively to international market signals. They argued that this strategy would lead the economy to excessive specialization. Without adequate diversification, it would be excessively exposed to risks of price changes on international markets. Moreover, short-term price signals would be unlikely to steer investment toward areas with the most promising developmental potential. These signals, for example, take no account of the opportunities for learning and for developing managerial and innovative capacity presented by some investments. Product-price signals also failed to take account of externalities, such as pollution. Outside owners will be less sensitive than domestic ones to the effects of externalities. Moreover, there is the fear that outside investors will use their economic power to influence the domestic political process in ways contrary to the interests of citizens.

Theorists warned that in small, open economies, investment would tend to pour disproportionately into sectors such as natural-resource extraction and manufacturing of commodities. These sectors are subject to volatile product prices. They provide relatively poor learning opportunities for workers because they involve capital-intensive manufacturing with dedicated machinery, which often requires thin and rigid skill sets. In contrast, more flexible manufacturing processes require more extensive and more readily adaptable skills. In addition, resource extraction and manufacturing have a relatively high potential to generate pollution, and these industries tend to create concentrated economic organizations controlled by outsiders.

51. Jane Jacobs, *Cities and the Wealth of Nations* (1984). See also Persky et al., "Import Substitution." For the debate in the context of national economic policy, see Robert Packenham, *The Dependency Movement* (1992), a critical view based on the Latin American experience, and Robert Wade, *Governing the Market: Economic Theory and the Role of the Government in East Asian Industrialization* (1990), a more positive view based mainly on Taiwan.

The import-substitution strategy proposed that nations develop a fairly broad range of advanced industries capable of satisfying domestic demand. States had an advantage in supporting industries producing for local demand because they could use trade restrictions (tariffs and import quotas) to aid them. They could and did give support through subsidies, too, though these could have been used for export producers, as well. It was also assumed that producers would often have a relative advantage in serving domestic demand, in terms of both transportation and communication costs and perhaps also in understanding of consumer needs. And for some, producing for local need desirably lessened dependence on the international economy and vulnerability to its fluctuations.

The countries most associated with the import-substitution strategy—mostly in Latin America—have not been successful economically, and their experience has produced a backlash. Critics find that relative failure in these nations has vindicated the basic commitment of conventional economic theory to trade. By striving for diversification of their industrial bases, these countries sacrificed the benefits of specialization. Their businesses did not reach the scale at which they could take advantage of state-of-the-art technology, and they did not develop the innovative technical cultures more likely to emerge in more extensive industries. In addition, they did not experience the strong competitive pressures that are the most effective inducements of both efficiency and innovation. The domestic market could not sustain a large enough number of producers to create effective competition.

To the extent that the strategy avoided the political disadvantages of absentee ownership, it led to distinctive problems of its own. The domestic-owner class it created was both fairly small and dependent on the state for subsidy and protection. Under these circumstances, the owners readily constituted a cohesive, well-endowed interest group with incentives to lobby the state to entrench its subsidies and protection and to minimize performance standards and social responsibilities. The nationalistic economic policy could contribute more to oligarchy than democracy.

Import substitution, however, looks considerably more promising when it is associated with the highly successful economies of the Pacific Rim—notably, Taiwan and South Korea. The practice (if not the term) appears to have played a role in the development of these economies, but with two major differences from the Latin American cases. Although many successful South Korean and Taiwanese industries started out producing for local demand, as they grew, they sought successfully to become competitive as exporters. This happened in part because the governments of these countries evaded capture by the owners and were able to hold the industries to performance standards and to cut back subsidies and protection as they became internationally competitive.

American state and local governments are forbidden by the Constitution to restrict trade directly through tariffs and quotas, but they have broad discretion with respect to subsidies. The economic and political arguments for import substitution resonate strongly with the CED perspective. The horror stories of "smokestack chasing"—such as that of the Seaboard Corporation's pig processing plant in Albert Lea, Minnesota—involve exactly the type of bad consequences that the import-substitution strategy is designed to preclude.

However, the basic economic objections to import substitution obviously apply more strongly at the local than at the national level. A community of, say, 50,000 people cannot by itself support businesses of major scale. In many lines of business, an enterprise that cannot compete with outside businesses would be unlikely to serve local demand very efficiently. And the danger that the beneficiaries of local subsidies might become an interest group with potential to entrench its subsidies by capturing some element of the local political process has been often observed in CED contexts.

We see such complaints in connection with local procurement preferences. Detroit's rigid and demanding preference for small and Detroit-based businesses is said to have impeded important public projects because of the difficulty of finding qualified contractors.[52] In some cities with large minority electorates, procurement preferences for minority or "economically and socially disadvantaged" businesses are said to have benefited small, permanent groups of politically influential people.[53] Another common criticism is that beneficiaries become dependent on

52. Palacios, "Detroit's Public Contracting Policies," 248–52.
53. See Tamar Jacoby, *Someone Else's House: America's Unfinished Struggle for Integration* 401–3, 458–62 (1998) which chronicles failures and abuses of racial construction-contracting preferences in the construction of the Atlanta airport. A further problem is "fronting," the use of a person who qualifies for the preference as a figurehead for a business dominated by nonqualifying people: See ibid., 400–4.

the program and never learn to compete with mainstream enterprises in unsheltered situations. This criticism has been extensively documented in connection with the federal government's Section 8(a) preference for socially and economically disadvantaged businesses, which federal law mandates for federally supported state and local contracting, as well.[54]

The most that the import-substitution idea can mean plausibly at the local context is a vague preference, other things being equal, for this type of investment. Moreover, the presumption should be employed with sensitivity to the lessons of comparative national experience. The preferences should not be rigid; they need to take account of the capacity of local businesses in specific contracting areas.[55] They should try to make their costs as transparent as possible. In this regard, Chicago's practice of allowing a 2 percent price advantage to local businesses seems preferable to Detroit's rule that a fixed portion of contracts goes to preferred businesses. At least in business with substantial growth possibilities, import substitution should be a station on the way to export capacity, and subsidies should be transitional. Reforms in the Section 8(a) program mandating technical assistance to and setting "graduation dates" for benefited firms are examples of possibilities.[56] And institutions should be structured to avoid capture by a small class of subsidy beneficiaries. The preferences should be administered by agencies that have missions beyond simply supporting local business and that are accountable to constituencies that have a stake in the performance, as well as the allocation, of public contracts.

Of course, even without these problems a generalized policy of self-reliance at either the national or the community level could have enormous costs. If a community's efforts to capture the beneficial effects of its activities provoke similar efforts on the part of others, the community risks loss of the benefits of outside activities.[57]

---

54. See General Accounting Office, *Status, Operations, and View on the 8(a) Procurement Program,* B–201884, 24 May 1988.

55. See Persky et al., "Import Substitution," for ideas on how to do this.

56. Thomas Jefferson Hasty, "Minority Business Enterprise Development and the Small Business Administration's 8(a) Program: Past, Present, and (Is There a) Future?" 145 *Military Law Review* 1, 69–79 (1994).

57. The Maoist regime instituted a policy of community self-reliance across rural China in the 1960s. Carl Riskin, *China's Political Economy* 201–22 (1991). It may be unfair to portray it as an unmitigated disaster. It seems to have played some role in creating a

It seems unlikely, however, that concerns about retaliation or emulation will often weigh strongly against import-substitution strategies for low-income communities. More affluent communities have shown little interest in such strategies. Poor communities tend to feel, often plausibly, that they have been bypassed by the beneficial externalities of outside development. Some of their most important development assets, such as political control over land use and public spending, may lend themselves distinctively to import-substitution strategies.

Three CED developments illustrate that aspects of the import-substitution idea are still prominent—Michael Porter's widely noted strategy of inner-city business development, the "time dollar" plan of local service exchange, and a series of debates over chain-store outlets.

MICHAEL PORTER AND COMPETITIVE ADVANTAGE

Michael Porter, a Harvard Business School professor and one of the nation's best-known business consultants, turned his attention to inner-city business development a few years ago. His conclusions were reported (with what many CED insiders considered off-putting grandiosity) in an article in the *Harvard Business Review* and have become the basis for a network of urban business-development projects known as the Initiative for Inner City Competitiveness.

Although Porter never uses the term "import substitution," a substantial measure of his argument resonates with this framework. He is critical of the softer forms of import substitution, those that contemplate production only for local demand and permanent subsidization. He insists that, to make a serious contribution to economic development, businesses need to be competitive, which in most cases means that they should produce for outside as well as inside demand. He is also skeptical that local ownership is a feasible or desirable criterion. However, he argues that satisfying local demand is an important category of opportunity for inner-city business generation. Indeed, he suggests it includes the most immediate opportunities.[58]

Porter rejects the common view that the competitive advantage of inner-city communities will usually lie in relatively inexpensive land or

---

foundation for the rural industrial sector that boomed in the 1980s and 1990s. However, it was clearly vastly more extreme than necessary to achieve this benefit, and it brought tremendous costs.

58. Porter, "Competitive Advantage," 58.

labor. Inner-city land is often more expensive to develop than neighboring suburban land. Usually, the inner-city neighborhood will have a good deal of vacant land and land with low-value uses. But the costs of assembling large parcels, securing regulatory permissions, remedying contamination, and building new structures will often be considerably higher in even the poorest city neighborhoods than in the suburbs. So will security costs.

Nor does the high unemployment typically found in inner-city neighborhoods necessarily bring about the low labor costs that would make these neighborhoods attractive sites for labor-intensive businesses. Because the workers often lack skills and employment experience, training, supervision, and absence costs are high.

By contrast, Porter finds potential competitive advantage in producing for local demand for two reasons.[59] For one thing, the ratio of retail purchasing power to seller capacity tends to be much higher in low-income inner-city neighborhoods than elsewhere. Purchasing power relative to space in low-income neighborhoods is often comparable to that of high-income neighborhoods because higher density compensates for lower incomes. In the 1960s and 1970s, many large retailers abandoned the inner city. There was much debate about whether such decisions were based purely on costs and profitability as opposed to prejudice or monopolistic practices. Whatever the explanation, the trend seems to be reversing. Suburban markets seem saturated, and the inner city now seems a relatively desirable opportunity. Supermarkets such as the Jamaica Plain Stop 'n Shop, initiated by CDCs for communitarian reasons, have turned out to be exceptionally profitable for their owners. Many such opportunities appear to exist. "In Los Angeles, for example, retail penetration per resident in the inner city compared with the rest of the city is 35 percent in supermarkets, 40 percent in department stores, and 50 percent in hobby, toy, and game stores," Porter writes.[60]

Second, inner-city entrepreneurs and employees may have a relative

---

59. Porter's other major category of competitive advantage is proximity to downtown businesses or industrial clusters. The idea here is to focus on supplying products and services where quick delivery is key—such as catering, document storage, and laundry. (This idea presupposes relatively low costs for inner-city land relative to downtowns and industrial clusters rather than relative to the suburbs.)

60. Porter, "Competitive Advantage," 58.

advantage in understanding the tastes of local customers. Many successful inner-city businesses have focused on product design and marketing for fellow members of ethnic groups. Porter mentions Universal Casket (funeral homes), Parks Sausages, Johnson Publishing, and numerous beauty-care companies focused on African American customers; and CareFlorida (a health maintenance organization), and America's Food Basket (a grocery chain) as companies oriented toward Latinos. Porter is especially attracted to ethnic markets that have some export potential. The entrepreneur has an initial competitive advantage at the local level by virtue of proximity to and knowledge of some distinctive demand. But because there are other groups in other areas with similar tastes and identities, there is a potential for growth to reach these outside markets. Ideally, import substitution is an initial step on a road to export-oriented growth.[61]

COMMUNITY CURRENCY AND BARTER SYSTEMS

"Dudley Dollars" are basically discount coupons used in a marketing scheme. They differ from conventional money in at least two major respects. First, they are not legal tender; no one is obliged to accept them. Second, they can be used only within the community. Considerably more elaborate systems involving instruments of this sort have been proposed, and several experiments are in process.

For some CED practitioners, the idea of community currency is appealing as a form of symbolic commitment to local relationships. "Once a local money system is in place," writes Michael Shuman, "participation becomes a sign of good citizenship."[62]

There may be an economic rationale as well. The government sets the national money supply with a view to satisfying national needs for liquidity, but needs may vary among localities. Low-income communities are exceptionally dependent on cash because they have limited access to substitutes, such as checks and credit cards. They also typically have underused resources, especially labor. The national government

61. The economy of the Cuban neighborhoods of Miami, sometimes called an "enclave economy" because of its reliance on local hiring, credit, and consumer relations, has produced many businesses that started catering to distinctive local demand and matured into major exporters. See Alejandro Portes and Alex Stepick, *City on the Edge: The Transformation of Miami* 123–49 (1993).

62. Shuman, *Going Local*, 133.

could not increase the money supply to accommodate only these communities without causing general inflation. But to the extent that local demand could be satisfied by the underused resources in these communities, a local currency might induce beneficial exchange without threatening inflation.[63]

A variety of nonprofit groups currently operate local currency programs. In Ithaca, New York, in the 1990s, some 1,300 people and businesses engaged in transactions for a wide variety of goods and services using "Ithaca HOURS." These are distinctive green bills with the motto "In Ithaca We Trust" emblazoned on them. They are printed by Barter Potluck, a nonprofit group that also publishes *Ithaca Dollars,* a periodical listing all those in the community who have agreed to accept the currency and what they have to sell. The program has been replicated in at least twenty communities across the country.[64]

A program called "Time Dollars" conceived by Edgar Cahn and supported by the Robert Wood Johnson Foundation has been instituted at 200 sites, including several public-housing projects. The program is designed to promote labor exchange by retired or underemployed people. "A retiree might earn Time Dollars by tutoring young people—one Time Dollar for every hour put in. He or she might redeem credited hours when sick and needing help buying groceries or walking the dog, for example."[65] In Pittsburgh, a nonprofit consignment store accepts

63. Jacobs's better known but not widely credited argument for local currency is different: *Cities and the Wealth of Nations,* 156–81. In contrast to the proposals described above, she argues for a currency that is both legal tender and convertible into other currencies. She is concerned with the function of relative currency values in signaling imbalances between exports and imports. Relative currency values measure the extent to which a nation's exports are paying for its imports, and they can be adjusted to rectify imbalances. But because these adjustments operate only at the national level, the danger exists that they will be inappropriate for particular localities. A strong currency might be right for a nation with booming exports, but it sends the wrong signals to a city that is lagging. The high currency values make it relatively easy to import and harder to export, thus reducing the pressure to develop import-substituting production. Local currencies might alleviate this problem, but they would involve huge coordination problems for the myriad monetary authorities and large transaction costs for interlocality transactions.

64. See the E. F. Schumacher Society's Web site at http://www.schumachersociety.org/frameset_local_currencies.html (visited 22 June 1999); Lewis Solomon, *Rethinking Our Centralized Monetary System: The Case for a System of Local Currencies* 37–95 (1996).

65. Shuman, *Going Local,* 142.

Time Dollars for donated toys and clothing and pays its workers in Time Dollars. The District of Columbia Superior Court gives young people Time Dollars for serving as jurors in Youth Court.[66]

CHAIN STORE DEBATES

Chain stores present an interesting series of CED issues. Some of the proudest accomplishments of CDCs involve bringing chain outlets to their communities. Often these are grocery stores such as the Stop 'n Shop sponsored by the Jamaica Plain Neighborhood Development Corporation or the Pathmark sponsored by the New Community Corporation in Newark. Yet community groups often side with local merchants against chain store outlets. Discount department stores, especially Wal-Mart, are the most common targets. And sometimes activists within a community will divide. In 1998, one of Jamaica Plain's two CDCs sponsored a Kmart, while the other sided with a coalition that successfully killed it.

The obvious attraction of the outlets is that they make goods available more conveniently and more cheaply. But there are also potential harms, and some communities have plausibly believed that they are worse off as a result of the chains.

From a CED perspective, the harm falls into three categories:

First, the chains may put locally owned enterprises out of business or constrict the space for the development of locally owned businesses. The chains themselves are owned by absentees, and they typically are supplied by outsiders. At the time they first emerged in the years following World War I, the chains were vigorously opposed largely on this ground.[67] The desire to protect locally controlled business fueled a barrage of anti-chain tax and antitrust legislation, but most of the laws were eventually repealed or struck down by the courts. The recent cri-

66. Ibid., 142–3.
67. See Michael Sandel, *Democracy's Discontent* 227–31 (1996). According to Sandel, the case against the chains was expressed in basically Republican terms:

> The chain store threatened self-government by producing great concentrations of economic power, destroying local communities, and undermining the status of independent shopkeepers and small businessmen. Independent retailers such as the local pharmacist traditionally served communities as leading citizens of "intelligence and character." But the chains reduced the pharmacist to the status of a "drug clerk" beholden to a distant corporation, and so deprived the community of a trusted figure.

tique represents a revival of this debate, which has been dormant since the 1930s.

Second, there may be powerful externalities. Discount stores do not pollute like smokestack enterprises, though they may cause traffic congestion. The most prominent objection, however, focuses on their effect in reducing the volume of traffic (foot and car) in competing areas to the point that they are no longer viable commercial districts. The chain stores often locate away from established commercial districts, perhaps because of space and parking considerations. The older businesses suffer both because of price competition from the new store and because people no longer find it worth their while to visit the old district. So vacancies go unfilled, and property values decline. Had the chain located in the old district, its competitive effect might have been even stronger, but it would have left open, or perhaps even enhanced, the possibilities for nearby merchants to develop complementary businesses. By locating on the fringe, it undermines these possibilities (perhaps capturing the benefits itself if it controls the land surrounding its outlet).

And third, there is the potential loss of what the economists call consumer surplus from established businesses put under by the new outlet. Scale, amenity, and style often make small local businesses more enjoyable places to shop than the chains (the premise of the movie *You've Got Mail*). Because the management better understands its customers, local businesses may be able to provide products or services, such as credit and delivery, that the chains cannot provide. There is a tendency to respond that, if the customers value these local benefits enough to continue paying for them at the current high price, the store will survive, but that is not necessarily true. It would be true if all costs were variable—that is, proportional to sales volume. However, to an important extent, costs are fixed. Costs for personnel, rent, and publicity do not vary across a broad range of sales volume.

Thus, it is possible that a new business can put an old one under because the old one can no longer cover its fixed costs, even though a large fraction of the old one's customers would still prefer to pay the latter's higher prices. And it is possible that such a shift could leave the community worse off even in conventional pecuniary terms. This is most likely when the customers attracted by the new outlet have only a slight preference for it, while the loyal customers are deeply attached to the old store.[68]

Whether losses exceed benefits will vary with context. The common intuition that supermarkets are more likely to be beneficial than department stores seems plausible. People spend more on food than other retail purchases, so the value of lower prices can be great. Some residents may have been traveling outside the community to shop at supermarkets prior to the arrival of the new store, so to that extent the new business does not come at the expense of local merchants. And a supermarket, unlike a department store, leaves a fairly wide range of retail

68. Here is an example: A Mom-and-Pop store beloved by some has fixed costs of $1,000 (for renting, furnishing, heating, and lighting its space and paying someone to run it) and variable costs of $1 per item sold. People value the store because of the quality of its products and because it's a pleasant place to shop. Some of them would be willing to pay a premium just to buy at this store because of its attractiveness and convenience. Specifically, two hundred people would be willing to pay up to $4 per item; two hundred would be willing to pay up to $3 per item; and four hundred would be willing to pay up to $2.25 per item. So the store faces the following cost and demand conditions:

Price	Items Sold	Cost	Revenue
$4	200	1,200	800
$3	400	1,400	1,200
$2.25	800	1,800	1,800

Cost equals the $1,000 fixed cost plus $1 per item sold. (These figures include a minimal profit.) The store charges $2.25 because at any higher price it cannot generate enough volume to cover its costs.

Now suppose a Kmart opens and starts selling goods that resemble the Mom-and-Pop store's for $2. The marginal customers of the Mom-and-Pop (the ones who would not pay more than $2.25) regard the Kmart products as nearly as good as those at the Mom-and-Pop and are indifferent to atmosphere and amenities at the Mom-and-Pop. The infra-marginal customers regard the Kmart products as inferior or hate shopping at Kmart. They either would not buy the Kmart product at any price or would not pay a cent more than $2. Under these circumstances, the marginal customers will shift to the Kmart, and the Mom-and-Pop will go under because it cannot cover its costs. The marginal customers will benefit by $.25 each, for a total gain of $100 ($.25 × 400). The infra-marginal customers will lose the opportunity for a transaction in which each received a surplus of either $1.75 or $.75, for a total loss of $500 ($1.75 × 200 + $.75 × 200). So losses exceed gain.

I have adapted this argument from one made in a different context by Edwin Baker, "Giving the Audience What It Wants," 58 *Ohio State Law Review* 311, 328–30 (1997).

opportunities for other stores. A new supermarket can even create opportunities for new adjacent businesses, such as restaurants, laundries, and video stores, which might be locally owned. Sometimes the local small food stores can adapt to the arrival of the supermarket by specializing their goods more or focusing on hours when the supermarket is closed. All of the existing food stores in Jamaica Plain, whose owners had opposed the Stop 'n Shop, appear to have survived.

Note that the effort to protect local merchants has some of the troubling political dynamic associated with Latin American-style import substitution. The merchants and their most loyal patrons often constitute cohesive interest groups with strong incentives to oppose entrance by outsiders. The benefits of the new store are diffused throughout the community, and the stakes of the beneficiaries of change are individually smaller than those of the supporters of the status quo. This is the classic situation in which interest groups often seem to triumph over broader collective interests. The status quo supporters also benefit because, as locals, their claims also resonate with the CED commitment to local ownership. CDCs are supposed to serve as vehicles of countervailing power for underorganized segments of the community, but there is always the risk that they themselves will be captured by the special interests.

A controversy in Jamaica Plain in 1996 over a proposed CVS pharmacy at Eggleston Square illustrates how difficult these issues can be. A study suggested that the chain outlet would fill 4,000 prescriptions a week. The outlet would displace a local businesses that was filling about 800 prescriptions a week. The CVS store's prices would be considerably lower than the local pharmacy's. On the other hand, the CVS would not provide the credit and delivery services that the old pharmacy offered to a portion of its long-standing customers, many of them residents of a nearby housing project for the elderly. Some customers would miss the personal contact with the staff of the old pharmacy. The local owners and some of their customers organized to defeat the land-use permissions needed for the new outlet and to save the old pharmacy. However, CED practitioners remain divided about whether this result was a good one. Some customers of the old pharmacy would have lost significant consumer surplus from the change. But the aggregate benefits to the community—in terms of lower prices for those who had been patronizing the old pharmacy and more convenience to those who had been traveling to more distant discount stores—seemed large. And there is the suspicion that the outcome may have depended on the fact that the stakeholders in the status quo were more vocal and organized than the prospective beneficiaries of the new store.

Local Knowledge as a Community Asset

Knowledge of the creditworthiness of a loan applicant, or the reliability and skill of a prospective employee, or the viability of a local commercial investment are kinds of knowledge with economic value.

As noted earlier, the current relative distribution of knowledge and wealth disadvantages relatively poor and culturally marginal people in two ways. First, it is more difficult and costly for people with money to lend and invest to acquire this kind of information about those who are socially distant from them. Second, people with personal wealth can make investments on their own initiative that give information to others that increases the others' willingness to make investments in them. They can put their own money at risk in a business or pay for advanced education, thus giving others evidence of their confidence in their own projects and abilities. People who lack their own resources cannot do this.

Thus, a common thrust of many CED-related programs is to try to enhance the communication of information that facilitates investment. There are many approaches, but the one that resonates most with the core CED themes attempts to institutionalize local knowledge as a community asset. It does so by subsidizing community-based organizations in, first, the acquisition and formulation of local knowledge, and second, in the translation of that knowledge into reputational capital vis-à-vis outside institutions. Reputational capital is a kind of social capital. In a variety of programs, it performs the role of enabling local institutions to make credible commitments on behalf of the community to outsiders.

For example, a CDC sets up a job training program. It draws on its members' knowledge of the unemployed people in the community to identify job openings for which they might be trained, to screen local applicants for the most plausible candidates, and to configure the training program to help the trainees qualify. It then refers the trainees to employers, perhaps with a promise to give them continuing social support and training on the job.

One reason the organization may be able to induce the employer to accept its referrals is that it has reputational assets at risk. It has been established in the hope of inducing a continuing stream of support from government agencies and the nonprofit sector. Referrals of unqualified trainees will damage these prospects. Successful referrals will enhance these prospects. When the organization has a successful track record, its reputational capital increases. The stronger the organization's reputation for reliability in training and certifying its people, the more it has to lose from poor referrals and, hence, the more readily outsiders are willing to trust its representations. It can "bond" its assertions by putting its reputational capital at stake.[69]

The same process can operate with community-based support for home-mortgage credit and business lending. Here, too, the local knowledge that facilitates identifying plausible opportunities, screening local applicants, and configuring training resources to their needs can be converted into reputational capital that enables the local organization to induce outside investment. Public programs that support community-based training and technical assistance promote this process of institutionalizing information as a local asset.

The distinctive character of the community-based strategy is highlighted by comparing it with two other approaches. One involves a direct subsidy to outside employers or lenders to take actions that benefit community members. The Empowerment Zone employer's tax credit is an example. Another is to transfer resources directly to individuals with a view toward allowing them to signal directly to outsiders their employability or creditworthiness. "Individual development accounts" are an example.

All three approaches have the potential to benefit low-income com-

69. See Paul Milgrom and John Roberts, *Economics, Organization and Management* 257–69, 331–2 (1992). For CED applications, see Peter Pitegoff, "Shaping Regional Economies to Sustain Quality Work: The Cooperative Health Care Federation," in *Hard Labor: Women and Work in the Post-Welfare Era* (Joel Handler and Lucie White eds. 1999) (Cooperative Home Care Associates of New York and affiliated enterprises); Lisa Servon, *Bootstrap Capital: Microenterprise and the American Poor*, 118–22 (1999) (describing the Women's Initiative for Self-Employment in San Francisco).

munity members both directly, by getting them jobs or credit they otherwise would not get, or indirectly, by inducing learning that increases the general willingness of outsiders to invest in the community. If the successful performance of the beneficiaries' subsidized training or lending is widely observed, it may lead outsiders to revise their premises in ways that make them more willing to invest in low-income communities. However, of necessity, some of the information produced by these programs remains private, and its value inures to particular participants. The programs differ in how they allocate the benefits of this nonpublic information.

An employer tax subsidy gives the benefit to the employer. The employer takes advantage of the subsidy to hire workers she regards as high-risk and learns from her experience which characteristics are associated with productivity. Outsiders will get some information about her experience, but she will have the most detailed and reliable information, and will get the most benefit from it. Little reputational capital will develop because the employer has neither an interest in developing, nor much opportunity to develop, a reputation for credible referrals to other employers.

With individual accounts, the distribution of learning and reputational capital is harder to predict. Individuals can use the resources in their accounts to develop reputational capital for themselves. Employers, lenders, and investors will learn from their dealings with individuals, but this knowledge is likely to be widely dispersed and may not attain a sufficiently critical mass in any locus to make much of a difference.

The distinctive feature of the community-based approach is that the accumulation of learning and reputational capital is concentrated in local nongovernmental institutions. This gives control over such capital to the community, and it has the potential to strengthen local ties in ways that have beneficial spillover effects on other community institutions.

Chapter 5 ⋮ The Community as Agent of Economic Development

A community has no conventional legal form or institutional structure. One of the tasks of CED is to invent forms and structures to facilitate the kinds of collective activities it promotes.

Municipal governments do have conventional legal forms and institutional structure. Community development is dependent on municipal government. But communities are not the same things as municipalities. They are usually smaller, and even where they are geographically co-extensive with municipalities, as with East Palo Alto, they involve different sorts of relations. These relations are broader, more diverse, and less formal than those of municipal government. Thus, the conventional form and structure of municipal government needs to be supplemented for communities to act as agents of their own economic development. The CED Movement has refined a distinctive set of institutions for this purpose.

In this chapter, we survey the basic tools available to communities for economic development, then examine the distinctive institutions that facilitate collective grassroots use of these tools. The most central of these institutions is the CDC, a variety of charitable nonprofit corporations. Cooperatives play an important and revealing role. Churches also have played an important role in many areas, and their traditional organizational forms have proved well adapted to CED.

Tools

Six basic tools are available to community-based organizations (CBOs) in economic development. These tools include governmental powers that are sometimes delegated in various fashions to community-based organizations. When they cannot exercise these powers directly, these organizations can often influence their exercise.

The first tool is financial assistance. CBOs have privileged access to some sources of finance, and they can use these resources to support projects they undertake themselves or they can make them available for projects undertaken by others. Dozens of government programs and hundreds of private for-profit and nonprofit organizations are focused on financing housing, job, and business development in low-income areas through community-based organizations. Assistance to CBOs and by CBOs to others can take the forms of grants, equity investments, loans, and loan guarantees. Financial support sometimes comes at nominally market rates, but usually involves subsidy or liberality un-available to conventional borrowers. However, the level and form of the subsidy has many variations. It may involve a lower interest rate, ex-tended payment terms, a lower down payment, less or no collateral, or a willingness to extend credit where it would be commercially unavailable (for example, to borrowers who cannot satisfy conventional underwrit-ing criteria).

Although it is not really financial, the provision of tangible property on favorable terms can also be included under this heading. The most important example is land. Urban municipalities often have title to a good deal of land in low-income neighborhoods that has reverted to them because of defaulted tax payments or was acquired for public facilities that are no longer in use. This is the principal source of the free land CDCs sometimes get for affordable housing development. Many of the affordable housing projects at Dudley Street and the first one built in East Palo Alto sit on land contributed by the cities. Private charitable contributions of land also sometimes occur.

The second tool is technical assistance. The CBOs have myriad poten-tial sources of advice and training on economic development, and they provide myriad kinds of advice and training to the projects they sup-port. They train tenant management councils how to be landlords. They train owners in limited-equity cooperatives to run housing cooperatives. They teach accounting and business skills to entrepreneurs. They give job readiness and substantive skills courses to unemployed workers. CED activities tend to be training-intensive, because they are premised on grassroots participation. Resident board members of CDCs are typically inexperienced. They, as well as active rank-and-file members, should be trained in the fundamentals of an organization's structure, procedures, and finance and in the nature of its projects. Organizations that specialize in community planning, such as the Dudley Street Neighborhood Initiative, spend great time and resources to help community participants understand the issues and options involved in its projects.

We might distinguish institutional innovation—developing and demonstrating new organizational forms—as an especially important form of technical assistance. Some CED support organizations are engaged not simply in transmitting an established body of knowledge, but in actively developing a new one. The Local Initiatives Support Organization has developed and popularized new structures for affordable tax-credit supported housing. The Neighborhood Reinvestment Corporation has striven to elaborate and popularize a model of mutual housing. The Industrial Cooperative Association has devoted itself to experimenting with production cooperatives. These organizations have the expertise and the funding to engage in a kind of experimentation conventional CDCs lack, and their efforts help popularize and reduce the risk of new forms.

The third tool is tax concession. Municipalities often have the power to make property-tax concessions to businesses as inducements to increase or maintain local investments. State and local governments can sometimes confer federal and state income-tax advantages. The federal Low Income Housing Tax Credit, the single most important source of funding for affordable housing, is allocated through the states.[1] The Empowerment Zone program allows designated municipalities to confer federal tax advantages for the employment of workers within the zones.[2] The federal government has programs that permit state and local governments to issue bonds for development projects, with interest payments exempt from federal tax.[3]

At least when used alone, tax concession is out of favor as an explicit

1. 26 USC 42(h)(3).

2. 26 USC 1396.

3. See, for example, Bennett Hecht, *Developing Affordable Housing: A Practical Guide to Nonprofit Organizations,* 95–103 (2nd ed. 1999).

development inducement. The Clinton administration produced the neologism "Empowerment Zone" (and the accompanying smaller-scale version, "Enterprise Community") to distinguish its program from the "Enterprise Zone" programs tried in various jurisdictions here and abroad in the 1980s. The CED literature suggests that a program focused solely or principally on tax concessions is likely to attract the wrong kind of industry. Tax costs are not a major factor in location choice by most businesses. The businesses most sensitive to small cost differences also tend to be technologically stagnant and disinclined to invest in workers and the surrounding community.[4]

The Empowerment Zone program acknowledges this criticism and makes tax concession part of a broader package of tools, including educational and police services, to be employed in a process designed to induce the attraction to relatively desirable enterprises.

Tax law delegates to CDCs, as charitable nonprofits, the power to confer tax advantages in return for resources that can be used in development. With the approval and assistance of state or local government, charitable organizations can issue bonds that pay tax-exempt interest to fund their activities, though as a practical matter this is a power available only to very large organizations.[5] Charitable nonprofits of all sizes have the unilateral power to confer tax advantages on private people simply by accepting donations from them. These benefits can be large. A recent affordable-housing project in the San Francisco area was built on land donated to the CDC developer with a valuation of $20 million. The donor, of course, received tax advantages worth many millions of dollars. So the CDC was able to induce a major government investment in the project through its own, largely unreviewed initiative.

The fourth tool is the provision of public goods. Local governments routinely provide public services, such as police, fire, sanitation, and schooling, and physical infrastructure, such as roads, parks, and sewers. Community-based nonprofits have traditionally supplemented many of these activities.

The way these goods are allocated affects investment decisions.

4. See David Osborne, "The Kemp Cure-All: Why Enterprise Zones Don't Work," *New Republic*, 3 April 1989, 21; Margaret Wilder and Barry Rubin, "Rhetoric versus Reality: A Review of Studies of State Enterprise Zone Programs," 62 *Journal of the American Planning Association* 473 (autumn 1996).

5. Hecht, *Affordable Housing*, 95–103.

Almost any large building project will require some infrastructural changes. Increasing police presence in an area will often make it more attractive for a variety of types of investment. Adapting a job training program to a particular industry or employer may make a nearby location more attractive for its plants.

Agitation over public services is the most traditional kind of community action. Low-income and minority neighborhoods often feel short-changed by city governments in terms of services. As noted earlier, Dudley Street's first project was a campaign to pressure the city to close down an illegal garbage-dumping station, a critical prerequisite to attracting housing investment.[6]

The fifth tool is procurement preference. Local governments and CBOS can support enterprises by committing to purchase their output on favorable terms and persuading others to do so. They currently use a range of procurement preferences, framed variously in terms of criteria of residence, race and gender, or social and economic disadvantage.[7] We might also consider as a form of procurement preference commitments by employers to hire graduates of training programs they support. A simpler form, really more like an advertising campaign, is illustrated by the "Dudley Dollars" program.

The literature suggests that the softer forms of preference are unlikely to have a large impact by themselves. Exhortation and local loyalty can rarely sustain an otherwise uncompetitive enterprise.[8] The harder preferences can make a difference. However, they are subject to two kinds of abuse. Sometimes they go to people who are fairly well established and could get along without them. And sometimes they sustain in permanent dependence a class of businesses that never attain the ability to get along without them. In these cases, they seem an expensive and arbitrary subsidy. The challenge is to target the preferences to people who could not get along without them and to make them transitional, so

6. Peter Medoff and Holly Sklar, *Streets of Hope: The Fall and Rise of an Urban Neighborhood*, 67–88 (1994).

7. See Michael Schuman, *Going Local: Creating Self-Reliant Communities in a Global Age* 128–51, 236 (1998) (on municipally-initiated preferences for local businesses); 15 USC 637 (on federally mandated preference in federally supported state and local projects for "socially and economically disadvantaged business").

8. Jed Emerson and Fay Twersky, eds., *New Social Entrepreneurs: The Success, Challenge and Lessons of Non-Profit Enterprise Creation* 7 (Roberts Foundation, 1996).

they can be phased out after the business has had a chance to become self-sustaining.[9]

The sixth tool is land-use permission. Land-use regulation is the most extensive power of economic regulation that local government has. Any large-scale development will require zoning and building permits. The governing substantive norms will usually give the administering agency a good deal of discretion. Procedural norms will create opportunities for participation by affected citizens and organizations, as well as opportunities for administrative and judicial challenges to first-instance decisions they do not like.

As noted, local governments often own land in lower-income communities, so they can support or impede projects by cooperating or refusing to cooperate as landowners. Community-based organizations have sometimes been successful in raising money to purchase land to head off undesirable development.

This list of tools is not comprehensive. There are other candidates, such as regulatory concessions—for example, abatements of environmental requirements. However, municipalities rarely have much power in this area. An important exception, however, comprises federal and state "Brownfields" programs, which trade regulatory concession for developer exactions.[10] Under these programs, government agencies agree to waive strict landowner liability for contaminated sites in return for development commitments that have local support.

Another tool omitted from the list is rent control, though I suggested in chapter 4 that it might play a valuable role in some situations. However, the legislative and political obstacles to an effective program are high in most jurisdictions. Eminent domain is a unique combination of

9. See the material on the Section 8(a) set-aside program cited in chapter 4, notes 54 and 56. Such problems are exacerbated by the conflicting goals of most administering agencies, which are responsible both for getting a good product at a reasonable price and to seeing that the intended social benefits go to the beneficiary class. Once they find a contractor in the targeted class who can do a good job, there is a temptation to keep her on to avoid taking the risks of a new, untested contractor. A similar problem occurs in job-training programs built around sheltered enterprises. It is hard to let go of a really productive employee, even though that is what the social goals dictate. See "Rubicon Programs, Inc.," Emerson and Twersky, *New Social Entrepreneurs*, 24–37.

10. Jennifer Hernandez and Katherine B. Reilly, "A Practical Guide to Brownfields Transactions," 14 *Practical Real Estate Lawyer* 9 (July 1998).

land-use regulatory and spending powers. It is not often used, but it can be important in large-scale projects. The "Triangle" project, in which the Dudley Street Neighborhood Initiative exercised eminent-domain powers jointly with the city, shows how strong a role a CDC can play in its use.

Institutions: The Community Development Corporation

The central institution in the theory and practice of CED has turned out to be the CDC. Community Development Corporations have a fairly standard legal form that involves four basic characteristics. Many public and private programs require these characteristics (among others) as conditions of eligibility for support, but the characteristics are standard even among organizations that do not receive support from such programs.

The first characteristic of the CDC concerns its goals: It must have among its organizational purposes commitment to benefiting through development some geographically bounded community of disproportionately low-income people. The remaining characteristics are structural: It must be a charitable, or public-benefit, nonprofit corporation recognized as such under both state law and the Internal Revenue Code; it must have a governing board that includes representatives of the beneficiary community; and its membership must be open to the beneficiary community.

The goal characteristic differentiates the CDC from municipal government in that its purposes are more specialized. But governments have agencies, ranging from Redevelopment districts to little city halls or community boards, that have specialized purposes potentially similar to those of CDCs. To appreciate the most important differences between local government and the CDC, we need to consider the structural characteristics.

CDCs are free-standing corporations. Almost anyone can create a corporation by filing a small number of papers and paying moderate fees. In addition, CDCs are nonprofit corporations, a term that is somewhat misleading. Although nonprofit corporations are not devoted primarily to making profits, they can, and many do, make profits. The defining characteristic of the nonprofit corporation is not the limitation of profits but a legal constraint on distribution of resources to those who control it—the Nondistribution Constraint.[11]

The extent of the Nondistribution Constraint depends on which of two kinds of nonprofit corporation the enterprise is. If it is a mutual-benefit nonprofit corporation, the Nondistribution Constraint will prevent the distribution of current income. If it is a charitable or public-benefit corporation, the Nondistribution Constraint will preclude the distribution of income *and* assets. Mutual-benefit corporations are designed to benefit their members or customers and are usually controlled by them.[12] Examples are country clubs and trade associations. Charitable or public-benefit corporations may or may not be controlled by members, but they are always designed primarily to benefit people other than those who control it. Mutual-benefit nonprofits resemble cooperatives; public-benefit nonprofits resemble trusts.

The constraint on the distribution of income is a fairly minor, and perhaps anachronistic,[13] limitation on mutual-benefit corporations. They may distribute assets to their members, and their basic purpose is to provide ongoing benefits in kind to them. On the other hand, the strong Nondistribution Constraint on public-benefit corporations is fundamental.

As a matter of state law, a nonprofit can acquire the status of a public-benefit corporation in one or more of three ways. Under the more modern corporation statutes, the incorporators are required to elect explicitly either mutual-benefit or public-benefit status.[14] In addition or alternatively, an organization can commit to hold its assets for charitable purposes through an express trust. Finally, if it accepts donations

11. My discussion of nonprofits draws heavily on Henry Hansmann, "Reforming Nonprofit Corporation Law," 129 *University of Pennsylvania Law Review* 497 (1981), and James Fishman and Stephen Schwartz, *Nonprofit Organizations* (2d ed. 2000).

12. Hansmann points out that there is a distinct subcategory of "commercial entrepreneurial nonprofits" that are designed to benefit customers but are not controlled by them. Examples include the American Automobile Association and the Consumers Union. Although typically considered mutual-benefit corporations, he argues, they would be better treated as public-benefit corporations; Hansmann, "Reforming Nonprofit Corporation Law," 586–7.

13. Ibid., 582–94.

14. For example, California Corporations Code, sec. 5130, 7130.

for traditionally charitable purposes, an implied trust of those assets may arise.[15]

Under state corporation and trust law, the main consequences of charitable status are the requirement that the organization use its resources for its declared purposes and the consequent strong Nondistribution Constraint that forbids their distribution to those in control. Under federal and state tax law, potentially quite favorable consequences accrue to charitable nonprofits. Their income is generally exempt from income tax, though this advantage is also accorded most mutual-benefit corporations as well. However, other important privileges are available only to public-benefit nonprofits: Their supporters receive an income-tax deduction for donations. They can make donations without paying estate or gift taxes on them. And the organization's property is exempt from state and local property taxes and often sales taxes.[16]

The tax benefits do not follow automatically from state-law status as a public-benefit corporation. For federal-tax purposes, a corporation also needs to qualify as a charity under Section 501(c)(3) of the Internal Revenue Code.[17] State-tax benefits typically depend on a similar standard, and state administrators often piggyback on the Internal Revenue Service's determination of federal charitable status.

The federal standard for charitable tax status has not been coherently elaborated, despite a profusion of recent case law. Standards remain vague, cases inconsistent, and administration erratic. As the role of the nonprofit sector grows, this becomes an increasingly important area of legal development.

Section 501(c)(3) requires an applicant to subject itself to a strong Nondistribution Constraint. Beyond this, its central standard concerns the substantive character of the applicant's purposes and activities. These must be charitable in three general senses. First, they must have some connection to the traditional understanding of the scope of chari-

15. For example, *In re Los Angeles Pioneers Society,* 40 Cal. 2d 852, 257 P. 2d 1 (1953).

16. See John G. Simon, "The Tax Treatment of Nonprofit Organizations: A Review of Federal and State Policies," in *The Nonprofit Sector: A Research Handbook* (Walter Powell ed. 1987).

17. Charitable status for federal tax purposes does not require incorporation, although CDCs are invariably incorporated.

table activity. This includes religion, health, education, art, and "relief of poverty." Housing, job, and business development do not, per se, fall within this traditional understanding, however, and many beneficiaries of CDC activity are not strictly poor. Moderate income people, who are considered part of the core CED beneficiary class, may have up to 80 percent of an area's median income,[18] and entrepreneurs who receive CED subsidies may have assets valued considerably higher than that of the median household.[19] Thus, it is important that the IRS has recognized as sufficiently analogous to the core traditional fields activities that involve "combating community deterioration," "lessening the burdens of government" (i.e., providing benefits that government would otherwise have to provide), eliminating "prejudice and discrimination," and "lessening neighborhood tensions."[20] CED activities that are not targeted exclusively to poor people generally qualify under one or more of these headings.

A second aspect of the charitable character inquiry requires that benefits provided be diffused to at least a minimal extent. The beneficiary class need not be large, but if it is small, it must be one whose membership changes over time. An organization devoted to the benefit of a small number of designated people would not qualify. (A trust for the oldest citizen of Biloxi might qualify; one for Mrs. Johnson, the oldest citizen of Biloxi, would not.) The remaining aspect of the inquiry requires that the organization provide benefits of a kind or on terms not available from for-profit providers. This criterion is necessary to disqualify the many conventional for-profit businesses that provide such benefits as housing and medical care to poor customers. As a practical matter, it suggests (though this is not an explicit requirement) that at least some of the organization's benefits should be provided on a basis

18. 24 CFR 91.5 (HUD definition of "moderate" income).

19. For example, individuals with assets of $250,000 in addition to equity in their homes can qualify as "socially and economically disadvantaged" for the purpose of the major federal procurement preference program. 13 CFR 124.104(c)(2).

20. 26 CFR 1.501(c)(3)–1(d); for elaboration in CED contexts, see Revenue Ruling 74–587, 1974–2 *Cumulative Bulletin* 162; Revenue Ruling 70–585, 1970–2 *Cumulative Bulletin* 115; IRS, "Guidelines for Determining Whether Organizations Providing Housing Are Described in Section 501(c)(3) of the Code," *I.R.B.* 1995–20, at 18 (Announcement 95–37).

that is below both the organization's costs and the market price from for-profit providers.[21]

Two further requirements for 501(c)(3) status are important. The first is the "private inurement" rule, which provides that no part of the organization's earnings may "inure to the benefit of any private share-holder or individual." As applied to outsiders, this simply reinforces the requirement that the organization's operations be charitable or provide public as opposed to private benefits. As applied to insiders, it reinforces the Nondistribution Constraint, as well as the corporate and trust law duty of loyalty that requires dealings between the organization and those who control it be fair to the organization.

Finally, there is a fairly specific limitation of political activity: The organization may not engage in more than a minimal amount of lobbying and may not "intervene in any political campaign on behalf of or in opposition to any candidate for political office." This strengthens the effect of the general substantive requirement of charitable purpose and operation. Political activities are not considered charitable, so an organization devoted primarily or extensively to political activities could not qualify in any event. The more specific prohibitions make some secondary political activities disqualifying.

Nonprofit managers are policed at both state and federal levels. At the state level, the attorney general polices the Nondistribution Constraint. Although most attorneys general have staff lawyers who focus on monitoring charitable corporations, they have limited resources and information to do so, and enforcement is considered lax. If a nonprofit corporation has members, some states will permit them to bring derivative suits against managers to enforce duties to the corporation, but such suits are rare, many states do not allow them, and nonmember beneficiaries are generally denied standing.[22]

The more elaborate requirements of Section 501(c)(3), which em-

21. See Rev. Rul. 74–587, 1974–2 *Cumulative Bulletin* 162 (ruling exempt organizations providing capital to businesses in low-income areas that are "not able to obtain funds from conventional commercial sources" where the organization disposes of any equity interest it acquires "as soon as the success of the business is reasonably assured"). See also, for example, *Plumstead Theatre v. Commissioner*, 74 T.C. 1324 (1980); *Sound Health Association v. Commissioner*, 71 T.C. 158 (1978).

22. Hansmann, "Reforming Nonprofit Corporate Law," 606–15.

brace both the Nondistribution Constraint and the substantive confinement of activities within the scope of the charitable, are policed at the federal level by the Internal Revenue Service. The IRS's enforcement efforts exceed the aggregate efforts of the states, but they too are considered small in relation to the universe of 501(c)(3) organizations.

For the typical CDC, the most important benefit of 501(c)(3) status is not tax benefits but, rather, qualification for grants, subsidized loans, and other assistance from both government agencies and other private nonprofits, especially foundations, that make 501(c)(3) status an eligibility condition. In effect, these funding organizations piggyback on the federal standard for charitable tax benefits. They spare themselves the need to define this part of their own eligibility standards, and they get the benefit of the IRS's enforcement apparatus. The IRS requires a fairly lengthy application and conducts some (though rarely extensive) review before issuing a letter of determination of 501(c)(3) status. Organizations are also required to file annual reports. Although thorough investigations are rare, they can occur when problems come to the IRS's attention. Thus, an agency that incorporates 501(c)(3) status into its own eligibility conditions has some assurance that the applicant is operating in accordance with charitable purposes and the Nondistribution Constraint.

If we turn to the internal control structure of the public-benefit nonprofit corporation, we find that, as with the business corporation, general managerial power resides with a board of directors charged with appointing and monitoring managers, setting policies, and authorizing extraordinary transactions. In business corporations, directors are chosen by shareholders who have voting power in proportion to their holdings. Public-benefit corporations, however, almost never have shareholders (and even when they do, the shareholders do not necessarily choose the directors). Their directors are generally chosen in one or more of three ways, as specified in their articles or bylaws: Initial directors can be designated by an incorporator, and thereafter vacancies can be filled by the remaining directors. Outsiders designated in the organizing documents, such as a state official or another nonprofit organization, can be empowered to designate directors. And if the organization has members, the members can be charged with electing directors.

State corporation law imposes few limits on board composition.[23] Federal 501(c)(3) law imposes two minimal limits: A corporation controlled by direct beneficiaries may be held not to satisfy the substantive definition of a charity, and a corporation controlled by a small number of major financial supporters may be held to be a "private foundation" subject to less favorable tax benefits than other 501(c)(3) organizations. Funding sources, however, often insist on a degree of community representation, and CDCs invariably have a substantial amount. A study of 130 CDCs finds that, on average, 44 percent of board members are individual members of the community or beneficiary class; 15 percent are representatives of other community-based organizations, including churches; 12 percent are from local businesses; 3 percent are local government officials; 4 percent are donors; and 20 percent are "relevant professionals," people who provide services or advice to the organization.[24] Although the officials, donors, and professionals are typically not community residents, the members of the other categories are.

Neither corporation nor tax law requires a public-benefit nonprofit corporation to have members, but CDCs invariably do. The CDCs with a neighborhood focus offer membership to individuals and often businesses and organizations within the neighborhood. Sometimes various categories of outsiders who have an interest in the community, such as social services agencies and businesses with philanthropic or economic interests, are permitted as well. Members elect the community representatives to the board, and sometimes those from the other categories as well. By virtue of state law or articles and bylaws, members typically have the power to approve major organic changes in the organization, such as mergers or dissolutions. This function is rarely of practical importance, however. More important is the role of members as volunteers in working with the paid staff, which is typically quite small, to organize and conduct the CDC's activities.

I have suggested that the development activities of CDCs can be viewed both as a form of public-goods provision and as a form of

23. A notable exception is the California provision that no more than 49 percent of board seats may be held by "interested persons," who include employees, paid service providers, and their close relatives. California Corporations Code 5227.

24. Avis Vidal, *Rebuilding Communities: A National Study of Community Development Corporations* 39 (New School for Social Research, 1992).

political mobilization. With respect to the public-goods provision, they seem to be alternatives to government; with respect to political mobilization, they seem to be alternatives to political parties. We should compare their structural characteristics to the alternatives.

Unlike governments, nonprofits lack taxing and regulatory powers. To an important extent, CDCs are dependent on government for support that requires such powers. In other respects, however, they are independent of government, and this independence carries advantages.

Nonprofits are more flexible than government in several ways. They are potentially more decentralized, more specialized, and less procedurally restricted. When a CDC focuses on a subarea of a large municipality, it decentralizes decisions. By limiting its purposes and activities to a designated range, it specializes. A government agency or advisory commission might aspire to decentralization and specialization of this kind, but its powers would be legally dependent on the central administration.

The relative procedural flexibility of nonprofits can be seen in many areas. Nonprofits are not subject to public contracting rules, civil-service and public-employee labor laws and collective-bargaining agreements, open-meeting statutes, and a host of norms that make government operations rigid (though sometimes desirably so).

One of the most often remarked advantages of nonprofits is their superior ability to induce voluntary contributions of both services and funds. This is partly a consequence of specialization, which enables them to customize their programs in ways that appeal to volunteers. It is also a function of their procedural flexibility—in particular, their ability to use their governance structure to induce volunteerism. A business corporation gives control to investors as a way to reassure them that managers will make efforts to maximize the return to investors' financial interests. Nonprofits, of course, cannot give control to investors for this purpose, and this is a disadvantage in raising capital. On the other hand, they can give control in a variety of forms, including director and officer positions and chairs of program committees, to people who donate funds or services. Donors and volunteers can use this control to see that their contributions are put to the purposes they support. It seems likely that this control induces altruistic investments in a way that is analogous to the way corporate control induces business investments.

Governments have comparatively little ability to give such control to volunteers.

However, charitable nonprofits resemble government in that their control is supposed to be *disinterested.* In this, they differ from mutual-benefit nonprofits and business corporations. Members of mutual-benefit corporations and shareholders in business corporations are expected to use control for their own benefit. But members and directors of charitable nonprofits are fiduciaries for the organization's charitable purposes. In CDCS committed to benefit a particular neighborhood, member-elected directors are supposed to act for the benefit not just of the members, but of the community as a whole. And charitable non-profits are forbidden to give major control to direct beneficiaries—for example, recipients of grants, loans, training, or services from the organization.

A further important difference between government agencies and nonprofits is that nonprofits are not monopolistic. Anyone can set up a nonprofit and compete both for local support and the various outside resources available to CDCS. Dissatisfaction with a CDC can lead to the formation of a competitor.[25]

Thus, CDCS are subject to two explicit types and one implicit type of accountability mechanism. The explicit mechanisms are, first, judicial and administrative supervision by attorneys general, the IRS, and member lawsuits, and second, election of directors by members (coupled with fairly open membership criteria). The indirect mechanism is competition for funding and grassroots support.

The direct mechanisms seem weaker than the comparable ones in government and for-profit sectors. Participation and issue saliency in CDC elections are much lower than in local government elections. The immunity of nonprofits from statutory requirements such as competitive bidding, which was previously associated with the virtue of flexibility, has the cost of reducing their accountability in some respects. And CDCS lack a constituency analogous to shareholders of for-profit corporations that have both strong powers and incentives to monitor. On the other hand, the need for supervision seems less intense. Non-

25. The possibility of competition as a CDC accountability mechanism is discussed in chapter 7.

profits lack the coercive taxing and regulatory powers of government. Moreover, unlike for-profit businesses and other types of nonprofits, CDCs do not generally accumulate pools of discretionary capital. The CDCs tend not to have steady, extensive free cash flow (income not needed for current commitments) with which to finance new ventures, such as large for-profit businesses, nor do they have endowments, like universities or private foundations. They tend to live from hand to mouth on current support. This makes competitive pressures for such support a more powerful accountability device than it is with organizations that can support themselves on discretionary assets or endowments. It means that CDCs are always applying for fresh support and, in that process, triggering some review of their operations by support sources. One should not press this point too far, however. The largest support sources are governments and foundations that are often subject to weak accountability themselves. There are many stories of funders who have continued to support evidently weak CDCs because of inertia or parochial political considerations. Nevertheless, it seems likely that the continuing need to seek funding is an important inducement of performance. (On the other hand, it has its costs in terms of stress on staff and the diversion of internal resources from projects to fund-raising.)

The political dimension of CDC activities raises distinctive concerns. These are signaled by the Internal Revenue Code's restrictions on partisan activity by recipients of 501(c)(3) tax benefits. In general, politics is not deemed to come within the ambit of charitable activities subsidized by the tax system. A political party, for example, could not qualify. And an otherwise charitable organization is specifically prohibited from most direct intervention in the electoral process. The explanation for the exclusion is not that charitable activities cannot be controversial. An abortion clinic or a fringe religious sect can qualify. It is that the category of charity does not include activities primarily oriented to mobilizing people competitively over divisive issues.

From a corporate-law perspective, partisan political activity would also fit awkwardly with the CDC structure. Although political parties are legally sui generis, they generally permit a degree of member control over their goals that seems incompatible with a public-benefit corporation. Parties are subject to important procedural restrictions, but substantively their members are free to define their goals as they wish. Although parties always purport to speak in the public interest, they are free to pursue their members' selfish interests and are not subject to accountability for the purposes they pursue in the manner of a public-benefit corporation.

The CDCs can avoid challenges to their charitable or public-benefit status by steering clear of direct involvement in electoral politics. For most, this is not difficult.[26] The lobbying restrictions have been narrowly interpreted to apply only to legislative matters, not to decisions of administrative agencies,[27] and the campaign restrictions apply only to campaigns for office. Thus, the restrictions do not apply to decisions over matters, such as land use, that are made by regulatory agencies or to electoral referenda or initiatives on issues. Moreover, the rules on political activities do not reflect any strong notion that charitable organizations ought not to be involved in politics. They are merely intended to preclude the extension of the charitable tax subsidy to electoral political activity. There is no obstacle to a 501(c)(3) charity affiliating itself with a formally separate non-501(c)(3) engaged in lobbying or electoral activities prohibited by Section 501(c)(3). As long as separate accounts are kept accurately and expenses are fairly apportioned, it would not be objectionable that the two organizations had interlocking boards or shared staff and facilities.

In general, however, CDCs are rarely closely integrated with affiliates of this sort. Although they often have strong connections to political actors and institutions, they usually do not view the lobbying and campaign activities restricted by Section 501(c)(3) as an integral part of their mission. CDCs' political activity tends to take place outside the formal electoral and legislative processes and to focus on issues that are relatively local and ostensibly uncontroversial. The prohibited political activity is more likely to involve nonlocal matters and will nearly always involve controversial or contested matters. While local development issues can generate intense controversy, they need not, and the CDC premise of community assumes a strong measure of shared interest that should moderate controversy.

26. Fishman and Schwartz, *Nonprofit Organization*, 546–51, 566–67, 570.

27. An "insubstantial" amount of even legislative lobbying is permissible. The regulations create a "safe harbor" with a sliding scale of percentages of the organization's total charitable expenditures—20 percent of the first $500,000; 15 percent of the next $500,000; and 5 percent of amounts higher than $1 million. Expenditures within these limits are deemed permissible: 26 USC 501h(3)–(4).

The CDC's characteristic conception of their mission thus more or less incorporates the implicit distinction of Section 501(c)(3) between organizing and mobilizing activities compatible with charitable subsidy and more partisan activities that are noncharitable. This conception is pretty much the one Alinsky first articulated in the 1940s. Alinsky disdained involvement in electoral politics; his organizations have generally refused to endorse candidates and have been wary of alliances with them. He disdained ideology as prone to needlessly divisive symbolic and rhetorical posturing. He detached local issues from national and regional ones. He argued that it would be easier to achieve programmatic agreement by focusing on local issues and defining them in tangible, material terms.[28] These remain operating premises of contemporary CDCS.

Institutions: Cooperatives

When CED activities produce for-profit entities, they sometimes take the form of conventional business corporations. However, CED themes have a distinctive affinity with the cooperative form. Thus, one encounters cooperatives with some consistency in the CED landscape. For example:

—Credit. Borrower cooperatives are pervasive in low-income and moderate-income communities worldwide. The widely replicated Grameen Bank model involves two levels of cooperation: Each borrower peer group is a mini-cooperative on its own, and the Grameen institution as a whole is a cooperative. The most familiar form of borrower cooperative in the United States is the credit union, which provides deposit and lending services to its members and is controlled by them. More than 200 of the 6,500 or so federally chartered credit unions focus on community economic development. Many of them receive support from the Community Development Financial Institutions Fund.

—Housing. When CED groups produce housing for sale to residents, they often set up the housing in cooperative form. Even housing produced under the Low Income Housing Tax Credit, which must be rental property, is sometimes set up to evolve into cooperative ownership after the tax credits have been consumed.

28. Peter Skerry, *Mexican Americans: The Ambivalent Minority* 126 (1993); Saul Alinsky, *Reveille for Radicals* 76–88 (1946).

—Jobs. Some of the most notable CED efforts to create work opportunities through new enterprises have taken cooperative form. The outstanding example is Cooperative Home Care Associates of New York and its sister organization in Philadelphia.

Cooperative organizations benefit from a variety of public and private support. They receive favorable tax treatment under Subchapter T of the Internal Revenue Code.[29] They are eligible for credit from the National Cooperative Bank, a federally sponsored corporation with about one billion dollars in assets that lends to housing, worker, and consumer cooperatives and operates a subsidiary focused on economic development in low-income communities.[30] The Industrial Cooperative Association of Brookline, Massachusetts, is the best known of many private organizations offering technical assistance to worker cooperatives.

The fundamental characteristic of the cooperative is ownership by the organization's patrons.[31] Patron is a term of art that denotes a relation more active and personal than that of a capital supplier or contract creditor. In a "purchaser" cooperative, the patrons are the customers. The best-known purchaser cooperatives are retail or consumer cooperatives such as REI, the camping-goods seller, or the Harvard Cooperative Society and many other college bookstores, or the Kresge Community Natural Foods Cooperative of Santa Cruz, California, and other grocery sellers. Another variety of purchaser cooperatives consists of wholesalers, such as the Ace Hardware Corporation, which buys goods and resells them to the retail stores who are its patron-owners. Numerous cooperatives in the farm sector that buy or produce equipment, fertilizer, or power for their customer-owners constitute another variant. Housing cooperatives are also purchaser cooperatives; they are owned

29. 26 USC 1381 *et seq.* These provisions allow cooperatives a deduction from the corporate income tax for income allocated to members. Subject to compliance with specified procedures, they allow cooperatives to escape corporate-level taxation on their income.
30. See the National Cooperative Bank Web site at http://www.ncb.com (visited 31 May 2000).
31. See 26 CFR 1.1381–1; Revenue Ruling 82–51, 1982 *Cumulative Bulletin* 117 (defining cooperative for purposes of income-tax exemption); David Ellerman and Peter Pitegoff, "The Democratic Corporation: The New Worker Cooperative Statute in Massachusetts," 11 *NYU Review of Law and Social Change* 441 (1982–1983); Joseph Knapp, *The Rise of American Cooperative Enterprise* (1969). For references to a wide range of contemporary American cooperatives, see the University of Wisconsin Center for Cooperatives' Web site at http://www.wisc.edu/uwcc/ (visited 31 May 2000).

by the residents, who are in effect the purchasers of the housing services they generate.

In a "supplier" cooperative, such as Sunkist, Land O' Lakes, and Ocean Spray, the patrons are the suppliers, those who furnish the inputs—oranges, milk, cranberries—that the business then processes, markets, and resells. (Because marketing is frequently their most salient activity, these cooperatives are sometimes called marketing cooperatives, but if we focus on the identity of their owners, they should be understood as supplier cooperatives.)

Cooperative banks and insurance companies owned by their depositors or policyholders once occupied major segments of their industries, and many large examples survive. They are typically called "mutuals"— for example, Washington Mutual Savings and Loan or Liberty Mutual Insurance—but they are best understood as a hybrid of customer and supplier cooperatives. The depositors or policyholder-owners are customers, in the sense that they receive banking and insurance services, and also suppliers, in the sense that they supply the funds that the businesses then re-lend or invest. The credit union is a form of cooperative bank that typically restricts its lending to its depositors. Thus, its owner-depositors have a dual customer status; in addition to receiving banking services, they are the business's borrowers (credit customers).

The third major category is the "worker" cooperative. Here patronage means work. The Linnton Plywood Association of Linnton, Oregon, and the Alvarado Street Bakery of Cotati, California, are examples. Worker cooperatives have long had a small presence in the American economy, and a somewhat larger one in several European societies. The network of worker cooperatives in Mondragon, Spain, that has flourished for the past forty years and now involves about 20,000 workers has been an inspiration for many CED and labor groups, such as the Industrial Cooperative Association. They have also taken heart from the success of small business networks in the Emiglia-Romagna district of Italy, which includes about 200,000 workers in business mostly organized on cooperative principles.[32]

Patron ownership has two basic connotations. The first is democratic

32. On Mondragon, see Harvard Business School, *The Mondragon Cooperative Experiment* (case study, n.d.); William Whyte and Kathleen Whyte, *Making Mondragon: The Growth and Dynamics of the Worker Cooperative Complex* (1988). On Emiglia-Romagna, see Michael Best, *The New Competition* 203–26 (1990).

control by the relevant class of patrons. This excludes capital suppliers—the presumptive control claimants in the conventional business corporation. Moreover, control is presumptively exercised on a one person–one vote basis rather than in proportion to patronage. This is the control model associated with political entities, and again it contrasts with the conventional business corporation, where control is presumptively allocated in proportion to financial investment.

The second connotation is distribution of net income in proportion to patronage. The business-corporation model distributes profits in proportion to investment. The cooperative model makes patronage refunds in proportion to the relative amounts of product purchased, materials supplied, or work performed.

These two connotations mean that all forms of customer, supplier, or worker ownership are not cooperative. Many assume a conventional business-corporation model with the relevant patrons substituted for (or more commonly, added to) outside capital suppliers as shareholders. Thus, for example, in an Employee Stock Ownership Plan, the employees are partial or total owners of the enterprise, but control is presumptively exercised and profits are allocated not democratically or on the basis of patronage but in proportion to each employee's financial investment.

There is a good deal of flexibility in cooperative organization. For the most part, the statutes do not prevent an organization from compromising either democratic patron control or distribution by patronage. Worker cooperatives often have some non-owner employees; consumer cooperatives often sell to some nonmembers. We will see in chapter 8 an interesting compromise in the Cooperative Home Care enterprises that gives some control to nonpatron capital suppliers. However, an enterprise that departed too far from the basic principles would no longer be considered "operating on a cooperative basis" and, hence, would be ineligible for such support as favorable tax treatment under Subchapter T and for financial and technical assistance from various sources.[33]

As compared with conventional business corporations, cooperatives have two principal practical disadvantages. First, they have more difficulty raising capital. Because it is impossible (or at least not easy) for

33. 26 USC 1381(a)(2); *Puget Sound Plywood v. Commissioner,* 44 T.C. 305 (1965); Revenue Ruling 71–439, 1971 *Cumulative Bulletin* 321.

them to give ownership-type control rights to outside capital suppliers, they must finance themselves through inside equity—investments by patrons—or debt. In many contexts, including nearly all CED contexts, patrons will have slight ability to make financial investments. Even if they had some capital, investing a large fraction of their wealth in an enterprise in which they already have a nonfinancial investment as patrons leaves them with too many eggs in a single basket; it subjects them to substantial firm-specific risk they could avoid through diversification. And cooperative investments tend to be illiquid. This is true generally of small-business investments. But members of a cooperative of any size have an exceptionally limited resale market for their interests; they can sell only back to the cooperative or someone qualified to join the cooperative as a member. It may be hard for the cooperative to finance the repurchase, and it may be hard for the departing member to find a qualified purchaser.

Second, the diffuse control and reward structure that cooperatives require may be inefficient in some situations. Democratic control does not mean that day-to-day decisions are made by the membership as a group. Cooperative members can delegate control to a board of directors and professional managers as readily as do corporate shareholders. But the members must be able to make decisions effectively about electing directors and managers and about major strategic and policy issues. Some, including Henry Hansmann, believe that member groups of substantial size will find this difficult unless they have homogeneous interests.[34] Otherwise, they are likely to become mired in dissension and deadlock. Moreover, while there is no legal obstacle to a cooperative paying its managers well, the democratic culture will constrain dispersion in compensation to some extent, and one form of compensation that is important in some enterprises, stock options, is ruled out. Thus, an enterprise dependent on high-powered incentives for top managers will be uncomfortable in the cooperative form. The Mondragon cooperatives, for example, have had to steadily increase the disparity between top-manager and rank-and-file compensation over the years to retain their managers. Even though the disparity is now greater than that

---

34. Henry Hansmann, "When Does Worker Ownership Work? ESOPS, Law Firms, Codetermination, and Economic Democracy," 99 *Yale Law Journal* 1749 (1990).

permitted by the group's espoused principles, the cooperative continues to have difficulty retaining top managers.[35]

However, the cooperative form also has potential advantages. For one thing, it eliminates the conflict of interest between owners and patrons, which in some situations is quite costly. When the patrons would otherwise face a capitalist firm with monopoly power, or when patrons make large purchases of goods they cannot readily evaluate, making the patrons owners mitigates the potential for exploitation. Agricultural processing and marketing cooperatives were established by farmers seeking to escape the monopsony power of investor-owned agribusiness firms. Insurance and banking cooperatives were established on the premise that these businesses' retail customers have limited ability to evaluate an important aspect of their quality of service: the adequacy of their reserves for future liabilities. As public regulatory systems have developed to perform these quality-assurance functions, the perceived need for patron control has declined, and banking and insurance firms have been converting out of the cooperative form.[36] But in other areas, concerns about quality control still prompt patrons to organize cooperatively. Child care is an example. Consumer (parent) cooperatives in this area are quite common.

A related point of importance to the worker cooperative is that, although the cooperative is not well adapted to raising large financial capital, it is exceptionally conducive to engendering an important kind of human and social capital. This is firm-specific human capital.[37] It includes workers' knowledge, practices, relationships, and processes that are distinctively useful within the firm. Such capital does not increase workers' mobility outside the firm. Thus, they have material incentives to help develop it only if they know that their current firm will reward them for it. Firms often have self-interested reasons to do so, but workers may plausibly fear opportunism: that if they train new workers, the firm will play the newcomers off against them in salary negotiations, or if they share information with the employer that in-

35. Whyte and Whyte, *Making Mondragon*, 203–5.

36. Henry Hansmann, "The Organization of Insurance Companies: Mutual versus Stock," 1 *Journal of Law, Economics, and Organization* 125 (1985).

37. On this concept, see Paul Milgrom and John Roberts, *Economics, Organization and Management* 328, 333, 350–51, 363–64 (1997).

creases productivity, the employer will find it advantageous to cut back the workforce. Unionization can mitigate these problems, but it will not necessarily do so. If the employer finances the development of firm-specific capital—say, by paying for training—the union may preclude him from recovering his costs by insisting on extortionate wage increases. Firm-specific capital in a unionized firm creates a bilateral monopoly in which the distribution of returns depends on the relative success of the parties in bargaining. In this situation, the potential for expensive combat or deadlock is substantial. The cooperative form can mitigate all these problems greatly by eliminating the major axis of conflict between workers and owners.

Moreover, although the cooperative has difficulty creating high-powered incentives for top managers, it is well adapted to creating weaker but more diffuse incentives for the workforce as a whole. In businesses where performance among the rank-and-file is hard to monitor from above and where lower-level initiative is important, weaker but more diffuse incentive structures may be more effective.

The cooperative form fits snugly with the CED vision. Indeed, its defining principles incorporate two of the three basic CED themes. The idea of patron ownership, which requires that the prerogatives of residual control and financial rights be accorded to people who have an additional relationship with the enterprise, and the requirement that the relationship be a relatively personal one, as opposed to that of an absentee capital supplier, restate the CED principles of multistranded and face-to-face relations.

These assumptions are notably explicit in the Federal Credit Union Act, which provides streamlined regulation and tax exemption for credit unions—a form of depositor cooperative—but insists that "membership shall be limited to groups having a common bond of occupation or association, or to groups within a well-defined neighborhood, community, rural district."[38] By associating ownership with patronage, any cooperative creates a role with at least two dimensions, but the statute prescribes that the union be based on a further, independent dimension, such as common employment or residence in the same neighborhood. The Supreme Court recently held that this restriction may not be inter-

38. 12 USC 1759.

preted cavalierly, ruling the benefits of the statute unavailable to credit unions with memberships from multiple, unrelated enterprises.[39]

The cooperative form does not necessarily involve the third CED principle, geographical focus, but it can and often does. When the cooperative form is applied to housing, geographical focus is almost invariably involved. Credit unions and other financial cooperatives sometimes define their membership qualifications geographically; they must do so to qualify for benefits from the Community Development Financial Institutions Fund. Consumer and worker cooperatives rarely restrict membership explicitly along geographic lines, but they often draw their memberships from distinct residential areas and consider themselves committed in various ways to such communities.

Hybrids: Churches and Mutual Housing Associations

The key characteristic of the charitable nonprofit is the separation of control and beneficial interest. Those who control the organization are obliged to run it in the interests primarily of people other than themselves. By contrast, cooperatives assign control rights to one of three key classes of beneficiaries: customers, workers, or suppliers. These members are expected to use control in their own collective self-interest. (Mutual-benefit nonprofits are similar to cooperatives in this respect. Most of them could be considered a loose form of consumer cooperative, though they typically do not make profit distributions.) Some institutions active in CED mix these two principles. They assign major control rights to classes of beneficiaries and expect these beneficiaries to use control in their own interests, but they also assign rights to more disinterested people and expect the beneficiaries to give weight to interests other than their own. This is generally true of churches. It is also a feature of Mutual Housing Associations.

CHURCHES

As noted, churches are among the most important supporters of CED activity. Although there is activity across the denominational spectrum,

---

39. *National Credit Union Administrator v. First National Bank and Trust Co.*, 118 S.Ct. 927 (1998).

the efforts of the Roman Catholic church and some of the black Protestant churches are especially prominent. The Catholic church sponsors the New Community Corporation in Newark, New Jersey, one of the nation's largest and most successful CDCs. For decades, it has supported community organizing and development efforts in low-income areas across the country—for example, those of Communities Organized for Public Service (COPS) of San Antonio, Texas. Many urban black Protestant churches have undertaken major housing, commercial, and health care projects. The development work of the congregations led by Floyd Flake in Queens, New York, and by Kirbyjon Caldwell in Houston, Texas, have received a lot of attention.[40]

Churches are often the strongest nongovernmental institutions in poor neighborhoods. They are invariably involved in the production of relations of trust and cooperation. A church that extends its members' religious relations into the sphere of economic development engages in the kind of relational synergy that is a defining feature of CED. Churches also make strong place-based commitments.[41]

Faith-based CED takes many forms, but it is most often conducted through freestanding CDCs that receive additional support from public and philanthropic sources. These CDCs make benefits available to the community regardless of religious affiliation.

The specific legal form of churches varies from state to state.[42] Some states have special corporation statutes for churches. Churches can usually incorporate under general nonprofit corporation statutes. Or they can organize as noncorporate voluntary associations. However they are organized, they are generally understood to hold their property in trust for religious purposes. They are, however, much more loosely policed by the state than secular charitable trusts. The attorney general has no role

40. See the New Community Corporation's Web site at http://www.newcommunity.org (visited 14 November 2000). Skerry, *Mexican Americans* (on COPS); James Traub, "Floyd Flake's Middle America," *New York Times Magazine* (19 October 1997), 60; Lloyd Gite, "The New Agenda of the Black Church: Economic Development for Black America" (*Black Enterprise*), December 1993, 54.

41. See chapter 6.

42. See Note, "Judicial Intervention in Disputes over the Use of Church Property," 75 *Harvard Law Review* 1142 (1962); "Religious Societies," *Am. Jur. 2d.;* Eric Posner, "The Legal Regulation of Religious Groups," 2 *Legal Theory* 33 (1996).

comparable to that for secular charities, and courts intervene less often in churches' internal affairs.

The role of church members varies greatly by denomination. In general, the law defers to the denomination's own constitutional arrangements. In churches with a congregational organization, each parish governs itself by majority rule, and church property is subject to disposition by the majority. In more hierarchical church structures—the Catholics are the strongest example—the parish and its property are controlled by national or international denominational bodies. Yet the formal legal structure can be misleading. Regardless of how they are organized, most churches are intensely local in operation. Nearly all give substantial discretion to local clergy, and nearly all seek to involve parishioners in at least some aspects of governance.[43]

Although churches vary in the degree to which they are controlled locally and in the extent to which that control is exercised in an egalitarian fashion, nearly all resemble cooperatives and mutual-benefit corporations in expecting members to exercise the control they have in their own interests. To be sure, they are expected to place collective above individual and spiritual above material interests, but members, as a congregation, are expected to pursue the congregation's interests. On the other hand, to a far greater extent than cooperatives or most mutual-benefit nonprofits, church congregations are generally understood to have duties to outsiders. Most feel a strong general duty of philanthropy. Many have commitments to share revenue or governance with co-religionists in other congregations or encompassing church structures. The most important difference can be seen in the treatment of new members. A cooperative or mutual-benefit nonprofit with substantial assets, such as a social club, will almost always charge new members for the right to share in the benefits of those assets. Churches almost never do this.[44] Nearly all welcome newcomers without any membership charge, and many actively proselytize for them. In thus

43. Skerry, *Mexican Americans*, 169–70 (on decentralization and the principle of "subsidiarity" in Catholic governance).

44. However, they commonly do condition, either explicitly or implicitly, particular benefits or services on various forms of consideration. Some parishioners pay for the right to occupy a particular pew, and clergy often expect payment for private ceremonies. But the general principle is most often free access.

recognizing very strong duties to nonmembers, churches resemble the public-benefit nonprofit paradigm.[45]

MUTUAL HOUSING ASSOCIATIONS

Congress has charged the Neighborhood Reinvestment Corporation with promoting another hybrid model for affordable housing called Mutual Housing Associations.[46] These are corporations that own and manage affordable housing. They typically embrace a variety of separate developments, and they are usually also engaged in developing new housing.

Residents have "occupancy agreements" with the corporation that give them lifetime tenure subject to payment of rent and compliance with regulations. Their rent is usually limited in relation to increases in costs or in their incomes. They cannot freely transfer their residential rights, but they can nominate a relative to succeed them. They elect representatives to the association's governing board. In addition, they elect a resident council to manage the building. Proponents of MHAS describe the residents' status as a form of ownership, and HUD has held such projects eligible for programs supporting homeownership.[47] These residual economic and control claims make the organization look like a resident cooperative.

In fact, however, the association is organized as a public-benefit non-profit. The residents share membership, and control, with other constituencies. Potential residents—community members hoping to attain affordable housing—are also represented, as are representatives from the community, local government, and business. Net income is explicitly dedicated to developing new housing rather than to benefiting current residents.[48] Associations can and do use the existing units as collateral to finance new units. The board has duties to the broader charitable pur-

---

45. However, as noted in chapter 6, some cooperatives, notably Mondragon, subsidize new entrants heavily.

46. 42 USC 8107; see Martha Taylor, "What Is Mutual Housing?" 6 *Journal of Affordable Housing and Community Development Law* 131 (1997).

47. 57 Fed. Reg. 1558 (Jan. 14, 1992).

48. 42 CFR 4100.1(b)(2); Neighborhood Reinvestment Corporation, "Frequently Asked Questions About Mutual Housing Associations." Available from http://www.nw.org/network/strategies/mutual/mhafaq.html (visited 28 July 1999).

poses of the organization and cannot single-mindedly pursue the interests of the current residents, as a cooperative board would.

Thus, like churches, MHAS combine features associated with the paradigms of the charitable corporation and the cooperative.[49]

---

49. Although organizations with this combination of features have not been widely observed or analyzed, there are other examples, including the Grameen Bank. I am aware of no detailed descriptions of the bank's structure, but it is usually described as "owned" in part by its borrower–members, which resonates with the cooperative form, and in part by the government of Bangladesh, which resonates more with the public-benefit nonprofit form. See, for example, David Bornstein, *The Price of a Dream* 128–31 (1996). Presumably, member interests have special status, but control has to take account of broader public interests, as well.

Chapter 6 : Constrained Property: Rights as Anchors

We have seen that a distinctive CED concern is the economic basis of community membership. Sometimes the issue is displacement: Economic forces, especially rising rents, push people out. Sometimes it takes the form of speculation. Owners, viewing their property more as a financial investment than as a basis for membership, refuse to maintain or improve it. Sometimes the concern is apathy. To the extent that community improvements are capitalized in land prices, nonowners have limited incentive to work for such improvement, because their share of any benefits would be nullified by rent increases.

The CED Movement has drawn on and elaborated a repertory of distinctive property forms designed to strengthen membership in a geographically defined community. As in Republicanism, real estate investments have a priority of place because their immobility creates an interest tied to the geographical community. And as with Republicanism, ownership holds a prominent status. Ownership, on the other hand, is not an end in itself. It is the characteristics of ownership that contribute to political independence—especially security of tenure and residual claims—that are most valued. These characteristics are not unique to ownership and, indeed, the more conventional ownership forms do not incorporate them in the ways most conducive to CED values.

The most distinctive property forms in CED belong to a class I call "social-republican."[1] Social-republican property is distinguished from more conventional forms by two features: (1) transfer or alienation restraints that confine control of the property to active or potentially active participants in a community constituted by the property; and (2) accumulation constraints designed to limit inequality among members of such a community. These core features of social-republican property operate as restraints on the commodification and capitalization of relationships. They secure to the holder a share of the future benefits of community improvement, but they do so in a way that restricts her ability to monetize or liquidate her interest. They thus encourage her to view her interest as a stake in a long-term relationship. The result of these arrangements is a form of property that is neither private nor public and that has promise in addressing the disadvantages of bureaucratic management and conventional market forces.

The intuition underlying this type of property was recently taught to economists by Albert Hirschman but has been known to Republican political thinkers for centuries.[2] There are two basic ways of expressing dissatisfaction with a community or organization. One can leave— "exit"—or one can try to induce internal change through participation—"voice." The Republican insight is that a trade-off often exists between exit and voice. Ease of exit tends to reduce the likelihood of voice; obstacles to exit can encourage voice. From a Republican point of view, this can be desirable because participation is a good in itself. From the economist's point of view, it may contribute to the solution of a coordination problem. Voice tends to be undersupplied because it is a public good. One person's activism benefits similarly situated others, and thus there is a tendency to sit back in the potentially self-defeating hope of free riding on the efforts of others. Subsidy is a common prescription for public goods. Exit restraints implicitly subsidize voice by acting as kind of tariff on the alternative.

Another virtue of social-republican property is that it preserves a

1. William H. Simon, *Social-Republican Property,* 38 *UCLA Law Review* 1335 (1991). The term is intended to connote market socialism and republicanism, from whose convergent programs these forms arise.

2. Albert Hirschman, *Exit, Voice, and Loyalty* (1970); James Harrington, *The Commonwealth of Oceans* [1656] in *The Political Works of James Harrington* (J. G. A. Pocock ed. 1977).

measure of economic equality that may be essential to the viability of the community as a democratic polity.

Subsidized Housing

Residents of affordable housing enjoy substantial subsidies. A 1993 study of fifteen CDC housing projects in five major cities found costs per unit ranging from $40,581 to $204,869, with an average of $89,237.[3] If the housing is targeted to low- or moderate-income people, then they will have incomes of no more than 50 (low) or 80 (moderate) percent of the area's median. If the residents receive an ownership interest, it is rarely practical to charge them more than a few thousand dollars as a down payment. Guidelines for HUD and various state programs provide that residents should pay no more than 30 percent of their incomes for monthly housing costs. These amounts typically cover operating costs (maintenance, taxes, insurance, repairs). They typically are not sufficient to cover market-rate interest charges on the development costs, much less to amortize the principal in a conventional manner. Thus, in financial terms, residents receive housing benefits of considerably higher value than they pay for.

Sometimes the resident becomes the putative owner of his dwelling; sometimes he becomes a tenant. Either way, his interest will be structured to provide those features that serve CED values and to eliminate features that are dysfunctional from a CED point of view. Practitioners of CED generally prefer ownership, largely because of its rhetorical associations with independence and middle-class dignity. Although there are substantial variations in the incidents of residence in affordable housing, their practical effects depend very little on whether residence takes the nominal form of ownership or tenancy.

The desirable features are those that make the dwelling a base of community membership. The undesirable features are those that make it a speculative financial asset.[4]

The membership idea requires security of tenure. This follows more or less by definition with ownership, but it can be written into the lease

3. Abt Associates, I *Nonprofit Housing: Costs and Funding* ES 5–6 (HUD 1993).
4. David Kirkpatrick, *Legal Issues in the Development of Housing Cooperatives* (National Economic Development and Law Center 1981); Harvard Business School, *The Forest Glen Cooperative,* Case No. N9–395–057 (13 September 1995).

in a tenancy. The resident can be dispossessed only for failure to perform financial obligations or for specified forms of conduct that demonstrably harm the property or the interests of neighbors. She is also protected against inflation. Rent increases will be limited by contract (mortgage and occupancy agreements in the case of owners, leases in the case of tenants), generally to increases in cost (but the rent may not exceed 30 percent of the resident's income).

Most affordable housing is found in multi-unit projects, and ideally, residents should participate in management of the projects. Ownership units are often situated in cooperatives, perhaps the preferred form of CED housing organization. In the cooperative, a corporation owns the project as a whole; the residents own the cooperative collectively, each receiving a membership share. Each also has an occupancy agreement with the cooperative entitling her to possession of the unit. The cooperative board of directors manages the project's common facilities and areas. If the cooperative is subject to a collective mortgage on the entire project, the board will be responsible for seeing that each resident pays her share and that the mortgage is kept current. Voting in the cooperative is typically structured on a one-vote-per-household basis, an accumulation restraint that reflects the political values of CED, rather than in proportion to the price of market value of individual units, which is the rule in some conventional homeowners' associations.

If the housing is structured as a mutual housing association or a leasehold, the residents' participation rights need not but can be as strong as those in a cooperative. In the mutual form, the residents will share representation on the board with nonresidents, and the mission of the board will include community responsibilities extending beyond any particular project. However, the board is likely to delegate operating concerns to a residents' council composed exclusively of residents. And as I have noted, public housing policy now favors resident management through elected councils in rental projects as well.

However, a series of rights associated with conventional home ownership will be limited by transfer and accumulation restraints. The right to affordable housing is typically conditioned on occupancy. Unlike a private owner, a resident of affordable housing is not free to buy and hold the interest as a financial investment or to use it for income production. Her right to sublease is subject to two strong transfer restrictions: She may do so only for limited periods during temporary absences, and she may rent only to people who meet income and other eligibility criteria. Moreover, the residence condition also involves an accumulation constraint. The right-holder must occupy the dwelling as her primary residence. This may in part be a measure of need, but it is also a measure of commitment to the community. One who primarily resides elsewhere is less likely to become an active participant and indeed cannot exercise voting rights in local public elections.

Accumulation restraints will also limit the extent to which the owner-resident can improve her unit. A primary goal of ownership is to encourage residents to maintain their homes, and some measure of investment by way of improvement is desirable, but excessive improvement or "goldplating," jeopardizes the unit's future availability as affordable housing. If the resident must be compensated on departure for expensive luxury investments, rents will have to be raised or subsidies will have to be increased to finance the buyout, both of which would be undesirable. Thus, legal arrangements typically limit the resident's right to improve either by requiring prior approval by the board or some affiliated watchdog entity or by setting spending limits.

The most revealing restraints are those that govern the owner-resident's opportunity to liquidate her investment on departure. (Such restraints come automatically with tenancy, but they take considerable ingenuity to design into ownership arrangements.) A conventional owner typically may sell to anyone for any price she can get and keep the net proceeds after paying off the mortgage debt. If a resident of subsidized housing were allowed to do this, she could render the housing unaffordable and take the subsidy with her out of the community.

So the owner's rights on resale are restricted. She may sell only to certain buyers. Sometimes she is required to sell back to the co-op, mutual housing association, or CDC at a price set by formula or arbitration. If she is allowed to sell to a prospective resident, then that resident must at least meet the income and other eligibility conditions to which she herself has been subject. Most likely, the buyer will have to be of low or moderate income and a resident of the community (unless no otherwise eligible residents apply).

The rules may specify how the sales price is to be derived and will always determine the portion of the sales price to which the departing owner is entitled. Four classes of resources used in the creation of the housing are potentially relevant. First, the owner has made contributions by way of a down payment, monthly amortization of the mort-gage, and the cost of improvements she made herself. In the more deeply subsidized units, these payments will represent a tiny fraction of the total cost, perhaps less than 1 percent. Second, funds will have been borrowed in the form of "hard loans"—that is, transactions on conventional commercial terms with strict repayment obligations secured by first mortgages.

Third, funds will have been made available by government agencies, nonprofit organizations, and government-sponsored entities on concessionary terms. Though it is often styled as debt, this kind of funding can look more like capital subsidies. Such obligations are usually called "soft loans" but might also be termed "subsidy capital." The softest of these obligations provide for repayment of principal and interest only at some remote point—say, fifty years—or sooner if there is a breach of some condition on the use of the property. These soft obligations are typically secured by junior mortgages. Their purpose in part is to prevent the inappropriate use of the property by giving those who have provided the subsidies a right to foreclose in the event of misuse. It is expected that the claimants on these soft obligations will roll over the debt at the end of the period, as long as the property will continue as affordable housing. A fourth category of resources will have been donated by public or philanthropic actors who have not taken a debt claim on the property in return. Publicly contributed land may fall into this category in some projects, and most projects of nonprofit developers involve some donated professional services. One might call such resources "implicit subsidy."[5]

As under the terms of conventional ownership, the commercial lender with the first mortgage will have first claim to repayment of outstanding debt on its loan. Unless the project has failed, there will be a substantial

5. Where affordable housing is produced through inclusionary zoning or "density bonuses," the entire subsidy may be implicit. These programs typically involve for-profit developers who must produce rent- or price-restricted units as a condition of permission to develop market-rate units. The market-rate units cross-subsidize the affordable units, but there is no soft debt, and the amount of the subsidy may not even be clear. Montgomery County, Maryland, for example, requires that 12 to 15 percent of the units in all large developments be affordable, and ownership units are subject to equity limitations. See the Montgomery County Department of Housing and Community Affairs Web site at http://www.co.mo.md.us/hca/housing/MPDU/mpdu.htm. (visited 15 November 2000).

surplus after the hard debts are discharged. Some or all of this surplus will represent the return of the subsidy capital and the implicit subsidy. If real estate prices have increased substantially between the time of development and the time of sale, the sales price will include an amount in excess of these resources, which we can call appreciation.

How will the surplus be distributed? That depends mostly on how one treats the subsidy. If one views it as a capital investment, one will be inclined to say it should receive a percentage of the surplus equal to its portion of the total capital investment. Because the only other capital investment is that of the resident, and that typically represents a tiny fraction of the total, this would give most of the surplus back to the subsidy providers.[6] If one ignores the implicit subsidy and treats the explicit subsidy as debt, which is how it is typically designated formally, one will be inclined to give the subsidy provider a fixed payment—the original amount plus interest—and allow the resident to receive the remaining surplus (after payment of the first mortgage). If the interest rate on the soft loans is in the conventional commercial range and the surplus is large, this will often result in a very large gain to the departing resident. Still more favorable would be to ignore any unpaid interest on the subsidy and simply require repayment of the principal. And most favorable would be to forgo repayment of the subsidy principal as well.

At a minimum, then, the departing resident could get back only her down payment and the cost of approved improvements. At a maximum, she could keep everything after the hard loans are repaid. Neither of these extreme approaches is unknown, but both are rare.

At the stricter end of the spectrum, it is common to permit the departing owner to recover, in addition to down payment and improvements, the portion of her monthly payments that went toward amortizing the mortgage and to adjust all these payments by an annual percentage representing interest, inflation, or a return on investment. The Consumer Price Index for the area is one candidate; an index focused on residential real-estate price increases is another. Another approach involves determining the total amount invested by the resident as a per-

6. Note that the resident's amortization payments are made only with respect to the "hard" first mortgage. This is often possible only because neither interest nor amortization need be paid of the "soft" loans. If the resident's down payment and monthly amortization payments were reduced by the market interest rate on the "soft" debt, her investment would often be negative.

centage of total investment in the property and to allow the resident a similar percentage of the amount by which the sales price exceeds all contributions. Because the resident's payments usually will make up only a small portion of total payments, these approaches give the resident only a small portion of the surplus.

Toward the other end of the spectrum, one finds with some frequency arrangements that permit the owner to keep a specified substantial fraction of the surplus—say, 40 percent. This means that she keeps 40 percent of both the amount that represents the return of the subsidy capital and the amount that represents appreciation in excess of invested resources. Alternatively, the owner might be required to repay the subsidy capital but permitted to retain all or a substantial portion of the appreciation.

The Hyde Square Co-op in Jamaica Plain exemplifies the strict approach. These units were built in 1993 at a cost of about $140,000 each (not counting the value of the land donated by the city). Residents made an initial payment of about $1,000. If and when they sell, the price is limited to the sum of (1) their initial payments; (2) an annual adjustment based on the Boston area Consumer Price Index but capped at 5 percent in any given year; and (3) the value of improvements made by the resident and approved by the co-op board, but only to $1,000 or $250 times the number of years the seller has been in residence, whichever is lower. The arrangement at Charlotte Gardens in New York City's South Bronx is more generous to the owner. The equity limitations phase out after ten years of occupancy.[7]

The federal HOPE for Homeownership program, which supports local initiatives to develop home ownership for public housing tenants and others, mandates a hybrid limitation. For the first six years, an owner who sells can receive only her equity contribution, adjusted for inflation. After that, she must pay back the explicit subsidy but may keep any remaining surplus.[8]

7. Barbara Stewart, "Market's Nod to Rebirth: In South Bronx Enclave, Rising Property Values and Suburban Living," *New York Times,* 2 November 1997, sec. 1, 37.

8. 42 USC 12875(d). The Montgomery County, Maryland, program cited earlier restricts the owner's share of the resale price to adjusted equity contribution for ten years, then requires that the surplus be shared 50–50 between the seller and the county housing program.

Table 1. Resale Rights in Owner-Occupied Affordable Housing: An Illustration

Assume the initial costs of making an affordable home available were as follows:

Construction and Development	$200,000
Land	25,000
Donated services	25,000
Total	$250,000

Only the $200,000 for construction and development represents monetary costs. (Development costs include payments to architects, lawyers, accountants, and the developer.) The land was donated by the municipality. The "Donated services" were provided without fee. Typically the resale determination will ignore the donated factors, which I call "implicit subsidy."

The $200,000 was financed as follows:

Down payment by owner	$5,000
First mortgage	70,000
Soft loans (subsidy capital)	125,000
Total	$200,000

The first mortgage is amortized over thirty years at an 8 percent interest rate. The soft loans do not require interest or principal payments prior to resale.

Owner occupies the home for ten years. At the end of the fifth year, she makes one approved improvement for $10,000. At the end of the ten years, the unit is sold for $400,000. How much of this amount may Owner keep?

1. A STRICT APPROACH

Down payment + Principal portion of first mortgage payments + Cost of approved improvements, all adjusted annually by the Consumer Price Index. If we assume a steady 5 percent CPI, this yields a share of $38,400.

2. A GENEROUS APPROACH

After ten years occupancy, owner's only obligation is to repay the first mortgage. Her share is thus $330,000.

3. TWO INTERMEDIATE APPROACHES

A. Same as the second approach, except Owner keeps only half the surplus after repayment of the first mortgage. Thus, she keeps $165,000.
B. Owner must repay soft debt (subsidy capital) with accrued interest in addition to the first mortgage. Depending on specifics, this might leave her with $150,000.

The relatively generous provisions have been common in the past and are still seen, but the recent tendency seems to be toward the stricter ones. Yet, intense controversy remains about which point on the spectrum is most plausible. Arguments in favor of generosity include:

1) The only explicit equity stake is the resident owner's. The other interests (usually) take the form of debt.[9] The conventional inference from this structure is that the resident owner is the residual claimant and entitled to the gains left over after fixed obligations have been discharged.

2) A basic CED purpose is to give the owner incentives to maintain the premises. The bigger her residual claim, the greater her incentive.

3) Ownership without a strong residual claim is not real ownership and will not be experienced as ownership by the resident or regarded as ownership by others. Equity limitations radically different from those to which middle-class homeowners are subject will degrade the idea of ownership. They will be experienced as an indignity. The spirit of this objection was expressed recently by opponents of a California bill designed to facilitate the enforcement of equity limitations on subsidized housing; opponents objected to such limitations as "enslaving" the homeowners.

4) Even if one views the surplus as a subsidy, allowing the resident to keep it means that it will go to a person who was certainly of low or moderate income when she bought in and more than likely will be when she cashes out. Even if she moves out of the community, she will more than likely continue to reside in some poor community. Creating individual wealth in poor communities serves an important social function. Individual wealth has beneficial spillover effects, not only as it is spent, but in the way it enables those who hold it to serve as role models and spokespeople.

On the other hand, there are counter-arguments in favor of strictness:

1) The owner makes no real investment beyond the often tiny and always small down payment and amortization payments. She has no effective personal liability for the financial obligations of the project. The loans are non-recourse either explicitly or effectively (because she is

9. This is not true, formally, in Low Income Tax Credit projects of the sort discussed in chapter 8, where corporate investors have nominal equity interests. However, it approximates the informal understanding of the participant even there.

judgment-proof). They can be enforced only against the property. Nearly all the risk is assumed by the providers of subsidy capital. If they have styled their interests as loans, it is for legal or tax reasons unrelated to the question of fair division of the surplus. In practical terms, they are the residual claimants.

2) The generous exit provisions give far more than is necessary for desirable maintenance and incentives. Most of the surplus is not due to any effort of the owner. Most obviously, some represents a return of the subsidy capital. Above that, some represents a return to the implicit subsidy—donated assets or services not reflected in claims. Most importantly, the Georgian perspective discussed in chapter 4 suggests that much of the surplus is due to improvements in the surrounding community and, hence, is most appropriately claimed by the community, not by the departing owner. The generous provisions allow the departing owner to appropriate the scarcity value of the site. By contrast, the strict provisions operate like Georgian land taxes.

3) It may not be necessary to give all the conventional attributes of middle-class homeownership in order to generate the psychological associations of dignity and security. Moreover, because most middle-class people pay a lot more for these attributes than do most subsidized owners, it seems inconsistent to insist that the attributes depend on giving the owner all the benefits but do not require that she bear the costs proportionately. Even if the psychological point is correct, one can still object that achieving these satisfactions is too expensive.

4) Individual wealth creation comes at the expense of community wealth. To the extent that the departing owner captures the surplus, she takes the subsidy with her. Either the home she sells will no longer be part of the low-income housing stock, or the buyer will require a fresh subsidy that could have gone to support someone else. There is no guarantee that the departing owner will be low or moderate income at this stage, and, most importantly, she, more than likely, will leave the community. The subsidy's intent was to benefit her as a community member.

One can argue that the strictness of the subsidy should vary with the nature of the community at the time the new housing becomes available. In a desperately poor neighborhood with extensive deterioration and little new investment, attracting moderate-income people may be difficult. Such people may be important both because they have enough income to support the operating costs and make some contribution to capital costs and because they may add valuable income and social diversity to the community. Less impoverished communities may be attractive to these people with smaller subsidies. Such considerations may explain the differences between Jamaica Plain and Charlotte Gardens. The South Bronx was barely recovering from years of desolation at the time Charlotte Gardens came on board, whereas Jamaica Plain was a mixed-income community undergoing significant new private investment, with signs of gentrification.

Finally, there is a fifth consideration that some consider a point in favor of strict limitations and that others see as a point against them. The strict provisions inhibit the owner's mobility by preventing her from liquidating or fully transferring the economic value of her home. As long as she remains a resident, she enjoys its full value in kind at a bargain price. But she can't take this value with her. In many—perhaps most—cases a comparable subsidized unit will not be available. Thus, if she moves, she will have to increase her payments or accept lower-quality housing.

Whether this point weighs for or against strict resale limits depends on your premises. From a conventional economic point of view, it is an argument against them. The limitation of mobility is inefficient. It prevents transfers that would make transferor and transferee better off. It may exacerbate unemployment because people are more reluctant to move to where job opportunities arise because the loss of housing benefits is too large. It can inhibit the optimal reallocation of housing in accordance with the progress of the life cycle. Older people with empty nests who would be happy to move to smaller units that are socially less costly refrain from doing so because, given the loss of the subsidy, it is personally more costly for them. Others will object to the lock-in effect as an infringement of liberty.

But in terms of the distinctive themes of the CED Movement, these effects have a positive dimension. They anchor the resident in the community. If the value of the dwelling appreciates, the resident can enjoy that appreciation, but only in-kind and on a current basis. That is, the resident enjoys the increased value as long as she remains a member of the community, but she cannot take it when she leaves. Like a conventional homeowner, she has a stake in public improvements in the community, because such improvement will enhance the value of her interest. Arguably, however, her limited equity interest is even better calculated to induce desirable political behavior. A conventional home-owner might be an absentee or short-termer with no commitment to the community, holding in the hope of a quick capital gain. Such a person would be unlikely to work collectively for improvements with long-term payoffs. The lock-in effect that some deplore as a constraint on mobility performs a valuable role in thickening the owner's relation-ship to the community and, hence, her inducement to participate in its collective processes.

Another desirable feature of equity limitations is that they may miti-gate the coordination problems that cause downward spirals and spec-ulative bubbles of the sort discussed in chapter 3. The illiquidity of the limited-equity owner's investment means that she will not be vul-nerable to pressure to sell out before things get worse. She can take so little of the value with her that only the most enormous prospective declines would push her to leave. And to the extent that others are locked in, this is mutually reassuring. At the same time, these property arrangements impede speculation by slowing turnover and, most im-portantly, blocking sales to speculators through the residency and in-come requirements.

To the degree that one favors strict equity limitations, the differences between ownership and rental approaches to subsidized housing dimin-ish. The strictest equity limitations create interests fairly close to those in tenancies with rent control and just-cause requirements for eviction. Nearly all subsidized rental housing has these features. If ownership eliminates the opportunity to capture economic appreciation, then its main differences from subsidized tenancy are threefold. First, the owner makes a (usually modest) contribution toward the capital costs and hence has a slightly greater incentive to maintain. Second, the owner can recover some improvement costs and hence has a greater incentive to improve. And third, the owner reaps the social and psychological bene-fits associated with the symbolism of ownership. But as long as the tenant has the right to occupy the apartment at a below-market rent, she has the type of property interest that serves as a strong basis for republi-can political membership. She has an interest that will be enhanced by community improvement and that she can enjoy only as long as she remains a member of the community.

Enterprises: Cooperatives

Enterprise subsidies are somewhat different from housing subsidies. Unlike housing, business enterprises do not necessarily involve land values that accrue scarcity rents. Moreover, although the goal of preserving affordable housing often leads to constraints on the residents' ability to improve their dwellings, there is no comparable interest in constraining entrepreneurs' investments in their enterprises.

However, as with housing, agencies will want to structure subsidies to businesses to insure that they are used consistently with their public purposes. They will want to protect any funds they have lent or invested and insure that the enterprise is operated so as to produce the anticipated community benefits—for example, developing local entrepreneurial talent, creating jobs for residents, or providing locally needed goods and services to consumers. In most situations, these goals can be accomplished with an enterprise structured as a general business corporation. The CDC can draft loan contracts or take stock that will give it both financial and control rights.

Nevertheless, cooperative corporations have a special prominence in CDC. They are not the most common form of CDC-supported business, but they are the form that, many practitioners believe, best incarnates the distinctive values of the movement. They build in commitments to multistranded relations and economic democracy. The cooperative thus becomes a microcosm of the larger community envisioned in CDC doctrine.

Cooperatives invariably entail the transfer and accumulation restraints that typify CED property rights. Because a cooperative is owned by its patrons—in the case of production co-ops, its workers—ownership rights usually cannot be transferred to nonpatrons. A departing worker must sell back to the cooperative or to someone acceptable to the cooperative as a worker. Accumulation restraints potentially take two forms. The most straightforward concerns decision-making. Cooperative governance is conducted on a democratic basis. The presumptive rule is one person, one vote.

The other potential type of accumulation restraint is a limit on economic rights. As in housing co-ops, the most salient issue concerns restrictions on the price for which a departing patron may sell her interest. The spectrum of possibilities resembles that in housing. Most parsimoniously, the seller could be limited to what she paid or to the book value of her shares, which will often approximate her payments. (Payments would include the portion of cooperative income allocable to her but retained in the business instead of distributed.) More generously, the payments could be adjusted by some interest factor. Assuming the enterprise is successful, she would do still better if she were allowed to sell for the allocable fraction of the estimated current value of the enterprise's tangible assets. The most generous provision would allow her to capture the full fair market value as measured by an asset appraisal or by an estimate of discounted future earnings. The latter provision differs from the provision based on tangible-asset appraisal in that it includes "goodwill" or going concern value in excess of tangible-asset value. Goodwill embraces a variety of intangible assets, such as good employees and work relations, product reputations and customer relations, and proprietary knowledge about production processes and products.

The debate about these alternatives resembles that about affordable housing, but there are differences. Much of the disputed value in housing involves land, to which, on Georgian principles, no individual has a strong claim. In a production cooperative, however, the dispute concerns the going concern value of a successful enterprise to which the departing patron will often have made an important contribution, both through putting capital at risk and through effort and ingenuity. To be sure, a venerable tradition holds that returns to capital of any kind are illegitimate and that the only morally acceptable basis for distribution of enterprise earnings is work. This belief has often been inferred from the labor theory of value by Marxists and from the principle of the primacy of labor by Catholic social theorists. The former influenced the industrial system of Yugoslav Communism, in which enterprises took a cooperative form until the reforms of 1988. Catholic social theory has influenced the Mondragon cooperative network in Spain, which has inspired the efforts of the Industrial Cooperative Association and other American proponents of cooperative forms.[10] However, even most cooperative proponents today find the stronger implications of the primacy of labor implausible, and Mondragon itself has institutionalized it only in a

10. See Harold Lydall, *Yugoslav Socialism: Theory and Practice* (1984); David Ellerman and Peter Pitegoff, "The Democratic Corporation: The New Worker Cooperative Statute in Massachusetts," 11 *N.Y.U. Review of Law and Social Change* 441, 461–63 (1983).

compromised form. In its stronger forms, the principle denies reward for saving and taking investment risk. Most people find this wrong as a moral matter, and as an economic matter it runs up against the need to motivate investment in the cooperative.[11] Moreover, enterprises need capital to sustain them, and cooperatives have limited ability to attract outside capital. Insiders will be reluctant to invest or refrain from disinvesting (that is, paying out earnings as dividends rather than leaving them in the business) if they do not anticipate adequate returns.

On the other hand, the generous formulas, while providing an inducement for investment, risk instability. If the enterprise is successful enough to generate large capital gains, then allowing departing members to capture their share introduces an inequality between the founders who remain and the newcomers. The newcomers will have paid more for their investment and consequently receive a lower return on it than the old-timers. To be sure, the old-timers took risks and expended effort before the newcomers arrived, but even if the newcomers acknowledge the justice of their differential treatment in principle, it may compromise their sense of solidarity with the old-timers and, consequently, the ability to cooperate with them. The cooperative form is likely to be especially advantageous in enterprises that depend on voluntary, informal cooperation among workers. The inequality that comes with sharply differential economic returns may contaminate the atmosphere that sustains such collaboration.

As the value of the enterprise increases, the desire to liquidate capital gains may put overwhelming pressure on the cooperative form. Even if the organization permits the departing member to sell for whatever a purchaser will pay, purchasers who are willing and qualified to join as workers may not be able to pay full value. In order to capture this value, the founders may find that they have to compromise the cooperative form, or convert out of it entirely. Successful cooperatives have frequently met this fate. The founders sell to outside owners and become

11. Another moral objection is that, however egalitarian distribution according to work is *within* the firm, it can lead to great inequality *among* firms. If workers capture the returns to the firm's capital, then the more capital-intensive the firm is, the more the workers will benefit. At least to the extent that capital comes from outside the firm (which it must in enterprises of major scale), this seems arbitrary. Workers in more capital-intensive firms do not seem more deserving than workers in less capital-intensive ones.

employees, though perhaps affluent employees. For example, the Sunset Scavenger Company, for decades a cooperatively owned garbage-collection firm in San Francisco, sold out to a national, corporate waste-disposal firm in the 1980s when it had difficulty finding new recruits who could purchase its retiring members' shares.

From the founders' perspective, conversion in these circumstances may be acceptable and even desirable. On the other hand, if an outside agency contemplated subsidizing the enterprise out of an ideological commitment to the cooperative form or in anticipation of beneficial social externalities, it would view such a conversion as a defeat and might seek to prevent it. This was effectively the situation in much of the pre-1988 Yugoslav economy. The government provided financing to the firms. The workers had both control rights and residual income rights to the firm's assets. But they had no capital rights that could be transferred or liquidated on departure.[12]

The model adopted in Mondragon and promoted in the United States by the Industrial Cooperative Association takes a position between the Yugoslav denial of capital rights on the one hand and the fair market value option on the other.[13] In Mondragon, the buyout price is based on book value as reflected in internal capital accounts. As with partnership accounting, each member has an account that reflects the amounts she paid for her membership and her share of retained earnings—that is, earnings allocable to her that, instead of being paid out as dividends, were left in the firm. These amounts are reduced when the firm suffers losses. When the firm is successful, the amounts are increased, first, by a fixed-interest factor, and second, by an amount that approximates tangible-asset appreciation.

The capital-account adjustments do not take account of goodwill or going concern value. Moreover, about 30 percent of the firm's income is not allocated to the individual capital accounts at all: It is allocated to one or more collective accounts. These accounts fund a variety of collective benefits for the workers, such as recreation and education. They also function as a reserve that protects the firm from financial pressure in the event it has to repurchase several shares at a time.

New members buy their shares in Mondragon at prices considerably

---

12. See Lydall, *Yugoslav Capitalism*, 92–100.

13. See Ellerman and Pitegoff, *Democratic Corporation;* Harvard Business School, *The Mondragon Cooperative Experiment* (case study, n.d.).

below the present value of their pro rata share of the firm's anticipated income. The lower price is partly a reflection of the limited capital rights attached to the shares. It is partly a subsidy by incumbents of new members. The reduced entry price broadens the pool of potential entrants and mitigates the inequalities between old-timers and newcomers.

Equity limitations of this sort (and *a fortiori,* the preclusion of equity in the Yugoslav model) make ownership rights in the cooperative a kind of anchor. Ownership entails strong control and income rights (both to dividends and collective consumption) that can only be enjoyed as an active member of the enterprise. On departure, the individual can take part of the capitalized value of future income rights, but she leaves part behind. She can maximize her economic benefits only by staying with the enterprise.[14]

Community-Based Nongovernmental Organizations: The Nonprofit Corporation

As noted, the central actors in CED, community-based charitable corporations, tend not to accumulate tangible property. Nevertheless, they often have some tangible assets, and successful ones have large intangible assets: human capital in the form of able employees and volunteers, social capital in the form of ties to the community and outsiders, and reputational capital that outsiders will rely on. These assets are valuable both intrinsically and because they can be used to gain access to material resources.

Thus, property rights in these organizations can be significant, and it is important that they take a legal form analogous to the one we have

---

14. Equity limitations are sometimes found in business corporations in connection with employee compensation arrangements. A common form is "vesting" constraints on stock rights that provide for forfeiture in the event of departure before specified times. Equity limitations in the Mondragon cooperative model differ from the characteristic versions of such provisions largely in being (a) permanent, rather than short-term, and (b) more pervasive within the enterprise, because all cooperative workers presumptively have ownership rights, whereas only a few do in the conventional business corporation. Of course, the rationale for equity limitations may differ as between the two types of enterprise. In the business enterprise, they are likely to be purely a matter of incentive. In the cooperative, they may reflect an ideological belief that active community members have a stronger claim on the returns to its assets.

observed in other areas. They are subject to strong transfer and alienation restraints.

Transfer restraints are core features of the charitable corporation. Such a corporation holds its property in trust for specified charitable purposes. In the case of a community-based corporation, these purposes will usually invoke some dimension of the welfare of the residents of the relevant geographical area. By definition, a trust separates control rights from beneficial rights. The trustee (or board of directors) controls the property. She may not use it for her own benefit and must use it only in the interests of the beneficiaries. When the trust can no longer operate effectively, the trustee's only right and duty is to transfer the assets to another organization that is willing and able to put them to the relevant purposes.[15] Typically she cannot transfer her control rights. When she leaves office, her place will be filled by remaining co-trustees or directors, by member election, or by nomination by a specified person or a court.

For their part, the beneficiaries of a charitable trust have only indirect interests in its assets, but these interests can be quite important. The assets of charitable enterprises generate major subsidies for concert audiences, university students, and users of parks, as well as for those who receive housing, job, and business benefits from CED projects. All of these people have interests in the assets that generate these benefits. None of them, however, have any transfer rights over these assets. They cannot effectively capitalize their expectation of anticipated benefits.

The requirements for charitable tax exemption under Section 501(c)(3) operate as powerful accumulation restraints. At the beneficiary level, the public-benefit requirement mandates that benefits be spread among a class of some breadth. Where benefits are excessively concentrated on a small group, they will be characterized as "private," and the organization will be disqualified. At the control level, the limitation of control by beneficiaries in the private-inurement doctrine precludes a specific kind of accumulation.[16]

---

15. See, for example, IRS, Rev. Proc. 82–2, 1982–1 *Cumulative Bulletin* 367.

16. *E.g.,* Rev. Rul. 75–286, 1975–2 *Cumulative Bulletin* 210 (organizations to preserve and beautify public areas within city blocks are nonexempt because both control and benefits are too concentrated), for example, Revenue Ruling 69–545, 1969–2 *Cumulative Bulletin* 117 (hospital is nonexempt where control is concentrated among doctors practicing

Grant-making agencies, as we see in chapter 7, often impose more demanding requirements along these lines. But tax doctrine creates a general public baseline for all public charities.

The effect of these doctrines is to create property rights that are not transferable by the holder of either the control or the beneficial rights and that can be accumulated only within severe limits. To the extent that the organization has defined its purposes in terms of a geographically based community, these property rights should have an anchoring effect. Beneficiaries will enjoy them by virtue of their status as community members, but they will not be able to take these rights with them when they depart.

Churches: Mobile versus Immobile Membership

Church organizations typically incorporate transfer and accumulation restraints of the sort described earlier. Church members have virtually no capital rights, and control is usually diffused among parishioners.

Gerald Gamm has suggested that a significant difference exists among denominations in a factor that bears on transferability of interest. His analysis, though based on a single case, resonates with our concerns.[17]

In the 1930s, a Jewish community numbering 77,000 persons spanned the Dorchester and Upper Roxbury sections of Boston. One hundred thirty-six thousand Irish Catholics lived in adjacent neighborhoods. By the 1970s, the Jewish community had vanished. It had been replaced for the most part by much lower-income African Americans. Their neighborhoods had physically deteriorated and suffered high crime rates. By contrast, most of the old Catholic neighborhoods continued to be occupied predominantly by Catholics and were faring better in terms of amenity and safety.

One interpretation sees these events as an urban renewal failure.[18] An

---

there); Rev. Rul. 79–360, 1979–2 *Cumulative Bulletin* 236 (health club is nonexempt where membership is excessively restricted). The "private foundation" rules of the Internal Revenue code, discussed in chapter 7, impose additional accumulation restraints.

17. Gerald Gamm, *Urban Exodus: Why the Jews Left Boston and the Catholics Stayed* (1999).

18. This is more or less the thesis of another book on these neighborhoods: see Hillel Levine and Lawrence Harmon, *The Death of an American Jewish Community: A Tragedy of Good Intentions* (1992).

alliance of government and business elites set up programs designed to make credit available to first-time African American homebuyers and targeted the Jewish neighborhoods of Dorchester and Upper Roxbury as plausible places to encourage them to buy. Reckless underwriting practices by the programs extended credit to buyers who could not afford to maintain property. Racial fear fanned by blockbusting real estate agents encouraged disinvestment and flight by whites. And the city government's indifference to its African American citizens starved the neighborhood for services. In this interpretation, what accounts for the different fate of the Catholic neighborhoods is their greater political clout and perhaps also their greater racial intolerance. Local political leaders were less inclined to risk the displeasure of these neighborhoods, which contained core constituents, so they steered the newcomers away from them.

Gamm, however, points to more general factors. "Catholics," he writes, "have been especially likely to remain in traditional urban neighborhoods."[19] He suggests that this tendency is encouraged by characteristics of the Church and its organization: "What primarily distinguishes Jews from Catholics is . . . a different attachment to territory. Catholics have a strong sense of turf, regarding their neighborhoods as defended geographical communities."[20] These distinctions are reflected in the physical embodiment of the two communities: "The Catholic church is a permanent structure, consecrated to God and built around a permanent altar, and the territorial parish's relation to its neighborhood is inalienable. . . . Jewish neighborhoods, in contrast, do not take their identities from religious buildings. In Jewish law, the Torah is holier than any synagogue structure, and Torah scrolls are entirely portable."[21]

According to Gamm, Catholics feel a stronger commitment to terri-

19. Gamm, *Urban Exodus,* 13.

20. Ibid., 15–16.

21. Ibid., 18. Gamm elaborates:

For a church to be consecrated, both the altar and the building must be symbolically rooted and physically immovable. No church without an "*immovable* or *fixed* altar" can be consecrated, according to a 1957 textbook on canon law. Stone is the only material permitted for the table and base of an immovable altar and the entire table of the altar "must consist of a single natural stone." The church, too, if it is to be consecrated, must be built of either brick or stone; a church constructed of wood or metal may be blessed but not consecrated. Canon law does not permit the celebration of the Mass at an altar that has not been consecrated or in a church that has not been consecrated or blessed. Ibid., 131.

torially defined neighborhoods than do Jewish congregations. They view their institutional presence in the neighborhood as permanent, and they strongly resist pressure to disinvest or leave.

Organizational differences are pertinent here. Like congregational Protestant churches, Jewish synagogues tend to be self-supporting and self-governing membership organizations. By contrast, the Catholic Church is a unitary international organization with substantial centralized government and finance. It is thus able to support its doctrinal commitment to the permanence and stability of neighborhood parishes by providing resources to parishes in troubled or declining neighborhoods.

Most importantly, the two communities have very different membership rules. As in many Protestant denominations, synagogue membership typically has no strong territorial basis. More than one temple sometimes competes within a neighborhood for members, and temples often draw their members from across neighborhood boundaries. By contrast, Catholic churches are community-based organizations. They have a strong and explicit geographical organization. The diocese divides its territory into parishes, and Catholics are called to worship at the church in the parish in which they reside. Gamm shows that the territorial membership rule has been strictly enforced. At least in many areas, Catholics have no choice about where to worship.

Gamm sees these distinctive characteristics of Catholicism as mitigating the "coordination problem" in neighborhood investments.[22] In its most severe form, the problem leads to a downward spiral in which fears of decline become self-perpetuating as each wave of disinvestment and flight motivates a new wave. The advent of a new group of lower social status is a classic trigger for such situations. In Gamm's account, Catholic doctrine and organization mitigates the problem in two ways.

First, the Catholic Church's reputation and practice of making and standing by tangible physical investments is a stabilizing force. The church itself has a commitment to the community that leads it to resist pressure to flee. It also sustains a variety of networks and relationships. The church continued to make new investments in Dorchester and Upper Roxbury, and it continued to induce a substantial level of par-

22. Ibid., 22.

ticipation in its activities throughout the period of decline for many Boston neighborhoods.

Second, the church's membership rules create "high barriers to exit"[23] that make collaborative options seem more important. This is the Harringtonian Republican point that an immobile investment attached to a particular jurisdiction is more likely than a mobile investment to lead to responsible participation. The membership rights of Catholics are immobile in the following sense: A Catholic has a right to membership in his local parish conditioned on continued residence within its boundaries. When he moves out, he loses this right. He gains a right to participation in the parish of his new neighborhood, but if he has strong ties to his old parish, the new right may be considerably less valuable.

The situation is different for Jews. They can move to a new neighborhood and continue their membership in their synagogue. Gamm shows that this was in fact the tendency for Jews migrating from Dorchester and Upper Roxbury. They did return to worship, at least at first. As migration increased, the synagogues eventually followed their members and relocated in their new communities. Jews were able to maintain their membership and social ties after moving. Migration entailed little cost in terms of religious-membership rights.

Thus, Catholic as opposed to Jewish (and some Protestant) membership rights have a distinctive characteristic of social-republican property: transfer restraints. Of course, all religious membership rights are nontransferable in the sense that holders cannot sell or give them to others. But the rights in the Jewish congregations can be carried across boundaries. Catholics' rights cannot. The result is that Catholics bear nonmonetary costs of mobility that Jews do not. This contributes to the same sort of situation as the more conventional transfer restraints. Catholic membership rights involve benefits that can be enjoyed only while the holder remains a member of the community.

23. Ibid., 221.

Chapter 7 Induced Mobilization

Community Economic Development involves efforts by outside institutions—governments, businesses, and philanthropic organizations—to encourage and support grassroots organizing in low-income communities. These efforts can take a variety of forms.

Some programs provide support directly to community-based organizations. The HUD-administered HOME program and the Massachusetts Community Development Finance Agency, for example, make loans or grants to CDCS.

Some programs require government agencies to support community-based organizations as a precondition of particular activities. A local government applying for benefits under the federal Empowerment Zone program must demonstrate the participation of community-based organizations in the formulation and planned implementation of its proposal. Local governments distributing federal Community Development Block Grant funds must give community-based organizations an opportunity to participate in the grant-making process. A local Redevelopment authority in California must insure that a project area committee is formed of affected residents, businesses, and landowners, and provided with financial support.

Rules that provide citizen powers that are best exercised by community organizations indirectly encourage such organizations. Powers to challenge land-use decisions in court under zoning, planning, and environmental laws are examples.

Another form of indirect support comes from programs that subsidize activities that do not themselves involve political mobilization but have synergies with mobilizing activities and thus lower the cost of mobilization through cross-subsidy or economies of scope. The original idea of the Community Action Program of the 1960s was that giving community-based organizations responsibility for administering social service programs would encourage political organizing and activities. The routine service-administration activities would contribute to an organization's fixed costs. It would also provide occasions for regular contact with community members that would facilitate recruitment of members and learning about the community. Although this idea no longer survives in the comprehensive and ambitious form of the Economic Opportunity Act, many CED organizations administer service programs, such as job training and placement, immigration counseling, tax advice, and educational enrichment.[1]

From the perspective of the aspirations of the CED Movement, these efforts court dangers. First, there is danger of outside capture, that the outside providers of support—government, business, or philanthropic—will dominate the community organizations to serve their own interests. This is the danger exemplified by the disasters of Redevelopment in the urban renewal era. Second, there is danger of internal oligarchy, that the board and managers of the community-based organization will use their control in their own interests rather than those of the community. This might mean self-dealing and outright corruption. It might mean patronage and cronyism. Or more modestly, it might mean simple efforts to avoid accountability and evaluation. Third, there is the danger of factional control or takeover, that an unrepresentative minority will assume control of the organization and steer it in directions that are not in the interests of the larger community.

The prohibitions against private benefit and private inurement in the

---

1. The Dudley Street Neighborhood Initiative runs a variety of service programs, including programs concerned with teaching entrepreneurship to teenagers, mentoring high-school seniors applying to college, cleaning up neighborhoods, conducting outreach and education programs on lead-paint poisoning and solar energy, operating a community greenhouse, and counseling on the Earned Income Tax Credit.

tax law and corporate law mitigate these dangers, but only vaguely, and these doctrines are not strongly policed.

Community Economic Development institutions have two further types of responses to these dangers. One is explicit, the other implicit. The explicit response is *ex ante* and structural: a series of requirements designed to make the organization accountable to its membership and through the membership to the larger community. The implicit response is in the spirit of what Michael Dorf and Charles Sabel call "democratic experimentalism," a competitive process in which organizations achieve rewards by demonstrating their ability, among other things, to mobilize and represent their constituents.[2]

The Ex Ante *Structural Approach*

The structural approach conditions benefits on attributes of the applicant. The two most important examples of this approach are the "private foundation" rules in the Internal Revenue Code limiting the benefits of charitable tax exemption and a variety of specific governance conditions in CED support programs. The former focus primarily on financial support. The latter focus primarily on formal control.

PRIVATE FOUNDATION RULES

The private foundation rules were added to the tax code's charitable exemption in 1969 in an effort to encourage charitable nonprofits to attract public support for their activities. A core group of traditional charities, including churches, schools, and hospitals are excluded, but the rules apply to a very broad range of organizations. The rules are animated by concerns of popular participation and accountability that resonate with CED ideology. However, their demands are fairly modest by CED standards, and their implementation tends to be formulaic. It is doubtful that they are a significant force for institutional democracy in the CED context, and they are sometimes a bureaucratic nuisance. Nevertheless, they are an interesting example of an effort to induce popular mobilization by conditioning public benefits—in this case, tax benefits.

These rules are largely a response to the problem of internal oligar-

2. Michael C. Dorf and Charles F. Sabel, "A Constitution of Democratic Experimentalism," 98 *Columbia Law Review* 267 (1998).

chy. They were promoted by Congressman Wright Patman, a Texas populist who styled himself as the scourge of Eastern corporate and banking interests. Patman thought charitable organizations controlled by small groups of wealthy individuals or by corporations were undeserving of tax subsidy. As enacted, the rules single out a category of 501(c)(3) organizations called "private foundations" for less favorable tax treatment than "public charities." They limit the tax-deductibility of very large donations to foundations and impose an excise tax on investment income.[3] They also impose a categorical accumulation restraint, requiring the foundation to spend a minimum fraction of its assets annually (about 5 percent).[4] The rules police self-dealing and private inurement more strictly for private foundations, and they require more extensive record keeping and reporting.[5] The restrictions on large donations, investment income, and asset accumulation are irrelevant to most community-based organizations, but all of these organizations strive to avoid the burden of the stronger record-keeping and reporting requirements.

Characterization as a public charity or a private foundation turns on the balance of public and nonpublic support in the organization's income statement. The rules treat as public support small donations (measured as a fraction of total income), membership fees, and grants from government agencies and other nonprofits that have established themselves as public charities. Nonpublic support includes large contributions, investment income, and unrelated business income (that is, income from activities unrelated to the organization's charitable purposes). An organization can qualify as a public charity by showing that public support makes up at least a third of its total support.

The test looks to income sources as evidence of broad public approval. From the fact that the organization received a substantial part of its income in the form of small donations and membership fees, the rules infer that its mission and activities are approved by a substantial range of people. Resources from government agencies and public

3. 26 USC 170(b)(1)(A) (contributions to private foundations are deductible only up to 30 percent of a donor's income, as opposed to 50 percent for public-charity contributions); 26 U.S.C. 4940 (2 percent excise tax on private-foundation—investment income).

4. 26 USC 4942(e).

5. 26 USC 4941–4963, 6033(c), 6104.

charities, which are assumed to be themselves accountable to or supported by broad segments of the population, are taken as indirect evidence of broad approval. By contrast, dependence on contributions from a few wealthy donors, earnings on assets contributed in the past, and business income are not considered evidence of broad, current support for the organization's charitable activities.[6]

As long as it can show at least 10 percent public support, an applicant that cannot show that a third of its support comes from public sources may qualify under a "facts and circumstances" test.[7] This involves a much broader inquiry. It looks not only to the amount of public support but to the identity of the supporters. Donations from dispersed, unrelated individuals are better than donations from people with family or business connections. Efforts to attract public support, especially in a new organization, are favorably weighed. In addition, the breadth of distribution of benefits and of control are important. These factors are pertinent to the public-benefit requirement for 501(c)(3) status. Presumably, the expectations are higher for 501(c)(3) organizations that

6. 26 USC 509(a). See generally James Fishman and Stephen Schwartz, *Nonprofit Organizations,* 602–700 (2d 2000). This "traditional charities" test entirely excludes related business income, treating it as neither public nor nonpublic. The statute provides an alternative quantitative test that allows inclusion of "gross receipts" from related business activity as public support. However, to qualify as a public charity under this test, the applicant must satisfy not only the requirement that public support (now including related business revenues) exceed a third of total support, but also an additional requirement that no more than a third of total support come from investment and unrelated business income: ibid., 509(a)(2). This "gross receipts" test was designed for charities such as orchestras and museums that have traditionally derived a major portion of support from ticket sales. In effect, the statute treats such related business revenues as an indication of popular support but a weaker indication than small donations, membership dues, or government grants. Payments by beneficiaries of the charity show some satisfaction with its activities, but because the payer receives a material benefit in return, they are not disinterested in the way that the more heavily weighted forms of support are. Thus, such revenues can be included as "public support," but only at the cost of showing that the organization relies to a more limited extent on investment and unrelated business income than other public charities would be permitted to do. CDCs usually qualify under the "traditional" test without reference to related business income. However, some with relatively large amounts of related business income rely on the "gross receipts test." See Irwin Boroff, "Escaping the Perils of Private Foundation Status," *National Economic Development and Law Center Report* (winter 1983), 43.

7. CFR 1.170A–9(e)(3).

qualify as public charities. With respect to control, the regulations encourage boards with public officials and people appointed by public officials, community leaders and people representative of constituencies in the community, and people elected by a broadly based membership.

The democratic intention of the private-foundation rules is unmistakable, but their practical effects are not clear and have been surprisingly little studied. The rules undoubtedly function to single out for less generous subsidy and stricter regulation a class of charities that are controlled by narrow groups or rely largely on endowment income or contributions from a small number of wealthy individuals. On the other hand, the rules seem arbitrary and vague. The multiple avenues to escaping the private-foundation designation, the low thresholds of the quantitative tests, and the ad hoc vagueness of the "facts and circumstances" test amount to a tendency toward under-inclusion. Many organizations without meaningful public support easily escape private-foundation status. No doubt, the rules have some influence on the conduct of some organizations, including CED organizations, that serves their democratic purpose. They encourage CDCs at the margin to try to attract members, to raise small donations, and to avoid excessive reliance on foundation grants and donations from wealthy individuals. On the other hand, much of the resulting support may involve very small gestures, such as one-time donations responding to mail solicitations or infrequent attendance at meetings, that do not involve substantial participation.[8] The rules also encourage legalistic manipulation of

8. For example, the last time I was at the Metropolitan Museum of Art in New York, I noticed that the $10 I paid for admission was characterized not as a fee, but as a "donation." Most people seemed to be paying it automatically, and they may well have thought of it as a fee. They did not appear to be making a considered decision as to whether they wanted to support the museum as a charity. Yet although the financial consequence of this terminological choice may be negligible, the legal consequence is that the payments will be counted as "public support" under the "traditional test" rather than as "related business income," which could be used only under the "gross receipts" test. Recall that the advantage of the traditional test is that it does not place a direct limit on investment and unrelated business income.

For some, this example may call into question not just the implementation of the private foundation rules, but also their underlying purpose. The Metropolitan Museum is a great institution, and many might wish it to receive all the benefits of charitable exemption even if it is basically an elite institution in terms of its governance and sources of support. Democracy is not the only important value, and it is not one we

organizational forms that raise transaction costs without contributing to the goals of participation and accountability. For example, lawyers stand ready to show CDCs how to put activities that generate related or unrelated business revenues in subsidiaries so that such revenues will not put them at a disadvantage. The IRS generally has been tolerant of such maneuvers.[9]

On the whole then, the rules do not seem to be successful in inducing or rewarding popular participation and accountability. This is due in part to their inadequate specification—they are both too mechanical and too ad hoc—but it would not be easy to correct these problems. The rules' overemphasis on quantitative measures of financial support seems a response to the difficulty of measuring participation and accountability directly.

CONDITIONS OF CED PROGRAM GOVERNANCE

A more tailored variation of the structural approach can be seen in the frequent conditions on programs providing CED support regarding the governance structure of applicants. Most programs supporting CED require that applicants have a board that is "representative of," "responsible to," or "accountable to" the community or its low-income members.[10] In fact, all CDCs have boards with at least ostensible community representation.[11]

---

should insist on in every quarter. Nevertheless, democracy clearly is the underlying concern of the rules, and if their disadvantages can be avoided by such a largely formal move, it is questionable whether they are being coherently implemented.

9. See Boroff, "Perils," 48; Fishman and Schwartz, *Nonprofit Organizations,* 827–29.

10. 112 Stat. 2702, sec. 676B. (Head Start funds); 42 USC 9904(c)(1)(B)(3) (boards of applicants for CDBG funds must have a third of members chosen with "democratic selection procedures adequate to assure they are representative of the poor in the area to be served"); 13 CFR 124.3 (CDCs eligible for minority small business assistance must be "responsible to" community residents); 12 CFR 1805.201 (eligible Community Development Financial Institutions must have board "accountable to residents . . . through representation on its governing board").

11. On average, CDCs in Vidal's study allocated 44 percent of board seats to "residents/clients" and 11 percent more to representatives of other community-based organizations. Local business, religious, or government leaders got another 19 percent. The principal categories of non-local representation were "relevant professionals" (20 percent) and "funders" (4 percent): Avis Vidal, *Rebuilding Communities: A National Study of Community Development Corporations* 39 (New School for Social Research, 1992).

Sometimes the rules attempt to elaborate the idea of representative-ness with more specific requirements. A response to the danger of out-side capture is to prohibit or limit certain types of outside repre-sentation on the board. The Massachusetts Community Development Finance Agency prohibits applicants from having representatives of business or government on their boards.[12] Under HUD's regulations for the HOME program, a Community Housing Development Organization may have no more than a third of its board seats occupied by govern-mental or business sponsors.[13] Another approach is to require represen-tation of multiple outside constituencies, perhaps partly on the theory that they will check one another. An organization applying for assis-tance under the 1998 Human Service Reauthorization Act must have a board on which a third of the members are public officials and another third represent "small business, labor, religious groups, education, or law enforcement."[14] Community Services Block Grant applicants need boards on which one-third of the members are public-sector represen-tatives and one-third are from "business, labor, religious," and other interested groups.[15]

The common response to the problem of internal oligarchy is to require election of directors by members of the community. Regulations occasionally specify that the organization be a membership organiza-tion, with members empowered to elect at least some of the directors.[16] In fact, most CDCs are membership organizations. Nonmember CED organizations have other forms of community representation. Eligi-bility for assistance as a "Community Development Bank" from the Community Development Financial Institutions Fund requires that at least half of the governing board be appointed from nominees submit-ted by a "Community Investment Board" of community leaders. The investment board is appointed initially by the bank's governing board; as vacancies occur, they are filled by remaining investment board mem-bers. A federally supported community health center requires a board

---

12. Massachusetts General Laws, c. 40F, sec. 4.

13. 24 CFR 92.2.

14. 42 USC 9910.

15. 42 USC 9904(c)(1)(B)(3).

16. For example, Massachusetts General Laws 40F, sec. 2–3 (requirement for support from the Massachusetts Community Development Finance Corporation).

with a majority who are patients of the center (though not necessarily elected by patients).[17]

Some programs dictate a minimal frequency for board meetings. Federal health center rules require at least monthly board meetings.[18] Community Development Financial Institution rules require Community Development Bank boards to meet at least every three months.[19] When a CDC sponsors a socially disadvantaged enterprise for federal procurement preferences, the Small Business Administration requires that it have a board that meets at least quarterly.[20] Some programs address the range of the board's powers. The federal health-center rules require that the board have authority to "select the services to be provided by the center, schedule the hours during which the services are to be provided, approve the selection of a director for the center and . . . establish general policies."

Explicit responses to the problem of factional takeover or domination are rare. The requirement of the Massachusetts Community Development Finance Agency that membership be open to all community members may be directed to this concern.[21] However, if the danger were a serious one, this provision might actually exacerbate it by compelling an organization with a small or inactive membership to admit a group of insurgents bent on taking it over for parochial reasons. In the past, CDCs have adopted selective membership provisions, requiring applicants to persuade a membership committee that their admission would, say, contribute to the goals of the organization. Such provisions seem to have been adopted to give the organization defenses against a factional takeover.

Another response to this concern sometimes found in CDC bylaws is to have special rules regarding the replacement of directors. The rules sometimes require a super-majority member vote or decisions at two successive meetings in order to remove a director.

Funders of NGOs have developed checklists to assess the adequacy of the governance structures of community-based organizations. A list

17. 42 USC 254bj(3)(H).
18. Ibid.
19. 12 USC 1834b(b).
20. 13 CFR 120.823.
21. Massachusetts General Laws c. 40F, sec. (2)–(3).

recommended by an Aspen Institute study directs attention to the board's representativeness with respect to age, race, occupation, social class, intracommunity geography, and skills. It also identifies such matters as conflict-of-interest policies, training and orientation for board members, membership communication, and conflict resolution.[22]

In fact, member factionalism has not proved to be a major problem. Nor, however, does member or community election appear to be a serious check on outsider capture or insider oligarchy. The explanation for both phenomena is the same: member or community indifference to the governance process. For all the rhetoric and ceremony of democratic process, most people concede that most CDCS, good and bad, are dominated by a small number of senior managers (often one) or a few dedicated board members. The basic internal political distinction among CDCS is between staff-driven (or CEO-driven) CDCS and board-driven CDCS.[23] There are few member-driven CDCS.[24] When members are important, it is usually as a source of volunteers to perform organizing and service tasks, not as an internal political force.

Membership rarely embraces more than a small fraction of the community, and participation in member and community-wide elections for board seats is consistently low. So is participation in matters of governance generally. The Dudley Street Neighborhood Initiative, justly considered one of the outstanding recent successes of community organizing, typically gets about 250 people to vote in its board elections—about 10 percent of its membership. Board elections in CDCS are rarely contested, and when they are, the contest is usually not on programmatic grounds.

A telling indication in most CDC bylaws is the quorum requirement for member meetings. Business corporations typically require 50 percent shareholder representation for a quorum, and statutes often prohibit them from going below a third.[25] A typical CDC requirement for a membership quorum is 5 percent. Experienced lawyers advising inex-

22. Sharon Milligan et al., "Implementing a Theory of Change Evaluation in the Cleveland Community-Building Initiative." Available from: http://www.aspenroundtable .org/vol2/milligan/html, table 2 (visited 20 May 2000).

23. I take these terms from Arthur Johnson.

24. Skerry suggests that COPS of San Antonio may be one. *Mexican Americans: The Ambivalent Minority* 151–93 (1993).

25. For example, California Corporations Code, sec. 602.

perienced NGO organizers commonly find themselves challenging their clients' optimism about member participation when it comes to discussing the quorum provision.[26]

This is not to say that CDCs do not engage in genuine representation and mobilization. When substantive issues are at stake, they can often tap great energy and ingenuity. They can pack a zoning hearing, turn out people for a neighborhood cleanup, and get community views on a housing plan. Membership plays an important role in inducing contributions of effort and getting information about the community. But membership and the electoral process generally do not play a strong or consistent role in governance accountability.

One reason is that pure governance issues are not salient or exciting enough to most community members. Controversial issues about projects emerge only episodically at times that may not coincide with elections. Another is that the participatory demands of the electoral process are in some respects exceptionally exacting. Although participation by small subconstituencies is sufficient for many tasks, elections require a large proportion of the general constituency to act at more or less the same time.

Still another reason is that grassroots participation often depends on extensive staff work. When a crisis arises or an exciting issue is on the table, participation is easily and maybe even spontaneously mobilized. But more routine participation requires staff work to keep members informed, prepare and conduct events, and organize activities. For all their rhetorical homage to membership and participation, CDC managers are often ambivalent about them for reasons that have nothing to do with accountability. Managers may be ideologically committed to grassroots control. They know that funders like to see evidence of an active and representative membership. And they know that times will come when they will need to turn out a crowd or call on the efforts of a dedicated group. But often members are simply a drain on staff time

26. There is a similar but less severe problem with boards. Most effective CDCs have some dedicated board members, but many have trouble achieving regular attendance by a full board, or even a majority. CDCs are often advised to anticipate the problem of director attendance by providing in the bylaws that a director who misses a specified number of meetings in a year—say, more than three out of twelve—is automatically removed.

and resources. The care and feeding they require often seems to out-weigh their contribution to the organization's goals.

Moreover, even when members are a real asset, they do not neces-sarily function as an effective check on management or outsider domi-nation. Membership is too often dependent on the encouragement and support of staff who are under the control of the people the members are expected to hold accountable. Very few have the skills, information, or motivation to act independently in ways that would allow them to act autonomously.

The Ex Post *Competitive Approach*

The other approach to accountability relies on *ex post* assessment of the performance of the organizations in repeated rounds of competition for resources and authority. A key characteristic of the new social policy is the move away from monopolistic provision of services toward poten-tially competitive provision. The old monopolistic providers could be government agencies, such as local public-housing authorities, or they might be NGOs, such as the community action agencies, that were effec-tively granted monopolies in their neighborhoods.[27] The new programs put more emphasis on NGOs, but even when they leave a role for govern-ment agencies, they typically contemplate competition both among such agencies and between them and private organizations.

The providers compete on the basis of the quality of their proposals and the credibility of their commitments to implement them. The latter, of course, depends in substantial part on their past records. Competi-tion takes place across jurisdictions. It also, potentially and often in fact, takes place within jurisdictions. Given the ease with which nonprofit corporations can be formed, a CDC that performs poorly is often faced with a competitor.

Although it is rare for the board of a poorly performing CDC to be replaced by election, it is relatively common for such a CDC to find itself losing resources or authority for new projects to competitors. The Dud-ley Street Neighborhood Initiative was formed as an alternative to a pre-

27. There was no explicit limit of a single organization for a community, but this seems to have been the premise. The regulations explicitly contemplated a remarkable degree of entrenchment once an agency was designated. Termination or nonrenewal could occur only through elaborate procedures. 45 CFR Pt. 1067 (1971).

existing organization called the Greater Roxbury Neighborhood Association. The association had mostly African American members and officers. Some residents believed that it was unresponsive to the Latino and Cape Verdean communities and that it was excessively attentive to the interests of a group of African American construction contractors. The DSNI was designed to draw support from all four of the neighborhood's ethnic constituencies.[28] At about the same time, Boston's 5,000 resident Chinatown produced its second CDC, the Asian Community Development Corporation, which arose from dissatisfaction with the Chinese Economic Development Council. The founders of the new CDC considered its competitor's management ineffective.[29] The Harlem Urban Development Corporation—not a typical nonprofit but, rather, a state-chartered public corporation—acquired a reputation for patronage, ideological extremism, and ineptitude that eventually led to its dissolution by the state in 1995. Even before then, however, the city and philanthropic groups had begun to favor an emergent group of church-affiliated CDCs, including the Abyssinian Development Corporation and the Harlem Congregation for Community Development with support for residential and commercial development.[30] "It's worth noting," say Paul Grogan and Tony Proscio, "that none of the ministers [who started the newer CDCs] 'took on' the old Harlem UDC. Driven by necessity, they simply set out to do something credible themselves. By accomplishing that, they exposed the stark reality of HUDC."[31]

This form of ex post competitive assessment can be thought of as a form of democratic accountability in three senses. First, most of the organizations making the assessments are themselves subject to mechanisms of political accountability. Some, such as HUD and the Community Development Financial Institutions Fund, are government agencies accountable to elected officials. Some, such as the Neighborhood Rein-

28. Peter Medoff and Holly Sklar, *Streets of Hope: The Fall and Rise of an Urban Neighborhood* 92–96 (1994). A local offshoot of the national group ACORN (Association of Community Groups for Reform Now) sought unsuccessfully to enter the community in competition with DSNI. Ibid., 74–76.

29. Michael Liu, *Chinatown's Neighborhood Mobilization and Urban Development in Boston* 111 (Ph.D. diss., University of Massachusetts, Boston, 1999).

30. Tamar Jacoby and Fred Siegel, "Growing the Inner City: Harlem's Experience with the 'Third Way' Antipoverty Approach," *New Republic*, 23 August 1999, 22–4.

31. Paul Grogan and Tony Proscio, *Comeback Cities: A Blueprint for Urban Neighborhood Revival* 92 (2000).

vestment Corporation, are specially chartered, government-sponsored corporations that depend on legislative appropriations or periodic renewal of legislatively granted privileges, such as the ability to issue tax-exempt instruments. Some, such as the Grameen Bank and the Caja Popular Laboral, the principal bank at Mondragon, are organized as cooperatives in which the groups or institutions they support are members with ultimate control rights. Some are nonprofit public charities that depend in substantial part on their ability to mobilize a continuing stream of voluntary donations.

Second, the accountability of the organizations to their communities is in most cases an explicit criterion on which their performance is assessed. Third, and most importantly, the more tangible measures of CED's success depend on effective community mobilization. The three logics of community action all suggest that political mobilization will often be important for development that satisfies the general CED desiderata—benefits to residents, positive linkages with local institutions, minimal negative externalities, and local control. Thus, CDCs that succeed in terms of these criteria will be giving indirect evidence of their ability to organize political support in the community.

Two examples show the possibilities and limits of the *ex post* competitive approach to political accountability. The first concerns a development initiative for the Jackson Square area of Jamaica Plain, Massachusetts.[32] The successful supermarket project undertaken there by the Jamaica Plain Neighborhood Development Corporation has already been mentioned. Five major tracts of vacant or underused land remain in the area, four of them owned by state or local government entities. In 1995, Urban Edge, the other Jamaica Plain CDC, initiated a planning process to develop the area. It invited neighborhood residents and organizations to a series of community meetings. It also distributed through community newspapers a series of planning documents, each attempting to incorporate views expressed at the most recent meetings. The early documents were vague, however, and they did not present the participants in the discussion with clear choices and trade-offs. In September 1998, the group presented a proposal that was considerably more

32. This discussion is based on Michael Miramontes, "The Urban Edge Egleston–Jackson Strategy: A Case Study," unpublished, Harvard Law School, 2000.

specific and that appeared to depart from prior proposals in several ways, including a project of much larger scale incorporating a large Kmart.

Substantial community opposition emerged immediately. The local merchants' organization argued that the Kmart would put many small retailers out of business without providing any major compensating benefits to the community. Other community groups voiced concerns about traffic. Many worried that Urban Edge had a conflict of interest as planner, because it hoped to become a developer and thereby reap large fees when a plan became effective. Many organizations, including the Jamaica Plain Neighborhood Development Corporation, went on record in opposition to the strategy. More than thirty-five community-based NGOs from Jamaica Plain or neighboring areas of Roxbury and Dorchester participated in the controversy. At this point, the city government, which before the controversy had informally supported the Urban Edge effort, pulled the plug by assigning the Boston Redevelopment Authority (BRA) to conduct a new community-based planning process. Previously involved organizations immediately met independently to propose a procedure to the BRA for the new effort, and the BRA agreed in broad outline to many of their proposals.

The second illustration is the dispute among community groups in the merger in 1995 of Wells Fargo and First Interstate banks.[33] These were enormous banks with extensive operations focused in California. Bank mergers require specific regulatory approval, in this case from the Federal Reserve Board, and hence are among the principal levers for review and enforcement of Community Reinvestment Act duties. Among those filing statements in support of the merger was the Greenlining Coalition, a statewide organization speaking for community groups on finance issues. The merger application was opposed by the California Reinvestment Committee, another group with similar goals. The two organizations divided over the general effect of the merger on low- and moderate-income customers and the adequacy of the banks' past CRA performance and the commitments made in connection with the merger.

The Federal Reserve Board rejected the challenge and approved the

33. See Kenneth Thomas, *The CRA Handbook* 16–17, 82–84 (1999).

merger. Even those who do not feel qualified to assess the merits of the dispute have reason for concern about the decision. Of the major banking agencies, the Federal Reserve Board has shown the least commitment and sophistication in CRA matters. More specifically, some questioned the objectivity of the Greenlining Institute on the ground that it had benefited from various contracts with Wells Fargo. These critics suggested that the Institute might have traded support for Wells Fargo for substantial benefits for the organization. Kenneth Thomas reports that he asked the Greenlining Institute to disclose its contracts with Wells Fargo and the Federal Reserve Board to require such disclosure from participants in the regulatory process. Both declined.

With these illustrations in mind, consider some of the following issues in appraising the ex post competitive approach to accountability.

MONOPOLY VERSUS COMPETITION

The CED Movement is part of a trend to introduce competitive processes into the government and NGO spheres. The Community Action Program of the 1960s contemplated a single internally democratic but monopolistic organization in each neighborhood with broad responsibilities, including economic development. There are some advantages to monopoly. Competitive organizations may create more organizational and procedural costs than a single one. In addition, some tasks lend themselves to monopoly. Some projects are generally and broadly preclusive of others; hence, a single, unitary decision about them is required. Usually, we want a single, unitary set of criminal laws, street grid, or sewer system for a given locality.

Moreover, competition within the community has the potential to divide and weaken it in negotiations with outsiders. For example, the American system of collective bargaining requires that a single unit represent all the employees within any bargaining unit, in part on the premise that if the workforce were to fragment it would be at a great disadvantage vis-à-vis the employer. Even so, this system has been criticized for permitting too much competition at the certification stage among unions aspiring to become the workers' exclusive bargaining representative. The competitive certification process diverts resources and energy to disputes among workers that might be better deployed against the employer. Thus, it has been suggested that workers would sometimes do better with a monopolistic system in which the state assigns a union to represent them at each workplace.[34]

Peter Skerry makes a related argument in the CED sphere in an effort to account for what he sees as the more extensive activity of Catholic, in comparison with Protestant, churches. Catholic organization is monopolistic. Parish boundaries are centrally determined, and only one church is allowed within each parish. By contrast, Protestant organization is more competitive. Protestants are often free to defect from their congregations and form new ones whenever they wish. Because exit options are more limited in the Catholic church, the relative incentives for participation ("voice") are greater. Skerry sees two further consequences. Catholic parishes tend to be more inclusive and diverse. They are thus likely to represent a broader range of the community. Moreover, the internal processes of governance require a kind of diplomacy and mutual accommodation that better prepares both clergy and active lay parishioners for community politics.[35]

Although Catholic institutions do not compete with one another within a community, their CED activities may compete with those of other groups. The CED institutions tend to anchor people to the community, as shown in chapter 6, but within the community they seem compatible with a substantial array of competition.[36]

Several considerations favor competition. Smaller-scale, incremental planning processes that make room for multiple independent decision makers are often more attractive than detailed, comprehensive plans. Moreover, even when a single decision on a comprehensive plan is required, it may be more effective to have competing organizations present separate plans to an outside decision maker. And even in the absence of a single supervening decision maker, competing groups with a common stake in a single resolution may be able to come to agreement.

34. See Tamara Lothian, "The Political Consequences of Labor Law Regimes," 47 *Cardozo Law Review* 1001 (1986).

35. Skerry, *Mexican Americans,* 24.

36. Skerry's argument about monopoly should thus be distinguished from Gamm's argument about non-transportable membership rights discussed in chapter 6. Gamm emphasized the effect of Catholic organization in binding the individual to the community; Skerry emphasizes the effect in binding her to a particular institution within it.

The attractive feature of competition is that it provides a distinctive check on myopia, oligarchy, and inefficiency. Citizens with concerns about Urban Edge's Kmart plan or the Greenlining Coalition's relationship with Wells Fargo could have sought to raise their concerns within those organizations. But the structural guarantees of democracy in such organizations are often weak. There is no general assurance that such dissidents will get a fair hearing. Moreover, the narrow membership base of such organizations often means that those who share the dissidents' concerns are under-represented. It may be easier to mobilize people through a second organization dedicated to the dissidents' perspective than to oppose the established view within the first organization.

On the other hand, many activists take seriously the objection that the benefits of competition may come at the cost of weakening the community vis-à-vis outsiders. This may be illustrated by the Urban Edge Kmart story. On one hand, the story shows a project with inadequately considered costs to the community thwarted by organizational competition. On the other hand, one aspect of the result troubled some community members. In the absence of community consensus, an outside institution—the Boston Redevelopment Authority—intervened to run the process. To be sure, the BRA committed itself to conducting a community-driven process, and given the neighborhood-oriented politics of contemporary Boston, its presence may have been benign. But many residents remain suspicious of the BRA and considered its intervention a costly loss of autonomy for the community.

In some respects, the Dudley Street Neighborhood Initiative in Roxbury presents a contrast to Jamaica Plain. The distrust of outside institutions, especially the BRA, has been especially strong there, and this sentiment has led some to aspire for a monopolistic position for DSNI.[37] Purporting to be the only institution qualified to speak to the community on a range of issues, DSNI's most important move has been to confine its functions to planning, and to forgo development activities. It asserts that developers have a strong conflict of interest that impairs their ability to engage in planning and attendant mobilizing and advocacy activities. As Urban Edge's critics in the Kmart controversy

---

37. COPs of San Antonio appears to occupy a similar position. Alinsky's notion of an encompassing People's Organization that operated as an "organization of organizations" seems to have contemplated a monopolistic position. See Saul Alinsky, *Reveille for Radicals* 76–88 (1946), Skerry, *Mexican Americans*, 151–93.

pointed out, CDCs that do development have a self-interest in projects by which they can earn large development fees. Thus, unlike most CDCs, the DSNI contrasts itself, as a community planning organization, with the other CDCs in the area, which it considers developers. In its model, it sits as a forum in which the community can define its goals and choose among projects proposed by competing developers, both for-profit and nonprofit. When CDCs or for-profit developers initiate projects without seeking DSNI approval or collaboration, the DSNI is likely to sanction them rhetorically as trying to bypass the community and may oppose them actively.

The CDC developers have a claim to speak for the community, as well, but DSNI's point is not only that its participatory processes are more elaborate and extensive, but that having a single voice to resolve planning issues on behalf of the community increases the community's autonomy vis-à-vis outsiders such as the BRA. Of course, DSNI's position is a fragile one. It has no formal monopoly; in principle the regime is competitive. Thus, it could be subject to a challenge of the sort that Urban Edge experienced.

From the perspective of the institutional designer, the choice between monopolistic and competitive regimes depends in part on whether monopoly or competition is most likely to induce effective responses to organizational myopia, oligarchy, or ineptitude and on the importance to the community of unity in dealings with outsiders. One critical variable, of course, will be the character of the outsiders who are likely to intervene in the absence of unity. It is unlikely that a uniform answer exists for all communities.

BENCHMARKS AND INFORMATION

Competition implies comparative assessment, and this in turn implies both criteria and information about performance. Moreover, as its most ambitious proponents conceive it, the competitive process is not only a mechanism for the allocation of resources and authority but also a form of learning.[38] The process of articulating standards and assessing which programs have best met them is also a process by which participants learn how to improve their own performance. In some respects, the

38. See Dorf and Sabel, "Democratic Experimentalism," 316–23; Charles F. Sabel, "Learning by Monitoring," in *Handbook of Economic Sociology* 137–65 (Neil J. Smelser and Richard Swedborg eds. 1994).

competitive process is also a process of enforced collaboration. Organizations are forced to collaborate by sharing information with one another. This sharing sometimes leads to other forms of collaboration.

In the most interesting conceptions, the competitive process in social policy entails a distinctive type of norm, sometimes called a "benchmark." Benchmarks differ from market-price signals in being collectively specified and conveying a much broader set of information. They differ from bureaucratic rules in being neither fixed nor hierarchically promulgated. Rather, they are the expression of a process of continuous revision in which all the stakeholders participate. In CED, stakeholders include both the public and the private institutions allocating resources and authority and the community-based organizations applying for it.

The benchmarks set out a series of goals. Often the providers will have a good deal of discretion as to how to meet the goals. After a while, performance is measured in relation to the goals. But at the same time, the benchmarks are reconsidered in the light of both the experience of the particular project and experience of others on comparable projects. Experience may indicate that the benchmarks are unrealistic because they fail to capture certain costs or benefits. In this case, they can be revised to include the newly recognized variables. Comparison may suggest that other groups have performed better. In that case, the stakeholders consider why the comparison group has done better, and if the inquiry discovers some best practice that can be adapted by the current group, it will usually do so. To the extent that the comparisons suggest possibilities of greater productivity, the benchmarks can be revised upward. Of course, it is also possible that analysis will disclose reasons that the other organizations' circumstances or achievement are not strictly comparable to that of the one being assessed. This understanding may make possible refinement of the benchmarks to acknowledge the differences.

Benchmarking requires some effort to specify and measure the nonpecuniary costs and benefits of projects. There are two distinctive aspects to this problem. One has to do with the unpriced positive externalities that are the primary rationale for most CED. Traditional accounting skills can determine, though not without some difficult judgments, the financial cost per unit of affordable housing, per job created or obtained, or of subsidizing a business. But we need more creative measures of the contribution of a project to the reduction in crime, welfare, family breakup, neighborhood stability, or political efficacy. The other dimension of the problem is opportunity cost. Once the net benefits of a particular social investment have been measured, they need to be compared with the potential social returns in other areas. One manifestation of this issue is the pervasive "creaming" problem. It is easier to maintain affordable housing for residents with incomes at 80 percent of the median than for those with incomes at 40 percent of the median. It is easier to place job trainees who are well educated and have solid work histories. And it is easier to subsidize businesses run by those who have relatively good access to conventional finance. A program that focuses on the less risky prospects in the applicant pool will have a better track record in terms of the most easily measurable criteria. But the less easily measured social benefits are greater from serving more disadvantaged applicants. Such considerations have to be factored into the benchmarks.

The benchmarking process remains primitive in the CED field, despite some notable recent efforts.[39] Perhaps the most extensive efforts have come in connection with CRA enforcement. The CRA regulators have developed an elaborate set of categories designed to facilitate comparison of a broad array of performance data for banks. They use these data to generate rankings. Unfortunately, however, few observers find the system satisfactory. They complain that the regulators tend to be lax because they are unsympathetic to the statute, that standards vary erratically from region to region and even within regions, and that the regulators have not generated consistent criteria or plausible procedures for translating basic performance data into rankings.

39. Two notable examples: (1) The Roberts Foundation is working on calculating a "social return on investment" for its grants for low-income job training and business formation. An initial effort adds to traditional income and expense measures the social benefit of savings from welfare benefits that the beneficiaries would otherwise receive. See Graduate School of Business, Stanford University, *Asian Neighborhood Design* S-SB-195 (March 1998). (2) The Hartford-area Capitol Region Council of Governments designed standards for local government provision of affordable housing that take account of income and housing-price levels within each municipality, rent and resident income levels in affordable units, past efforts to remedy the problem, and indirect efforts, such as mortgage support. Lawrence Susskind and Susan Podziba, "Affordable Housing Mediation: Building Consensus for Regional Agreements in the Hartford Area," in *The Consensus Building Handbook* 773–99 (Lawrence Susskind, Sarah McKeanan, and Jennifer Thomas-Larmer, eds. 1999).

From the perspective of democratic experimentalism, the most fundamental defect of the process is the limited opportunity for stakeholders, particularly community groups, to participate. Stakeholders are invited to submit written comments to the bank's CRA file and, in the event of a regulatory proceeding, directly to the regulator. The regulators occasionally hold hearings on bank applications, and when that happens, community groups can be heard. Such opportunities are rare, however. Community groups have no active opportunity to participate in the regular CRA audits and no opportunity to engage the regulators in dialogue about appropriate criteria and enforcement.[40]

The benchmarking procedure is premised on the availability of information about the performance of community-based organizations. A requirement that organizations make such information accessible to their peers and community stakeholders seems an obvious entailment of the competitive approach. The requirement is surprisingly controversial, however. The organizers of DSNI began their efforts with a survey of local NGO service providers but gave up when they discovered that most of the organizations would not disclose detailed information about their operations.[41] This is a common experience. The Greenlining Coalition's refusal to disclose its relationship with Wells Fargo in the merger proceeding with First Interstate is another example. In 1999, Congress amended the Community Reinvestment Act to require disclosure of CRA-related contracts between banks and community groups. Although the measure was enacted on the initiative of Republican legislators who were unsympathetic to the CRA and was opposed by a broad range of community groups, it seems a valuable contribution to the goal of democratic accountability.[42]

In general, vastly more information is available publicly about banks' CRA performance than about the performance of community-based

40. There is no formal opportunity for community groups to contact the auditors, and informal contact is inhibited by the difficulty of finding out when the audits take place. Thomas, *CRA Handbook*, 186–9.

41. Medoff and Sklar, *Streets of Hope*, 102–3.

42. P.L. 106–102, sec. 48; 113 Stat. 1338, 1466–67 (1999). Some community groups continue to protest the requirement. See the Greenlining Institute's Web site at http://www.greenlining.org/pages/pressrelease5102000.html (visited 15 May 2000), which argues that the disclosure requirement violates the First Amendment rights of both community groups and banks (!). Taken at face value, the claim would seem to invalidate the entire CRA.

organizations under any of the programs that support them directly. Funders typically contract for access to information from those they support, and organizations often permit or are required by their funders to allow their work to be studied. But there is little by way of required routine disclosure of performance data, and although organizations love to volunteer selective information about their successes, they are often reticent about a vast range of less flattering information. Systems of mandated disclosure would enhance the evaluation process in many programs.

BACKGROUND RIGHTS AND SANCTIONS

Two types of pressure push organizations toward democratic accountability. First, to demonstrate good performance, organizations have to complete projects, and the three logics of community action suggest that CED projects will often require community mobilization. However, completion of projects by itself is not strong evidence of community support, as the urban-renewal horror stories emphasize. The degree to which a project gives evidence of mobilization or accountability depends in part on the background or blocking rights of community members who object to it. The stronger these background rights, the more the project's completion implies accountability. Second, the organization expects rewards for good performance and sanctions for bad performance. The calibration of sanctions presents some distinctive issues.

Background or blocking rights can take a variety of forms. Most states permit challenges by a single taxpayer or resident, or to a small group of them, to unlawful public expenditures, improper grants of land use, or other regulatory permissions. Rights of this sort have expanded in recent decades. Large projects are subject to procedural requirements of such complexity and vagueness that they are usually vulnerable to challenges of this sort, though how potent the challenge is varies among jurisdictions and situations. The stronger and more easily invoked this type of right, the more pressure on a CDC to insure broad community support for its projects.

Another form of blocking right arises at an earlier stage when an agency or NGO is deciding whether to grant resources or authority to a CED group for a particular project. The decision maker has to decide the level of community support that is needed in order to warrant the grant.

It might support a good proposal with substantial community support, even over strong opposition. It might insist on at least majority support. It might demand near-unanimity or complete unanimity. For example, when the BRA took over the Jackson Square planning process in Jamaica Plain, it announced as a precondition for any projects that "all of the community must be united in its request for the land."[43]

The closer the standard is to unanimity, the more successful completion of the project implies accountability. True, even the most demanding unanimity requirement applies only to active participants. If the community is inarticulate, passive, and unorganized, projects that are not viewed favorably by most community members might be able to win unanimous approval among a small number of activists. The hope is that successful CED projects in such communities will steadily induce participation both by demonstrating the possibilities of community action and by enhancing the participatory capacities of the residents. Jamaica Plain and the surrounding areas may be evidence of this. Recall that more than thirty-five groups had participated in the contentious process over Jackson Square prior to the BRA's intervention. Whatever the reasons for this density of organizational activity, the unanimity requirement is clearly a demanding one in this context.

Of course, there are drawbacks to the strong blocking rights that unanimity requirements create. It seems unfair that perhaps mildly felt opposition of a small group should preclude major benefits to most community members. Moreover, there is concern about bad faith or blackmail. People may exaggerate their dislike of the project simply to compel the others to bribe them into acquiescence with extra benefits.

Nevertheless, the core premises of CED support at least qualified use of the unanimity standard. This standard enhances the process's potential to induce learning and solidarity. The unanimity standard requires an organization with a project to address the concerns of every active constituency in the community. The premise of CED practice is that this be done primarily through face-to-face discussion. Practitioners of CED have great faith in the potential of such discussion to resolve differences. Part of the potential lies in conventional learning. As people understand one another's positions better and explore alternative ways to structure

43. Miramontes, "Urban Edge Egleston," 43.

projects, they often conclude either that their differences were based on misconceptions or that they can re-conceive projects to resolve them. Another part of the potential lies in the tendency of mutual respect and concern to induce feelings of cooperation and inhibit bad faith. Thus, an influential school of thought holds that unanimity should be an aspiration, but not a precondition. Social entrepreneurs with projects of broad impact should feel obliged to strive for consensus, although once they have made a serious try, something short of it should probably be sufficient to permit the project to proceed.[44] This may be the tacit meaning of the Boston Redevelopment Authority's statement that the "community must be united" on any Jackson Square proposal.[45]

Now consider the question of what happens to an organization that performs poorly. The basic sanction in the ex post model is the denial of new resources and authority. This approach assumes an indefinite series of repeat dealings. It probably works best when the size of the stakes remains constant or increases gradually from round to round. When a particular award is disproportionately large or lumpy, the incentive effects of later rounds may be dwarfed by the temptation to slack off or misbehave with the large award. For example, Redevelopment projects can take the form of a one-time negotiation for a single enormous contract between a government agency and a developer. The chances for the developer to profit opportunistically by shortchanging the project may dwarf the incentives of future dealings. The city may anticipate this by trying to tighten contractual specifications or by front-loading the community benefits—that is, requiring the developer to perform the parts of the deal that benefit the community most before the parts that are most profitable or beneficial to the developer. Although these tactics

44. Lawrence Susskind, "An Alternative to Robert's Rules of Order for Groups, Organizations, and Ad Hoc Assemblies That Want to Operate by Consensus," in Susskind et al., *Consensus Building Handbook*, 3, 6–7. See also David Straus, "Managing Meetings to Build Consensus," in ibid., 287, 289–90 (on "the value of face-to-face meetings").

45. The BRA added that "all the community must be involved in a thorough long-term process without leaving any one group out": Miramontes, "Urban Edge Egleston," 43. The multi-jurisdiction affordable housing negotiation described by Susskind and Podziba, in "Affordable Housing Mediation," proceeded initially under a legislative unanimity requirement, but when extensive negotiations produced a plan acceptable to most but not all participants, the legislature mandated the plan notwithstanding the holdouts.

can be useful, they are not conducive to the kind of ongoing participatory review and revision that democratic experimentalism contemplates. From the point of view of participation, a better approach would be to phase in the development in stages, leaving open the possibility of revising goals over time and, if necessary, switching developers (though not all projects will lend themselves to this).

One of the unsatisfactory aspects of the CRA enforcement process is that it often focuses evaluation on a single extraordinary episode with enormous stakes. The only regulatory sanction for low CRA ratings is the prospect that such ratings will cause an application for approval of a business change to be denied. Such applications are irregular and, for many banks, rare, and their timing is unrelated to the goals of CRA enforcement. The largest enforcement opportunities come in connection with large-stakes applications—mainly, mergers and acquisitions. Here banks have been willing to make large concessions to community groups. But the now-or-never quality of the proceeding limits participation and constrains follow-up. Once the applicant gets the regulatory approval, its incentive to perform faithfully is much reduced. Moreover, the temptations for community groups to behave opportunistically are large, given the size of the stakes and the rarity of the event. In addition, the opportunities for ongoing revision and community participation in the elaboration of the agreement are limited once the regulatory proceeding ends.

Another issue concerns the severity of the sanction. The typical sanction is a reduction in support or authority at the next round. However, such sanctions cannot be too severe or sudden. Under democratic experimentalism, a failure to meet goals is not automatically interpreted as default. It is an occasion to inquire into the problems and, ideally, correct them. An organization cannot benefit from this kind of learning if it is bumped at the first sign of failure. Moreover, an organization facing exile if it is determined to have underperformed is likely to behave defensively in the evaluation process and to try to conceal information. Some degree of security may be necessary compensation for the organization's duty to make information about its performance public.

The formal CRA sanction process is spectacularly ill-designed from this point of view. The only sanction is the denial of a regulatory permission of potentially enormous economic value. It would often be disproportionate to the noncompliance. However, informal process somewhat mitigates the problem. Because it seems disproportionate, the regulators almost never apply the sanction. Nevertheless, the potential stakes are large enough to motivate many banks to cooperate with community groups.[46]

46. Congress recently mitigated a similar problem in the enforcement of the private-benefit and private-inurement limitations in Section 501(c)(3) of the Internal Revenue code. In the past, the only sanction available to the IRS for violations of these provisions was revocation of the organizations's exempt status, and the IRS was reluctant to pursue such a draconian penalty for abuses that were not egregious. Section 4958 now imposes more graduated sanctions. Insider beneficiaries of "excess benefit transactions" are subject to a penalty tax of 200 percent of the excess benefit, and there are smaller sanctions for managers who authorize such transactions. See Fishman and Schwarz, *Nonprofit Organizations,* 511–18.

Chapter 8 ⋮ Institutional Hybridization

Community Economic Development institutions tend to take hybrid forms that breach conventional boundaries between levels of government and types of enterprise. The ubiquitous phrase "public–private partnership" only begins to capture this phenomenon. These structures rearrange organizational attributes in ways designed to respond to the problems of traditional social programs. They aim to improve coordination of public and private investments. More ambitiously, they aim to increase both support for and accountability of organizations that embody the CED themes of face-to-face relations, geographical focus, and relational density. They do so by cementing connections both among local organizations and between these organizations and more broadly based ones.

An Illustration: Hyde Square Co-op

The Hyde Square Co-op was developed in 1993 by the Jamaica Plain Neighborhood Development Corporation. It includes forty-one units in seventeen wood-frame, two-story buildings. The Hyde Square section of Jamaica Plain sits between a large, troubled, high-rise public-housing project and a gentrifying district of old but attractive single-family homes. The neighborhood was visibly distressed when the co-op project was undertaken and remains shabby in places, though there has been

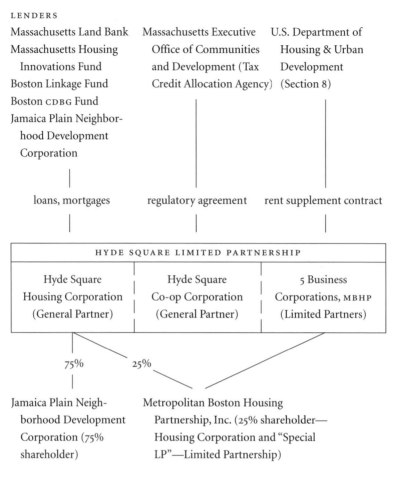

Massachusetts Land Bank   Massachusetts Executive   U.S. Department of
Massachusetts Housing   Office of Communities   Housing & Urban
  Innovations Fund   and Development (Tax   Development
Boston Linkage Fund   Credit Allocation Agency) (Section 8)
Boston CDBG Fund
Jamaica Plain Neighbor-
  hood Development
  Corporation

loans, mortgages   regulatory agreement   rent supplement contract

HYDE SQUARE LIMITED PARTNERSHIP

| Hyde Square Housing Corporation (General Partner) | Hyde Square Co-op Corporation (General Partner) | 5 Business Corporations, MBHP (Limited Partners) |

75%   25%

Jamaica Plain Neigh-   Metropolitan Boston Housing
  borhood Development   Partnership, Inc. (25% shareholder—
  Corporation (75%   Housing Corporation and "Special
  shareholder)   LP"—Limited Partnership)

Figure 3

notable improvement. The buildings are unobtrusive but attractive and have been well maintained. The project won a design award and is considered a model of new-style affordable-housing development.[1]

In most respects, the legal structure of Hyde Square is characteristic of nonprofit affordable-housing projects supported by the Low Income Housing Tax Credit, the largest source of support by far for projects of this kind. Housing projects tend to be more complex than other CED projects of comparable scale, and tax credit projects are often more

1. Pictures and a brief description can be found in Tom Jones, William Pettus, and Michael Pyatok, *Good Neighbors: Affordable Family Housing* 176–7 (1995).

complex than other housing projects. But all the features of the Hyde Square structure have analogies in other types of CED projects, and Hyde Square usefully illustrates a broad range of the distinctive institutional forms of the field.

The general structure of the project can be charted this way. (Figure 3) Although the project is known as "Hyde Square Co-Op," the owner is in fact a limited partnership. It has two general and six limited partners. One of the general partners is the Hyde Square Housing Corporation, a business corporation[2] of which 75 percent is owned by the Jamaica Plain Neighborhood Development Corporation and the other 25 percent by the Metropolitan Boston Housing Partnership, Inc. (MBHP).[3] As we've

2. The CDC subsidiary that acts as general partner in an affordable housing project is usually a for-profit corporation, though it is not clear that any practical purpose is served by this move. Some lawyers believe that a for-profit is desirable because it suggests the (largely fictional) possibility that profits might be earned and thus helps respond to a possible objection that the transaction violates the "business-purpose" doctrine. Under this doctrine, the IRS sometimes re-characterizes transactional structures whose main purpose is to produce tax benefits. However, the doctrine should not apply to structures like Hyde Square, since Congress seems to have specifically intended to support them. See 26 USC 24(h)(5) (nonprofit set-aside).

Unlike the practice elsewhere, in California the subsidiary general partner is invariably a nonprofit. This is because California has exempted tax-credit projects with nonprofit managing general partners from local property taxes. California Revenue and Taxation Code 214(a), (g).

3. Avis Vidal, *Rebuilding Communities: A National Study of Urban Community Development Corporations* 4 (New School for Social Research, 1992), found that three-quarters of the CDCs in her sample had subsidiaries, most of them for-profits. Subsidiaries have two kinds of potential legal advantage. The first is limited liability. The parent potentially shields its assets from tort claims arising from the project and from contract claims to the extent that other parties are willing to accept a commitment only from the subsidiary.

Second, the use of a for-profit subsidiary can sometimes obviate disadvantages under the tax laws. Nonexempt activities conducted by subsidiaries may not be attributed to the parent so as to jeopardize the parent's exempt status or trigger unrelated business income tax liability. Since there remains some doubt about the extent to which affordable housing development for the non-poor is exempt, this can be an important concern. Retaining business income in a subsidiary can also sometimes improve the parent's position in the "private foundation" calculations.

Subsidiary activities and finances are not attributed to the parent unless the subsidiary is "controlled" by the parent. For the purposes of the exempt activity and public charity determinations, the test of control is informal and turns primarily on "day-to-day" decision-making rather than ownership, though low ownership stakes strengthen

seen, the JPNDC is a community development corporation organized as a public-benefit nonprofit corporation. It is the entrepreneur who conceived the project, mobilized community support for it, secured the land-use permissions and financing, and supervised the design and construction.

The minority owner of the Hyde Square Housing Corporation, the MBHP, is also a public-benefit nonprofit corporation organized to support housing development in Boston's low- and moderate-income areas. The MBHP was formed at the initiative of leaders in the banking community and has a board that includes prominent figures from the banking, real estate, nonprofit, and government sectors. In 1993, its chair was chairman of State Street Bank and Trust, one of the biggest Boston banks. It administers a variety of housing projects; provides technical assistance to nonprofit developers; and channels both public and private funds into affordable-housing projects.

The MBHP plays a second role in the limited partnership: In addition to being a minority shareholder of a corporate general partner, it is a "special limited partner." As such, it has no financial interests, but it has the power to assume control in the event that the project fails to meet specified obligations to its limited partners, including timely maintenance and payment of outstanding debt.

The other general partner is the Hyde Square Co-op, a cooperative corporation owned by the residents. The residents do not buy their homes; they buy shares in the co-op. Each share comes with an "occupancy agreement" between the shareholder and the cooperative, giving the shareholder the right to possession of her unit. The co-op has an undivided ownership interest in the seventeen buildings, but initially this interest will be subordinate to the interests of the limited partners and the lenders. The co-op will, however, have an option to buy out the limited partners at a point in the future. The partnership agreement contemplates that the JPNDC will manage the property initially, but that the co-op will gradually assume this responsibility. The JPNDC has committed to providing the residents with training to facilitate the transi-

---

the case for non-control. See James Fishman and Stephen Schwartz, *Nonprofit Organizations*, 827 (2d ed. 2000). For the purpose of the unrelated business income tax, there is a more categorical test—more than 50 percent ownership establishes control. IRC 512(b)(13)(D)(i)(I). At the time of the Hyde Square project, the relevant threshold was 80 percent, so the subsidiary there would have been uncontrolled for this purpose.

tion. At the outset, the JPNDC is entitled to both managerial control within the limited partnership and representation on the co-op board. As the co-op demonstrates its capacities, the JPNDC representatives will depart from its board and cede managerial control (subject to the right of the special limited partner and lenders to intervene in the event of various defaults).

The remaining constituents of the limited partnership are five limited partners, all business corporations that have been induced to invest in the project in return for tax benefits. The tax credit program makes available to selected projects of this kind tax credits equal to a specified fraction of the construction costs. The credits are of no immediate use to nonprofit developers and investors, who pay no taxes, but they can be sold, or syndicated, to taxpaying corporations. A variety of intermediaries have evolved to perform this syndication role. In return for a putative equity investment in the property, the limited partners receive the credits as well as the benefits of artificial depreciation deductions associated generally with real estate investments. (The limited-partnership form was standard for real estate transactions until recently, principally because it permitted the pass-through of losses, especially depreciation, to individual investors. Today a limited liability company can also be used.) The taxpaying investors' ability to use the credits, however, depends on various conditions concerning the operation of the property, including compliance with resident income limits and affordability restrictions. The limited partners' interest in the project is purely financial; they have control rights only in the event of breaches of obligations of financial soundness and compliance with tax-credit conditions.

The limited partnership has a regulatory agreement with the Massachusetts Executive Office of Communities and Development, the state's tax-credit allocation agency. Federal tax credits are distributed through state entities of this sort. The tax code allocates to each state a specified amount of credits based on population. Some states supplement this allocation with state tax credits. The states award the credits to both for-profit and nonprofit projects. Allocation is made on a competitive application basis. Other explicit criteria focus on financial viability and social benefit, though political connections are sometimes thought to play a role. Affordability issues are among the most important criteria of social benefit. Other things being equal, a project that guarantees lower rents and, hence, affordability to low-income occupants for longer periods of time is preferred.[4] (At a minimum, qualifying units must go to households earning no more than 60 percent of the area's median income on terms that require these households to pay no more than 30 percent of their income for housing.[5]) Another factor is the length of time for which the applicant promises to keep the affordability restrictions operative. The federal statute creates a presumptive minimum compliance term of thirty years, although fifteen years is permissible in some circumstances.[6] Many states insist on thirty years and sometimes induce longer commitments. The regulatory agreement between the partnership and the state agency embodies these commitments and gives the agency a contract remedy in the event of breach.

In addition to the equity capital provided by the tax-credit investors, the project has been funded with loans. One is a conventional loan secured by a first mortgage, with monthly amortization and interest payments at a level close to the market rate. This loan comes from the Massachusetts Land Bank, a specially chartered public corporation with a social mission. The Land Bank's familiarity with this type of deal makes it more willing than some commercial lenders to participate, but the terms of the loan are fairly conventional, and commercial lenders commonly take this first-mortgage position as well.

The other five loans, however, are soft loans that would be made only by institutions with social goals. One comes from the Federal Home Loan Bank of Boston, a federally chartered public corporation that has

---

4. 26 USC 42(m)(1)(B).

5. More precisely, the project as a whole must satisfy one of two conditions: either 20 percent of the units must be restricted to people earning no more than 50 percent of the area median or 40 percent must be restricted to people earning no more than 60 percent of the area median. All subsidized units must be limited to people at no more than 60 percent. The income standards are scaled to take account of family or unit size.

Once in, a household's income may rise as much as 40 percent above the ceilings without disqualifying the unit. If its income goes higher during the first fifteen years, tax-credit benefits can be lost. In order to avoid having to reclaim the unit at this point, developers hope to forestall the loss by committing to rent another, previously unsubsidized, unit to qualifying families. At Hyde Square, only thirty-one of the forty-one units qualify for the subsidy. If one of the others became vacant, it could in theory be substituted for one of the thirty-one in the event it were disqualified by increases in occupants' income. 42 USC 42(g).

6. 26 USC 42(h)(6).

an affordable-housing program. Another comes from the Massachusetts Housing Innovations Fund, a state agency. Two come from Boston
city programs, one of which is funded by the city's "linkage" program of
exactions on office development, and the other by federal Community
Development Block Grant funds. The city also donated the land, having
acquired it through tax foreclosure. The JPNDC has also made a loan
from a small fund it has available for such purposes. Although these
contributions are called soft loans, they might more realistically be
called conditional grants. No interest or amortization payments are
required; instead, interest accrues, then comes due with the principal at
the end of the term, which ranges from twenty to fifty years. It is anticipated that each loan will be rolled over at the end of its term. The
funders' real concern is not repayment but compliance with affordability norms.[7] These concerns are reflected in covenants in recorded
mortgages that ostensibly secure the loans and in fact allow the lenders
to declare the loans in default and foreclose on the property in the event
of breach.[8]

Even with such extensive capital subsidy, the project cannot pay the
first mortgage's debt service and the operating costs while maintaining
rent levels that are affordable to low- and moderate-income people. It
thus requires additional support in the form of HUD Section 8 vouchers.
The JPNDC has persuaded the local housing authority that administers
HUD's Section 8 program to allocate vouchers to the first residents of
eight of the units. These vouchers will result in a contractual relationship between the agency and the limited partnership that obligates the
agency to pay, for each of these households, the difference between 30
percent of the household's income and the normal occupancy charges.

7. There is one additional consideration. The "loans" generate fictitious interest charges
that, through the magic of the Internal Revenue Code, generate real tax benefits to the
equity holders.

8. Development costs were about $6.2 million, or $150,000 per unit, financed as follows:

Tax Credit Syndication Proceeds	$3,198,792
Land Bank First Mortgage	517,470
Federal Home Loan Bank loan	312,467
State Housing Innovations Fund loan	500,000
City of Boston—Linkage	602,273
JPNDC loan	303,250
	$6,251,182

The residents' eligibility is subject to an income ceiling, and the partnership must keep its charges below a HUD-determined fair market rent and must maintain the building in accordance with applicable codes. This rent subsidy allows the project to support a larger amount of debt than it otherwise could. It also brings in an additional set of affordability restrictions.

The Hyde Square Co-op thus has started out as a co-op in only a limited sense. The residents are members of a cooperative corporation with rights and responsibilities to manage the property, but their occupancy rights take the form of tenancy. This is necessary in tax credit projects because the tax code makes credits available only for rental housing. In the conventions of real estate taxation, the limited partners' status (largely fictional) as owners is a premise of their entitlement to the benefits of depreciation and the credits. Thus, the project cannot provide for resident ownership at the outset.

At the end of fifteen years, however, the situation will change. The limited partners will exhaust their tax credits in ten years, but they must continue to participate for five more years (and disgorge their benefits to the extent that the project does not continue to comply with affordability restrictions).[9] At the end of the fifteen-year period, the statute contemplates, the limited partners will sell out. The statute creates a preference for projects that sell out on terms that preserve affordability. The purchaser might be a nonprofit CDC or land trust, but it might also be an organization of residents.[10] Hyde Square was one of the first tax credit deals to provide for sale to a resident cooperative, but this provision has become more common in recent years.

Thus, the limited partnership agreement gives the co-op an option to purchase the property after fifteen years for $1 plus assumption of the outstanding debt—the conventional first-mortgage and the soft loans. The buyer, of course, takes the property subject to the affordability restrictions in the mortgage covenants. The deal assumes that the building will have almost no conventional equity at this point; its market value will be offset by the debt. This outcome is more or less assured, regardless of surrounding real estate appreciation, because the afford-

9. 26 USC 42(h)–(i).

10. 26 USC 42(h)(6). The statute specifically permits granting a "right of first refusal" to an organization of residents ("whether in cooperative form or otherwise"). Ibid., 42(i)(7).

ability restrictions limit the effects of such appreciation. The cooperative thus has two transitional phases. Initially, the residents gradually assume management responsibilities; at the end of the fifteen-year compliance period, they assume (limited equity) ownership.

Almost everyone thinks that this structure is unnecessarily complex.[11] Nevertheless, its hybrid nature seems to serve several functions, including:

—Entrepreneurialism. The CDC is the entrepreneur. It has spotted the opportunity and shaped it to induce the support of the community, the land-use regulators, and the funders. In doing so, it has the advantages of flexibility and local knowledge. Its board and staff lack the high-powered material incentives of business corporations, but they have some material incentives. They derive fees from such projects, and their ability to attract foundation and other funding often depends on taking on such projects. At the same time, their ability to succeed in these projects requires that they have credibility with at least some of the activist segments of the community and with funders and land-use regulators.

—Information sharing and coordination. Part of the premise of organizations such as the MBHP is coordination and information sharing. Bringing NGO and government people together with banking and real estate people may facilitate coordination of public and private investments. It also allows the representatives of the different sectors to share expertise.

The recent history of these projects shows that learning across sectors is important and does not happen spontaneously. Some financing costs have fallen noticeably as private-sector actors have gained familiarity with the idiosyncrasies of these deals. Tax credit syndicators get a considerably higher price for the credits than they did some years ago,[12] and banks are more willing to make first-mortgage loans on limited-equity properties. In both cases, the effect seems due to learning. At the same time, NGO and public-housing developers, while rightly disdainful of some private-sector lending criteria (red-lining), have incorporated others into their own project assessments.

11. See Michael Stegman, "The Excessive Costs of Creative Finance: Growing Inefficiencies in the Production of Low-Income Housing," 2 *Housing Policy Debate* 357 (1991).
12. In the early years of the program, investors paid about 50 percent of the present value of the credits; now they pay about 80 percent.

—Intermediation. Another role of the MBHP is to reassure the limited partners, and perhaps some of the soft lenders, that the project will be managed in a financially sound manner. In doing so, the MBHP acts as an intermediary between local CDCs and regional institutions and between nonprofit and for-profit institutions. Its board has been constituted with people who have both local understanding and reputational credibility with national business institutions. To the extent that it achieves a successful track record, it should develop institutional reputational capital that is partially independent of the individual board members.

—Monitoring. The structure multiplies stakeholders with overlapping opportunities to monitor compliance with the project's social goals. This is most strikingly the case with respect to affordability restrictions. No fewer than thirteen public and private institutions have rights to enforce the affordability restrictions in various ways.[13] Some of these institutions, such as HUD and the state credit-allocation agency, do engage in systematic monitoring. Moreover, the grosser forms of violation, such as a resale at market rate, would require active cooperation by many stakeholders.

Pressures to allocate the subsidies initially with maximum efficiency are weaker. None of the actors with allocation responsibilities has the strong cost-minimization incentives associated with for-profit actors. The actors' incentives are mixed, and because the relevant social goals are mixed, their performance is hard to evaluate. Some of the actors' monitoring incentives are limited by commitments to particular constituencies. For example, the CDC is by design primarily responsive to the interests of current residents, though these interests may not coincide fully with social interests. Residents who have a secure place in the community typically want to limit the density and increase the quality of subsidized housing to an extent that, from a less parochial point of view, sometimes requires an excessive trade-off in quantity.

A potential virtue of the hybrid structure is that the biases of the different actors may offset one another. Specialized funding agencies with strong private-sector representation are likely to emphasize financial soundness. However, community groups that do not put capital at

13. The number of participants in the Hyde Square project is probably above average, but the typical number is still high. In a survey of twenty-four projects, Stegman found an average of five funders. Stegman, "Excessive Costs," 362–3.

risk and depend on their ability to demonstrate community support may have a compensating bias toward intangible goals.

There is some danger that the fiscal conservatism of the funders and the preference of local homeowners for gold-plating will converge to put excessive limits on development. A lot depends, however, on local conditions. If there is a substantial tenant constituency that fears displacement and it has influence on the CDC, it may exert countervailing pressure. For example, in East Palo Alto tenant organizations were recently able to pressure the local CDC to side with them against the CDC's regional-development partner to push for lower rents and income eligibility in a new project.

The large number of participants may prompt the concern that lines of responsibility will be blurred.[14] The danger also exists that each one will slack off, hoping that the others will mind the store—or, at least, that there will be someone else to blame if things go wrong. But if this is a problem, it would seem to be remediable simply by clearer assignment of responsibility among the participants. Business-securities offerings, for example, are often underwritten by a large number of investment banks, but one assumes explicit primary responsibility for vetting the investment.

Of course, there is no guarantee that even a well-designed structure will perform well. Many areas lack a developed nonprofit sector, an effective state and local government, or both. And there are gaps in monitoring responsibilities.[15] Still, the presence of overlapping stakeholders has the virtue of making difficult the cruder forms of misfeasance and making possible a variety of synergies.

—Risk-sharing. The multiplication of stakeholders in these projects is induced by funders' insistence that each provides only a fraction of the needed subsidy. The benefits provided by the tax credit program are

14. Ibid., 364–5.

15. For example, in a recent San Francisco area project, the CDC procured a zoning change for a private parcel to permit higher density in connection with a project combining affordable and market-rate uses. The owner then donated the parcel and took a tax deduction at a valuation nearly three times the pre-change value, thus profiting from the donation. This procedure resulted in an implicit tax subsidy, on top of various explicit ones, of several million dollars. Whether it was appropriate depends in part on the plausibility of the valuation. None of the explicit public or NGO stakeholders had any incentive to question the owner's valuation. Only the IRS had an incentive to do so, and it is weak in both resources and expertise to handle the question.

insufficient to fund projects of the quality and affordability that non-profit developers seek. Thus, additional subsidies have to be found. Nongovernmental funders are typically unwilling to fill by themselves the gap between the project's cost and the amount that can be raised through conventional borrowing and the sale of the credits. They prefer to participate with other NGOs.

A favorable view of this tendency is that it encourages the benefits of coordination, information-sharing, and joint monitoring. The funders, like charitable donors in other contexts, insist on matching grants conditioned on the participation of others in the hope of synergies from multiple participation.

It seems clear, however, that the practice is also driven by a desire of the individual funders to limit their risk. Funders do not want to jeopardize their organizations in the event of failure. Unfortunately, this risk-aversion has costs, most obviously in the form of transaction costs, but in the limitation of accountability as well. As noted, the dispersal of investments may dilute incentives to evaluate and monitor projects.

—Political expedience. The one group of stakeholders that clearly makes no social-policy contribution is the for-profit limited partner. Had the federal government been willing to fund the program through direct expenditures rather than tax credits, the for-profits' presence would be unnecessary. The tax credit approach reflects Congress's affinity for off-budget finance and the political advantages of social programs that provide benefits to private industry. This approach is quite expensive. The costs of marketing the credits is substantial, and the credits seem to sell at a substantial discount from their present value in part because a large segment of the market still lacks familiarity with them.[16]

Social Control, Opportunism, and Empowerment: Boundary Problems

Hybridization can generate synergies, but it can also produce dysfunctions. Participation by conventional for-profit businesses can enhance

16. Stegman estimates that, because of the high cost of syndicating tax credits and the higher cost of money to private investors than to the government, "a direct capital grant to the project sponsor equal to about half the government's tax expenditure would contribute roughly the same amount to development costs as does the syndication of the tax credit." Ibid., 371.

the financial and technical capacity of CED projects and induce spillover effects into private development activities, but it creates a risk of capture in which subsidies are diverted excessively to business participants. The problem has a distinctive form in efforts to develop business capacities and institutions among disadvantaged people. Here, giving control to the low-income beneficiaries can be an important part of the program, but it needs to be accomplished so that the public resources involved are not wasted or diverted in ways inconsistent with the program's goals. Finally, insiders in charitable corporations can compromise the operation of the programs or divert or dissipate social resources in their own interests.

These problems prompt the reassertion and redefinition of boundaries within the hybrid structures. Here we look at some doctrinal responses. First, we examine the very broad-based 501(c)(3) doctrine designed to constrain private capture of public subsidy and a more specialized SBA doctrine focused on a particular program. Second, we discuss the effort to combine NGO control with beneficiary empowerment in the transitional cooperative of the sort involved in Hyde Square.

CONSTRAINTS ON CAPTURE BY
CONVENTIONAL BUSINESS PARTICIPANTS

501(c)(3) Doctrine. In 1989 Jerry Harris, a California real estate developer, formed the nonprofit corporation Housing Pioneers, Inc. The corporation was designated as a public-benefit organization under California law, and its declared purpose was to develop affordable housing for low- and moderate-income people. The board included Harris, his brother and partner in various for-profit ventures, and nine people chosen for their interest in public housing and social services. Harris contemplated that Housing Pioneers would participate as a general partner in tax credit housing projects with various for-profit entities in which the Harrises were interested. The avowed goal of this plan was to qualify the projects for exemptions from local property taxes that were available to tax credit projects involving nonprofit developers. The limited-partnership agreements provided for Housing Pioneers to receive payments amounting to 50 to 60 percent of the anticipated savings from the property-tax exemption, which the organization was expected to use for further low-income housing development.

That public subsidies yield private windfalls is a common concern. Many programs have specific safeguards against private capture, an example of which will be examined shortly. The tax code provides a very general set of safeguards. These provisions are designed to protect the federal charitable tax subsidies, but they have a broader effect. As noted, many subsidy programs incorporate the tax code's safeguards by requiring that applicants for their assistance be exempt under Section 501(c)(3). The IRS thus plays a pervasive background role in policing opportunism in a variety of programs. The California property-tax exemption sought by the Harrises is an example: It is restricted to projects with a 501(c)(3)-qualified developer. The issue of the propriety of the Harrises' plan reached the courts in litigation not with the California tax authorities, but with the IRS.[17]

The increase in hybrid structures in a variety of fields—especially in health care, where the scale and volume of such projects is enormous—has prompted the IRS to elaborate doctrines that define the permissible role of for-profit businesses in nonprofit activity. Under this doctrine, an organization that engages in more than an incidental amount of nonexempt activity is ineligible for 501(c)(3) status. Whether activity is exempt turns largely on the distinction between "public benefit," on the one hand, and "private benefit" or "private inurement," on the other.[18] (Recall that before the "public-benefit" issue arises, the applicant must show that the organization satisfies the Nondistribution Constraint discussed in chapter 5. Housing Pioneers satisfied this by organizing as a public-benefit corporation under the California Nonprofit Corporation statute.)

In practice, there are three main aspects to the public-benefit inquiry. First, the organization's goals and activities have to fall within some broad category of traditionally charitable endeavor. Educational, health, and artistic activities readily satisfy this requirement. Housing, business, and job development programs will satisfy it only if they are also oriented to some additional goal, such as "relief of poverty," "combating

---

17. *Housing Pioneers, Inc. v. Commissioner*, 58 F.3d 401 (9th Cir. 1995).

18. The doctrine treats these terms as two separate requirements, sometimes conflating "private benefit" with excessive outsider benefit and "private inurement" with excessive insider benefit, but the usage is not consistent, and in practice the distinctions between the two are blurred. See generally Fishman and Schwartz, *Nonprofit Organizations*, 383–519.

community deterioration," or "fighting prejudice."[19] A sometimes tacit qualification to this substantive inquiry is that the activity should not duplicate benefits available from for-profit providers. A producer of Hollywood action movies would be unlikely to qualify under 501(c)(3) even if she organized as a charitable nonprofit subject to the Non-distribution Constraint and even if it were conceded that her activity was artistic. It is important that the service or product, or the terms on which it is provided, be of a kind or quality not available from conventional business organizations.[20]

Second, the organization should not provide benefits in amounts that exceed what is necessary to accomplish its public purposes. This applies both to beneficiaries and to insiders, such as employees, suppliers, and joint-venturers. An organization founded to provide affordable housing to low-income people appropriately provides decent, safe, up-to-code dwellings, but at some point, gold-plated units on large lots would raise questions, no matter how poor the beneficiaries. More commonly, the inquiry focuses on benefits to insiders, as with Housing Pioneers. In principle, the inquiry turns on whether the insider's services are necessary and are rewarded at no more than the "market rate."[21] Unfortunately, where the insider provides something other than a standardized commodity, the market rate is often hard to determine. This can be especially difficult in the CED sector. Many programs are designed to induce private investment in areas where it has not occurred in the past through subsidies. Because there has been no comparable private activity in the past, little data is available to determine a fair return in relation to risks. Because the excess-benefit inquiry makes large demands on information and expertise, it tends to be decisive only in fairly extreme cases.

19. Treas. Reg. 1.501(c)(3)–1(d)(2).

20. For example, *Plumstead Theater Society v. Commissioner*, 74 T.C. 1324 (1980) (the fact that the theater society produces "unknown playwrights" and "classics" not normally produced by commercial theaters weighs toward exempt status); Revenue Ruling 74–587, 1974–2 Cumulative Bulletin 162; *Living Faith, Inc. v. Commissioner*, 950 F.2d 365 (7th Cir. 1991) (vegetarian restaurants and health-food stores affiliated with Seventh-Day Adventist Church are non-exempt in part because they provide services indistinguishable from those provided by for-profit businesses).

21. IRS Ann. 95–25, 1995–14 I.R.B. 11 (a rural hospital's exceptionally generous physician compensation is not private benefit or inurement if the hospital might reasonably have believed the compensation necessary to attract doctors to the area).

Third, there is the question of whether the organizational control is confined sufficiently to disinterested decision makers. A strong or unconventional managerial role for interested participants is a red flag.[22] The main focus is on the board, which should not be dominated by employees, suppliers, private joint-venturers, or beneficiaries (though each of these groups may have some representation). This third criterion is in part a proxy for the second. Because precise determinations cannot be made about the reasonableness of the benefits provided, the inquiry shifts to the competence—and, in particular, the disinterestedness—of the organization's decision makers. The disinterestedness inquiry has an independent significance, however: It is part of the conventional understanding of charitable activity that is undertaken for altruistic rather than selfish reasons. Even if we were sure that a self-interested board was providing traditionally charitable benefits efficiently, we might view the organization as less worthy of public support than one with disinterested decision makers. Not only do we trust the disinterested decision makers more, but we find an intrinsic value in their altruism.

The District Court held the IRS's denial of 501(c)(3) recognition to Housing Pioneers erroneous, but the Ninth Circuit agreed with the IRS and reversed the decision. It made no attempt to assess whether the amount of property-tax benefits afforded the for-profit developers was more than necessary to induce their participation in the affordable projects, although there is real doubt on this issue. Certainly, many for-profit developers undertake tax credit projects in California without this inducement. However, it would have been open to Housing Pioneers to argue that these projects somehow involved greater difficulty, and that would have created a tough factual issue.

Instead, the court relied heavily on the control of the Harrises, who had an interest in the projects as limited partners and as principals of the for-profit general partner, Housing Pioneers. They were responsible for the formation of the organization and had two of eleven seats on the

22. Revenue Ruling 98–15, 1998–12 I.R.B. 6, compares two joint ventures between hospitals and physician groups and condemns one as incompatible with the hospital's exempt status in part on the ground that the hospital does not control the governing board of the joint venture.

board. Neither of these factors would normally be disqualifying. The control issue concerns the organization's current operations, not its formation, and two of eleven seats, at least formally, are not strong control. The court may have suspected that the nominally independent directors were under the Harrises' influence, though it mentioned no specific evidence to this effect.

The decisive consideration for the court seems to have been a judgment that the organization's activities in these projects were not substantively charitable. The court did not dispute that developing affordable housing for low-income people could be charitable; its concern was that the nonprofit's role in the projects was so passive that it did not seem to be doing any developing. In effect, it seemed merely to be renting its tax exemption to the for-profit participants. This court plausibly assumed that such activity should not be deemed charitable, even if the for-profits had returned the full value of the exemption to Housing Pioneers and even if Housing Pioneers had channeled the proceeds back into affordable housing. Because the joint ventures with Harris were the bulk of Housing Pioneers' activities, they could not be deemed merely incidental. If they were nonexempt, then Housing Pioneers was nonexempt regardless of whether it had other activities that were charitable. And the mere fact that the proceeds of an activity are used for concededly charitable purposes does not make the activity itself charitable.

Small Business Administration Procurement Doctrine. The federal and state governments and many local governments have programs that give preferences in public procurement to women, minorities, and sometimes other groups considered systemically disadvantaged. As noted in chapter 4, some local governments have procurement preferences for local businesses. The programs often set percentage targets in major public projects for participation by subcontractors from the relevant groups. Qualifying bidders are sometimes exempted from strict competitive bidding requirements, and prime contractors sometimes receive bonuses for using qualified subcontractors.

The resulting structures do not resemble the baroque labyrinths of the tax credit housing projects. They take the form of contractual relationships between governments and private businesses. However, they do represent a mix of public and social purposes characteristic of CED generally,[23] and they have at least one distinctive institutional wrinkle. The relationships between business and government are not the usual bilateral ones; they are typically triangular. In addition to the relationship with the contracting agency (or, in the case of a subcontractor, with the prime contractor), the business has an additional relationship with an agency that certifies and monitors its qualifications for the preference.

No economic-development program is more strongly associated with the capture problem than these. Reports of abuse have been constant and prominent. The typical report involves a minority person or firm "fronting" for an established white business. The token minority participant receives a payment simply for some titular role that enables the bidder to qualify for the preference, but most of the profits and all of the control over performance of the work remain with others. Such arrangements are viewed as unfair and wasteful: unfair because they give preferences to people who are not historically disadvantaged, and wasteful because they thwart the social purposes of the program to give members of the covered groups work experience that will enhance their capacity to compete independently. "Fronts" get no real work experience and remain dependent.[24]

The most sophisticated attempt to deal with this version of the capture problem is found in a recent revision of the sba's regulations for the largest of these programs—the Section 8a program, which governs much of the federal government's contracting. A similar program is mandated for state contracting on federally supported projects. The immediate impetus for the revision was the Supreme Court's decisions in *Croson v. City of Richmond* and *Aderand v. Peña*, which held that racial classifications are constitutionally suspect, even if they benefit

23. Strictly speaking, the federal and state programs do not fit the definition of CED. In particular, they are not decentralized or geographically focused on local communities. I discuss them here because their response to the capture problem is analogous to that of more canonical CED structures. In addition, these programs are compatible with CED institutions and sometimes provide support for CED projects, and, at one point, the sba program attempts explicitly to link with CDCs. See text accompanying note 27 below.

24. See, for example, Tamar Jacoby, *Someone Else's Neighborhood: America's Unfinished Struggle for Integration* 401–3 (1998).

historically disadvantaged minorities, and must satisfy an ambiguous but heavy burden of substantiation that they remedy directly specific past discrimination.[25] The Clinton administration responded by broadening the program criteria to embrace "socially disadvantaged" groups generally and making race merely one of many bases on which social disadvantage could be established.[26]

The regulations also address the capture problem by requiring that benefited firms be owned by people who meet the program definitions of social (and economic) disadvantage. These regulations are ambitious and, if conscientiously enforced, should go a long way toward addressing the problem. They begin by prescribing that a majority of the formal ownership rights—for example, shares in a corporation or interests in a partnership—be held by qualifying individuals. They then anticipate various legal devices other than formal ownership that affect control: options are to be treated as if they are exercised and minority interests are to be treated as controlling if they have veto rights because of, say, class or super-majority voting requirements. A majority interest is not to be treated as controlling if it is subject to redemption or option rights within the power of nonqualifying parties.

The regulations then look to informal sources of control. If the applicant's financing does not come from qualifying individuals or institutions, the regulations insist that the loans be made on terms that do not give the lender continuing control over the business's operations. The business must not be dependent on nonqualifying participants to meet bonding or licensing requirements. It must have the capacity to supervise and staff the work on its own. It cannot have any involvement at all by someone with more than a 10 percent interest in another firm in the same line of work.

The strictness of the rules limits the capture danger, though it does have a disadvantage: It precludes qualification by newer, weaker firms owned by members of disadvantaged groups who might have benefited from the program if they had been allowed to qualify in partnership with others. This disadvantage is mitigated by an exception. For firms supported by some CDCs, CDC ownership and control rights are not

25. *City of Richmond v. J. A. Croson Co.*, 488 U.S. 469 (1989); *Aderand Constructors, Inc. v. Peña*, 115 S.Ct. 2097 (1995).
26. 13 CFR Pt. 124.

disqualifying.[27] The exception makes sense. Capture of subsidies by a public-benefit nonprofit with goals overlapping those of the preference program does not present concerns comparable to capture by non-qualifying for-profit businesses.

CONSTRAINTS ON BENEFICIARY CONTROL:
THE TRANSITIONAL CO-OP

The Hyde Square Co-op has started out as a full-fledged co-op, fully owned by its resident patrons, but the co-op will acquire property interests only gradually, and these interests will remain subject to the equity restrictions expressed in various real estate and contract documents. The transitional nature of the co-op largely reflects the insistence of the various investors that the residents acquire the skills and demonstrate their capacity for management before assuming control.

A similar problem arises in some business development programs. There, however, the problem is sometimes aggravated by the fact that the business requires liquid assets at an early stage. Without anything comparable to real-estate transfer restrictions, the danger of opportunism is added to the danger of negligence.

The Industrial Cooperative Association (ICA) and the Paraprofessional Healthcare Institute (PHI) have responded to such problems by developing a transitional worker cooperative for some of the businesses with which they work. They arrived at this solution somewhat reluctantly. The ICA has been the leading American proponent of the Mondragon model. Like Mondragon, it has been influenced by Catholic social doctrine and its commitment to the "primacy of labor," which it once interpreted to entail that control and profit interests in the firm be awarded only to workers in proportion to work.[28] Over the years, however, some proponents of cooperatives have concluded that, for non-profit providers of support to protect their investments and reassure their contributors, they may need to retain some formal control over the enterprises they assist. The solution has been to modify the Mondragon

27. However, the definition of CDC is a limited one; it embraces only firms with grants from the federal Community Services Administration, which is a small subset of current CDCs.

28. See David Ellerman and Peter Pitegoff, "The Democratic Corporation: The New Worker Cooperative Statute in Massachusetts," 11 NYU Review of Law and Social Change 441 (1983).

structure to provide for two classes of stock: common or member shares held by workers and preferred shares held by a nonprofit funder.

The model was first implemented at Cooperative Home Care Associates of Boston.[29] Like the Hyde Square Co-op, this enterprise involved an affiliation between a member-controlled enterprise and a charitable corporation. The member-controlled enterprise is the cooperative providing in-home personal services to Medicare and Medicaid beneficiaries. The charitable corporation is the Paraprofessional Healthcare Institute, an organization that receives government and philanthropic funds to train indigent people, including recent welfare recipients, for the co-op jobs. The business plan calls for continuing training subsidies but eventual self-sufficiency for the co-op's service operation. Initially, however, the co-op will depend on a substantial investment from philanthropic sources. The preferred stock is designed to protect this investment.

As implemented at Cooperative Home Care, the preferred shares were issued to PHI in return for its investment before any member shares were issued. The principal financial advantage of the preferred shares is a liquidation preference. However, although such provisions conventionally provide for an interest that must be fully satisfied before any payment is made to the junior class, the CHCA's articles provide for payment first to members in the amount of the purchase price of their shares, followed by payment to the preferred shareholders in the amount of the purchase price of their shares plus accrued dividends, if any,[30] then distribution of any remaining assets to members.[31]

---

29. Cooperative Home Care of Boston failed in 1999, though its welfare-to-work training ideas continue to influence other programs. The New York organization on which it was based and replications in Philadelphia and Concord, New Hampshire, continue. The Philadelphia and Concord organizations have preferred-stock arrangements similar to the one described in the text. See generally Peter Pitegoff, "Shaping Regional Economies to Sustain Quality Work: The Cooperative Health Care Federation," in *Women and Work in the Post-Welfare Era* 100–6 (Joel Handler and Lucie White eds. 1999). My discussion of cooperative structure is based on the articles and bylaws of the Boston organization.

30. The articles provide for preferred dividends of 3 percent "as declared."

31. The embrace by leading cooperative proponents of the preferred-stock model represents a substantial evolution from long-standing premises. The worker co-op statute the ICA drafted to facilitate adoption of the Mondragon model initially precluded any

The control provisions provide for gradual phasing in of member control, with continuing veto rights for ICA. No member shares are to be issued until the firm has had three profitable quarters. At that point, the preferred class gets four board seats, and the members get two. This balance is altered each year in favor of members until, by the fourth year, the preferred class has only one seat, and the members have four. As long as the preferred shares are outstanding, however, specified major decisions require approval of both shareholder classes. These decisions include hiring a CEO, issuing new preferred stock, selling the company, expanding into new lines of business, and amending the articles. Thus, the preferred shares function a little like the "golden shares" that some governments have retained in once publicly owned companies that have been privatized. Such shares are designed less to confer financial rights than to give the government a veto over changes in corporate policy that might jeopardize public interests. (The State of Israel, for example, retains golden-share rights in the airline El Al to insure that the airline cannot stop flying routes that the government thinks serve vital public needs.)

The members have no right to buy out the PHI interest forcibly, and the PHI has no right to force the members to buy it out. Of course, the option remains open to the parties, should the enterprise become sufficiently stable, to agree on a buyout.

This structure is designed largely to prevent reckless or opportunistic behavior. It would not work to insure the funding organization a share in the economic gains of the enterprise. Presumably the principal gains expected are current returns on members' work rather than large capital gains. Were large capital gains a significant possibility, the structure could easily be modified to provide the funder a share. Stronger preferred dividend rights and a larger liquidation preference could accom-

---

kind of nonworker equity. However, in order to secure passage in Massachusetts, the ICA found it had to acquiesce in the insistence of the corporate section of the state bar association that co-ops be given the option of nonmember shares. When the ICA's counsel, Peter Pitegoff, who drafted the Massachusetts statute, filed the Cooperative Home Care of Boston articles with the Massachusetts Secretary of State, an official in the secretary's office initially refused to accept them on the ground that worker co-ops could not issue nonworker equity. Pitegoff had to point out and rely on the provision he had been forced by the bar to include in the statute.

plish this. In enterprises organized as conventional business corporations, the funders could take common as well as preferred stock. This
seems to be an increasing practice among NGO business-development
programs.[32]

32. For example, the Three Guineas Fund of San Francisco, which provides infrastructure and technical assistance at bargain rates to female entrepreneurs in high-tech
businesses, requires that a beneficiary company return 2 percent of its equity to the
fund. Marci McDonald, "A Start-Up of Her Own," *U.S. News and World Report* (15 May
2000), 34.

Chapter 9 The Limits of CED

Although the rhetoric sometimes implies otherwise, few regard CED as a panacea. It does not work in all neighborhoods. It is not viable without a substantial proportion of residents with at least moderate levels of civic competence, economic independence, and attachment to neighborhood. In some communities, it works only at enormous public cost. Moreover, where it works, it does so only as part of a broader set of institutions that links the community to surrounding state, regional, and national structures that support and coordinate local efforts.

We can get some sense of the limits of CED by considering four points that are sometimes phrased as critiques of the movement. None of them is plausible as a categorical objection to CED, but each is an important reminder of the limitations of this particular set of tools and strategies and of the complementary tools and strategies that would be required to vindicate the larger ambitions of American social policy.

Distributive Consequences

On average, CED programs are oriented toward groups at the top of or somewhat above the class to which traditional welfare programs have been directed. The shift from traditional public housing to the newer models has come at the expense of the poorest groups. In 1990, nearly a third of the residents of traditionally subsidized housing had incomes under 20 percent of median, and 80 percent had incomes below 50 percent.[1] By contrast, housing subsidized by the tax credit program can be allocated to people with incomes as high as 60 percent of the median, and it rarely goes to people much under 40 percent. Eligibility for housing supported by the HOME and related programs extends to people with incomes up to 80 percent of the median.[2] Boston's inclusionary zoning program produces rent-restricted units that can be allocated to people with incomes as high as 120 percent of the median. The Small Business Administration's preferences for "socially and economically disadvantaged" businesses are open to people with net-worths of up to $250,000, not counting home equity.[3] Resident management and ownership programs work best with people with higher income; business support programs work best with people who have capital and experience; and job programs work best with people who have better skills.

Even heavily subsidized home or business ownership is not a plausible option for most poor people. Many of them cannot benefit substantially from job training and placement without vastly more extensive support—whether in terms of therapy, basic education, child care, or transportation—than current programs contemplate. A serious commitment to a minimally decent standard of living will always require something like traditional welfare programs for a significant fraction of low-income people. For a larger fraction, traditional welfare programs are a cheaper short-term response than the new housing, job, and business development programs, and hence in an era of stringency may be more plausible.

There is no dispute that people in the lower–middle income ranges are plausible candidates for social assistance. If the benefits they received under the new programs did not come at the expense of people who were worse off, there would be no cause for concern. However, it seems clear that many of the new benefits do come at the expense of people who are worse off. In general, the new programs provide benefits that

1. See Michael Stegman, "The Excessive Cost of Creative Finance: Growing Inefficiencies in the Production of Low-Income Housing," 2 *Housing Policy Debate* 357, 360 (1991).

2. 42 USC 12704(9)–(10). The composition of traditional public-housing projects seems to be moving upscale, as well. Congress has extended eligibility to incomes up to 80 percent of the median and has created incentives to favor more affluent applicants: 42 USC 1437a(b)(2), 1437g(2)(b).

3. 13 CFR 24.104(c)(2).

are individually more expensive to smaller groups of relatively well-off people. Yet they are often portrayed by their political proponents as substitutes for the older programs.[4] The newer low-density, high-amenity style of subsidized housing produces more benefits for its occupants and better externalities for neighboring residents, but it also produces considerably fewer units. The reorientation of the Aid for Families with Dependent Children program from income maintenance to employment has improved the situation of some beneficiaries with better skills and less demanding family responsibilities, but it has worsened the situation of the most disadvantaged recipients. The general distributive effect of recent social policy may turn out to have been a massive shift of wealth from the bottom quintile of the income distribution to the one second from the bottom.

On the other hand, if one takes account of less measurable costs and benefits, a case can be made that extending subsidies upward benefits the worst off. Programs with middle-class constituencies are less vulnerable politically. And poor people can benefit from the presence in their neighborhoods of middle-class people. Benefits can take the intangible form of role models or social capital. They can also take the form of externalities and complementarities from tangible local investments.

Karla Hoff and Arijit Sen have shown theoretically in connection with homeownership programs that the poor will sometimes benefit more from a modest individual subsidy given to both poor and moderate-income people than from a larger subsidy focused exclusively on the poor.[5] It takes relatively less subsidy to move moderate-income people to the point where they have the kind of stake in the neighborhood that motivates civic activism and tangible investments. The loss to the poor in direct subsidy may be more than compensated by the spillovers from these activities. The argument may sound a little like the trickle down rhetoric of the Reagan era that CED practitioners disdain. Note, however, that the chain of causation in Hoff's vision is much shorter temporally, spatially, and socially. The beneficial effects are expected fairly quickly, and among them is a civic solidarity between the relatively advantaged

4. This was especially noticeable in HUD Secretary Jack Kemp's vision of converting traditional public-housing subsidies into ownership programs. See Michael Stegman's critique in *More Housing, More Fairly* (Twentieth Century Fund, 1991).
5. Karla Hoff and Arijit Sen, "Homeownership, Community Interactions, and Segregation" (unpublished 2000).

and disadvantaged groups arising from shared economic stakes in the same neighborhood. Moreover, the argument only works with a measure of income diversity, so the program is a natural complement to more direct efforts to maintain or achieve economic integration.

The Instability of Low-Income Communities

Community economic development institutions are designed to produce and maintain stable, long-term communities. Their participatory processes seem to assume a measure of long-term commitment, and their institutions are designed to attach people to the community on a long-term basis. In some respects, this program swims against a tide of both fact and aspiration that makes low-income neighborhoods transitional places for their most able residents. Low-income communities are places people are trying to get out of, it is said, and when people succeed, they leave.[6] The most skilled and motivated people in these neighborhoods do not view themselves as long-term stakeholders and will, in fact, leave if and when they are able.

It seems right that the more ambitious dimensions of CED programs require residents with long-term perspectives and residential stability. Neighborhoods that lack these assets are poor candidates for the more ambitious forms of CED—those that aspire to resident control and high social-capital development.

On the other hand, the objection may exaggerate the extent to which poor neighborhoods lack residents with long-term perspectives and ties and the possibility that the development of CED institutions will induce such perspectives and ties. Contrary to some impressions, there has been no general increase in residential mobility in recent decades. The average American adult has lived in the same locality for twenty-two years; this figure has not changed for many years. "Americans today are, if anything, slightly more rooted residentially than a generation ago," Robert Putnam writes.[7] On the other hand, aggregate data may obscure a trend toward greater mobility in low-income neighborhoods. William Julius Wilson has documented growth in the concentration of poverty

6. For example, Nicholas Lemann, "The Myth of Community Development," *The New York Times Magazine* (9 January 1994), 27, 30.
7. Robert Putnam, *Bowling Alone: The Collapse and Revival of American Community* 205 (2000).

that seems to result in part from an increase in out-migration of relatively successful residents from poor and minority neighborhoods.[8]

However, the question of whether this trend might be reversed by institutional development of the sort CED attempts is important. Wilson suggests that emigration has followed jobs out of the city. This suggests that local job development could make a difference.

It is also possible that emigration is influenced by the weakness of local institutions in leveraging individual economic improvements into community improvement. People who succeed are most likely to leave when they do not observe any corresponding improvement in the community. It may be that a noticeable level of community progress, even if proportionately less than the individual progress of the most successful members, would induce them to stay. Thus, modest initial CED success might induce the long-term perspective needed for more ambitious CED projects.

Neighborhoods such as ones served by South Shore Bank in Chicago and by Jamaica Plain Neighborhood Development Corporation in Boston have not been places that low-income people are trying to get out of. They have been places that low-income people are trying to hang on to in the face either of rising social disorder or gentrifying price inflation. These were stable and attractive areas whose declines were arrested with the help of CED efforts. They were never among the lowest-income or more deteriorated neighborhoods, but they had substantial proportions of poor and moderate-income people. Dudley Street in Roxbury and the Charlotte Gardens area of the South Bronx were far bleaker, but they have recently become areas that people try to get into, again with the help of CED institutions. To be sure, there are many counter-examples of failure, but we are far from having any definite sense of the limits of maintaining or enhancing stability in low-income neighborhoods.

The Limited Appeal of the Communitarian Ideal

Some people do not find the idea of a social setting defined by multi-stranded relations, geographical focus, and face-to-face encounters especially appealing. They persist in this view even while recognizing that

8. William Julius Wilson, *When Work Disappears* 25–50 (1997).

the CED notion of community differs from the romantic one of spontaneous and pervasive intimacy.

Some of these people reject the ideal of face-to-face collaboration. They prefer the strong impersonality of markets and bureaucracies. They do not like the idea of multistranded relations. They would prefer a larger number of more shallow relationships. And they would prefer policies that tend to spread their experiences across the largest possible number of contexts to those that tend to cluster their experiences in a common space.[9]

Others do not find the communitarian ideal unattractive in itself, but fear that, in the circumstances of contemporary America, CED policies are in tension with the goal of racial integration. Low-income communities are likely to be predominantly minority communities. Strengthening them means entrenching existing patterns of racial discrimination. By contrast, policies that enhance the capacity of such communities' residents to move to predominantly white areas further integration.

These are important points, but they show only that the CED strategy is a partial one, not a panacea. The most ambitious CED approaches will not work in all low-income neighborhoods. They do not respond to the aspirations of all low-income people. And, at their best, they do not touch important social goals.

But the ideal of rooted community seems attractive to a broad range of Americans. There is no reason to think that low-income Americans have weaker preferences for it than others. It seems more plausible to think that the greater instability of their neighborhoods reflects economic adversity and institutional underdevelopment of the sort that CED projects seek to mitigate. Moreover, mobility policies, such as housing vouchers and wage supplements, often have limited effects in inducing integration, and may even have bad effects in the absence of institutional developments. Providing individual benefits does not necessarily affect patterns of housing and employment discrimination. Moreover, individual benefits can exacerbate various coordination problems. Housing benefits can cause inflation in areas where beneficiaries are

9. Jerry Frug develops such an orientation under the rubric of the "Postmodern Subject" in "Decentering Democracy," 60 *University of Chicago Law Review* 253 (1993).

welcome and panic-driven disinvestment and exit in areas where they are not. The downward spiral of the Roxbury and Dorchester, Massachusetts, neighborhoods described by Gerald Gamm is an example.[10]

Moreover, such efforts can result in social and political isolation of the newcomers. Black and Latino high-school students in East Palo Alto, California, are bused to a school in the more white and affluent Menlo Park because of a court order in a desegregation case. Many residents believe that the students do not benefit from this mobility. As a group, they underperform the Menlo Park students substantially; they feel socially marginalized; and they are suspended and expelled far more often than the other students. Such stories suggest that it is sometimes rational for poor or minority groups to choose efforts to improve relatively segregated communities over efforts to provide mobility into more advantaged ones. They also suggest that mobility efforts often require institutional development that facilitates economic coordination and social inclusion in the destination communities. The institutional repertory of the CED Movement may prove useful for such purposes.

Unfortunately, there is no need to choose between CED and mobility policy. Neither shows any imminent prospect of massive success that would obviate the need for the other.

The Weakness of the Inside Game

David Rusk calls community-based urban strategies the "inside game," and he portrays them as weak.[11] Communities are dependent on outside institutions for resources. They have little control over the larger forces that affect them. At best, they achieve control over the municipal political process, but this process is at the mercy of political boundaries that more often than not allow the relatively privileged to segregate themselves outside the reach of the jurisdictions in which low-income com-

10. Gerald Gamm, *Urban Exodus: Why the Jews Left Boston and the Catholics Stayed* (1999), discussed in chapter 6. See also the discussion of the general limitations of housing vouchers in Jennifer J. Curhan, "The HUD Reinvention: A Critical Analysis," *Boston University Public Interest Journal* 239, 258–64 (1995).

11. David Rusk, *Inside Game/Outside Game: Winning Strategies for Saving Urban America* (1999).

munities are located. These governments have little capacity to re-distribute wealth or fund adequate public goods and services for their low-income residents. They lack the political reach to influence housing and school-attendance patterns toward economic and racial integra-tion. Their land-use policies tend to be swamped by centrifugal pres-sures that cause residential development to sprawl outward beyond their boundaries and undermine efforts to achieve denser, more socially desirable development within the city.

Rusk's response is the "outside game"—the effort to achieve more inclusive local government and to use it to implement metropolitan remedies for local finance, integration, and land use. He gives sev-eral examples of success in this game: Portland, Oregon; Montgomery County, Maryland; Minneapolis. In each of these cases, an inclusive government with a broad fiscal base oversees a land-use regulatory system that inhibits sprawl, encourages urban density, and disperses subsidized and low-income housing throughout the jurisdiction.

Few CED practitioners would argue with Rusk about the value of the kind of metropolitan government he prescribes, and Rusk acknowl-edges the value of CED as a complement to the outside game. Successful metropolitan government does not obviate the need for, or the desir-ability of, local implementation. But Rusk does suggest that an implicit political trade-off may exist between inside and outside approaches. As we have seen, the inside game has been popular across the political spectrum in recent years. The outside game has comparatively little support from national and state government, and it encounters fierce resistance in many areas from suburbanites who fear redistribution or integration or distrust strong government. It is easier for politicians and NGO reformers to play the inside game because the inside game is less threatening to middle-class interests and attitudes. The danger, of course, is that support for inside efforts relieves the pressure for outside reforms by deluding people about the efficacy of the former and encour-aging complacency about broader needs and goals.

It seems unlikely that there are substantial non-rhetorical differences here within the CED Movement. The best program is one that combines strong inclusive government with community-based implementation. However, the best should not be the enemy of the good. The need for metropolitan solutions is no reason to minimize the local achievements and potential of the CED Movement.

Conclusion

In its more extreme moments—when it flirts with autarchy—the CED perspective seems implausible. Yet most Americans seem to find attractive the idea of focusing a substantial range of their lives in a geographically defined local community. Some community control of many social programs makes sense on instrumental grounds. The importance of neighborhood externalities—for example, in residential housing markets—makes coordinated action at this level critical.

Moreover, the ideas of devolving decision making to a point at which groups defined by face-to-face relations can participate substantially and of leveraging these relations from one dimension to another seem broadly promising. This strategy does not require a geographical focus. Given the substantial degree of spatial mobility and the efficacy of communications technology, spatially dispersed groups can often develop dense personal relations. But to most people, local geography comes as a natural focus of effort and identity. Moreover, geographical focus is embedded in American traditions of political organization and in the organization of public services, such as schooling and policing.

The CED Movement has given such ideas new promise by elaborating a variety of institutional forms to implement them. Structures such as the CDC, the limited-equity co-op, grants conditioned on democratic self-organization, and the hybrid partnership are significant additions to the toolkit of social policy and democracy.

Index

William H. Simon is Saunders Professor of Law at
Stanford University. He is the author of *The Practice
of Justice: A Theory of Lawyers' Ethics.*

Library of Congress Cataloging-in-Publication Data
Simon, William H.
The community economic development movement :
law, business, and the new social policy / William H. Simon.
p. cm.   Includes index.
ISBN 0-8223-2804-6 (cloth: alk. paper)
ISBN 0-8223-2815-1 (pbk.: alk. paper)
1. Community development—United States.
2. United States—Social policy. I. Title.
HN90.C6 S557 2001   307.1′4′0973—dc21   2001047054